IMAGES
of America

CORSICANA

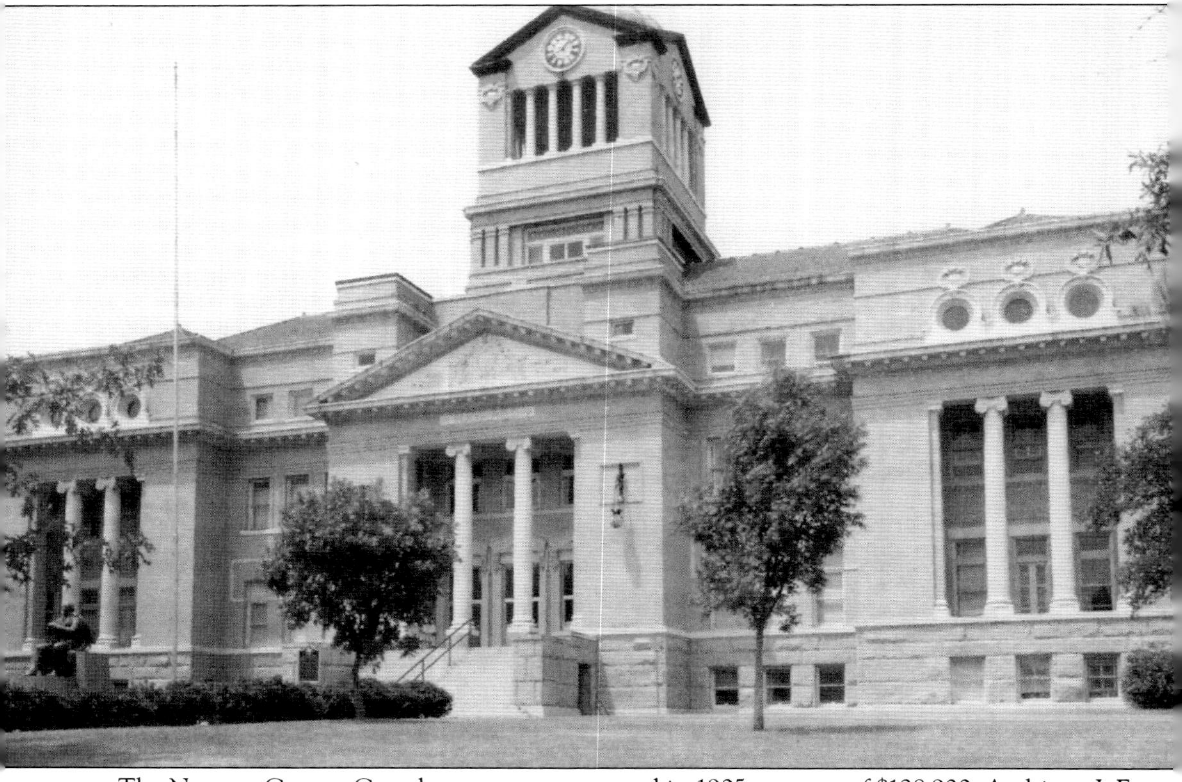

The Navarro County Courthouse was constructed in 1905 at a cost of $128,900. Architect J. E. Flanders designed the three-story Beaux-Arts building made of red Burnet granite and gray brick. Ionic columns mark the main entrance to the building. The four-sided clock was added to the tower in 1923. This is the fifth courthouse in the county's history. The exterior of the building has remained unchanged since its construction more than a century ago. (Courtesy of the Navarro County Historical Society.)

On the Cover: Navarro County employees gather outside the courthouse to enjoy a 12-inch snow that fell in 1929, a rare occurrence in Corsicana. (Coutesy of the Navarro County Historical Society.)

IMAGES
of America

CORSICANA

Tommy Stringer

ARCADIA
PUBLISHING

ISBN 978-0-7385-7878-1

Published by Arcadia Publishing
Charleston, South Carolina

Printed in the United States of America

Library of Congress Control Number: 2009932662

For all general information contact Arcadia Publishing at:
Telephone 843-853-2070
Fax 843-853-0044
E-mail sales@arcadiapublishing.com
For customer service and orders:
Toll-Free 1-888-313-2665

Visit us on the Internet at www.arcadiapublishing.com

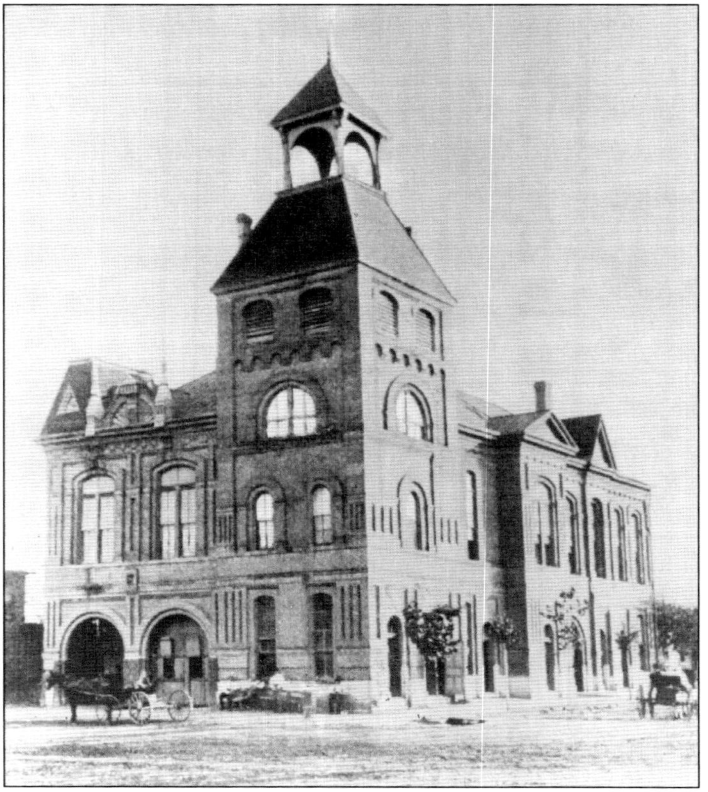

Old city hall, with its signature tower, was located at the corner of Main Street and West Fifth Avenue. It was constructed at a cost of $17,000. In addition to providing offices for city officials, the building also housed the fire department. It was built in 1886 during the administration of Mayor Robert Neblett. (Courtesy of the Navarro County Historical Society.)

Contents

Acknowledgments 6

Introduction 7

1. Judges, Legislators, and a Governor:
   Corsicana's Players in the Political Arena 9

2. Fruitcakes, Chili, and Oil:
   Corsicana's Businesses and Industries 31

3. Churches, Schools, and Clubs:
   Corsicana's Cultural Scene 69

4. Home Is Where the Heart Is:
   Historic Homes in Corsicana 117

ACKNOWLEDGMENTS

The extensive photographic archives of the Navarro County Historical Society, located at Pioneer Village, provided the majority of the images used in this volume. Unless otherwise noted, all images appear courtesy of the Navarro County Historical Society. Other individuals who provided additional images include Jon Ketcham, the Navarro County Oil Museum, Lona Hines, Nancy Weems, Babette Samuels, Kathryn Zack, Richard Parker, Lynda Green, John Barron, Al Hopkins, Janet Jacobs, Sidney and Jane Miller, Mabel Scott, Megan Vadasy, Tresa Darby, Steve Stroube, and Leonard and Seely Fuller.

In preparing the text and captions, the excellent publications of the Navarro County Historical Society were the most utilized sources of information, along with the *Handbook of Texas* and Corsicana city directories. Wallace Charlton's *History of Wolf Brand Chili* provided background information on that Corsicana business icon. Special thanks go to Bobbie Young of the Navarro County Historical Society for her efforts in locating appropriate photographs and providing background information on people, places, and events. Verna Bonner of the Navarro County Genealogical Society provided assistance as well. Larry Turner graciously shared extensive information on Corsicana's oil history. Heather Turner, archivist for the Pearce Collections museums at Navarro College, was invaluable in scanning images and advising the arrangement of the materials. Allison Chew, also of the Pearce museums, assisted with scanning and other technical matters. The *Corsicana Daily Sun* helped promote the project, and many local service clubs and community organizations graciously provided a pulpit to appeal for images and information, as well as to promote the project.

Because of their commitment and loyalty to the community, this volume is dedicated to the good people of Corsicana whose contributions have made this town unique. While a project of this nature tends to focus on buildings, businesses, and organizations, it is the people who have made Corsicana a special place.

To learn more about the history of Corsicana and Navarro County, contact:

Navarro County Historical Society
912 Park Avenue
Corsicana, TX 75110
903.654.4846

For tourist information, contact:

Corsicana-area Chamber of Commerce
120 North Twelfth Street
Corsicana, TX 75110
903.874.4731
Visitcorsicana.com

Introduction

Corsicana, Texas, has a rich history marked by icons that are synonymous with the Lone Star State. Cotton, railroads, oil, cowboys and Indians, chili, football, power broker politicos, and visionary entrepreneurs are all part of the community's heritage. The intent of this book is to provide a photographic record of the people and events that have shaped the legacy of Corsicana. Necessarily, a project of this nature poses problems. Because of space limitations, some worthy entries will be omitted, but every attempt has been made to provide a balanced presentation of the people, places, and events that have helped shape the town's history. The material will be arranged topically, rather than chronologically, grouping photographs into categories that will address Corsicana's political scene, various businesses, industries, and entrepreneurs, and the town's social and cultural institutions and recreational activities.

The first Anglo settlers arrived in the 1840s, attracted to the area by the liberal land policies first of Mexico and later of the Republic of Texas as well as the rich soil that was ideal for cotton production. They came primarily from the states of the Old South, bringing with them their slaves and the religious and political values of that region. The town was established in 1848 to serve as the seat of government for newly created Navarro County. When asked to name the new settlement, Texas patriot Jose Antonio Navarro, the county's namesake, replied, "Call it Corsicana for the island of Corsica, the birthplace of my father." When the Southern states began withdrawing from the Union, setting the stage for the Civil War, residents of Corsicana and Navarro County overwhelmingly supported the Confederate cause. Some 450 men from Navarro County served in the Confederate army during the conflict. Like many southern communities, Corsicana was occupied by federal troops during the Reconstruction era until Texas was readmitted to the Union. The arrival of the Houston and Texas Central Railroad (H&TC) greatly enhanced the town's future, providing dependable transportation to move both people and goods. The arrival of the St. Louis and Southwestern Railroad, commonly called the Cotton Belt, 10 years later provided the city with an east-west rail line.

Despite the advantages of a good climate, a reliable transportation system, and an adequate population for markets and work force, the community struggled in the 1890s. Because the economy was heavily dependent on cotton, Corsicana was on the brink of collapse when the cotton market declined in the early part of that decade. To attract new industry to diversify the agricultural-based economy, town leaders contracted with the American Well and Prospecting Company, a Kansas-based operation, to drill water wells to enhance the city's limited water supply. At a depth of 1,027 feet, workers noticed a black, sticky substance seeping into the drilling shaft. They had inadvertently discovered oil. Although the contractor was annoyed by the "intrusion," fortunately some local businessmen realized the potential value of the new discovery and focused their efforts on developing the oil reserves. By the end of the decade, as many as 1,000 oil wells were operating within the city limits, marking the state's first commercial oil field. Many of the petroleum industry's technological innovations and marketing strategies were developed in

Corsicana, and some of the industry's leaders began their careers here as well. In the 1920s, a second oil boom occurred with the discovery of the Powell field east of Corsicana. Boomtowns sprang up all over the county overnight, bringing economic prosperity but also an increase in crime and violence. The boom ended by the late 1920s, but oil continues to be a key component of the local economy.

Other businesses thrived as well. A German baker and his partner, an Irish cotton broker, established a bakery on Collin Street that would become internationally famous. In the 1890s, a farmer would come to town to sell a concoction from the back of his wagon parked in the downtown business district. Eventually he canned the product and called it Wolf Brand Chili. A Jewish immigrant started as a street peddler and eventually established a chain of retail dry-goods stores across Texas. Corsicana made significant contributions to World War II. An operation that had manufactured oil field equipment was converted into a bomb and munitions plant. From 1941 until its closing in 1944, more than 8,000 cadets received primary flight training as Army Air Corps pilots at the Air Activities of Texas on the southern outskirts of town. Mom-and-pop family-owned businesses lined the downtown streets, providing goods and services to the local residents.

Politics and politicians have been a vital part of the Corsicana's history. From the outset, local citizens were "yellow dog Democrats," and it was not until the 1980s that Republicans had any success in local elections. Corsicana has contributed a number of political figures who have wielded power on the state and national levels. The only Texas governor to die in office was a graduate of Corsicana High School, and his father had earlier served as the state's lieutenant governor. A late-19th-century U.S. senator had practiced law in Corsicana prior to going to Washington, and the ranking member of the U.S. House Committee on Foreign Affairs during the perilous days of World War II was a Corsicana native son. A blind man represented Navarro County in the state legislature and later served as county and district judge, giving literal meaning to the term "justice is blind." A chief justice of the Supreme Court of Texas grew up in the Corsicana State Orphans Home.

The development of social institutions is an indicator that a community is coming-of-age. Corsicana established schools for its young people and civic organizations and service clubs for the adults. A first-class junior college was established in 1946, utilizing the abandoned Air Activities of Texas facilities for a temporary campus. The initial student body consisted largely of returning servicemen using the recently enacted GI Bill to fund their education. The Merchants Opera House and movie theaters provided entertainment and cultural events, while the YMCA, the public library, the Kinsloe House, the Pioneer Village, and the Pearce Civil War Museum and Western Art Gallery all enhanced the quality of life in the community. Hospitals, clinics, and dedicated physicians and health care professionals provided medical care to the citizenry, and churches met the spiritual needs of the community.

These are only a few of the many examples of the fascinating story of Corsicana, Texas. Hopefully, the photographs included in this volume will provide the reader with a greater understanding and appreciation of this special community and its rich history.

One

Judges, Legislators, and a Governor

Corsicana's Players in the Political Arena

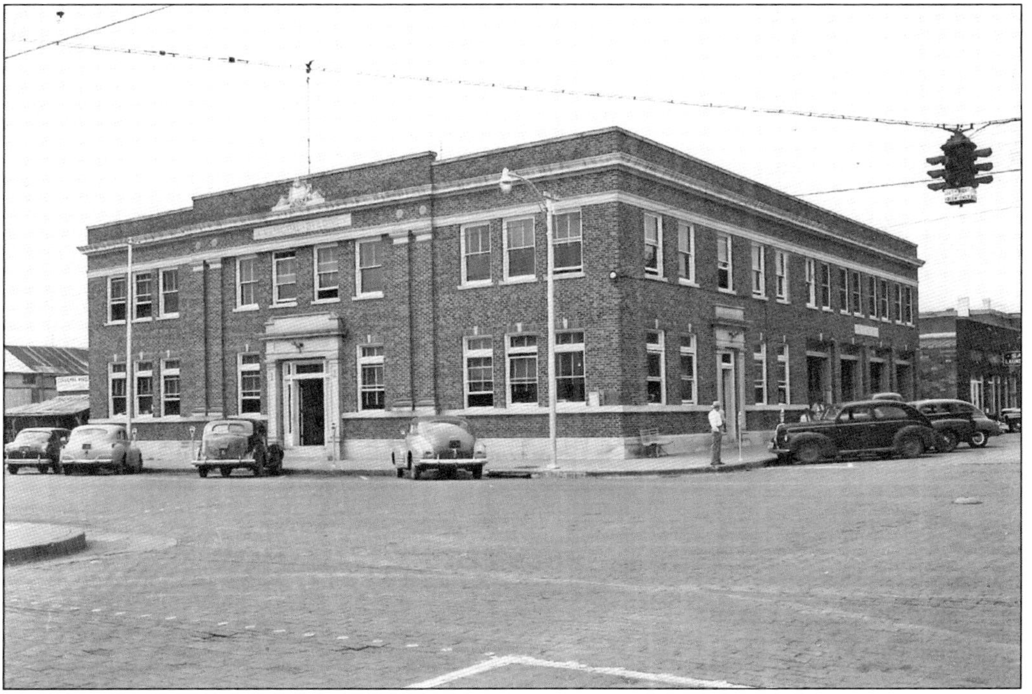

The Corsicana Municipal Building was constructed in 1923 during the administration of Mayor J. S. Eubanks. Taking advantage of the oil boom that was underway in the county at the time, Eubanks sold water to the oil companies for their drilling operations, generating enough revenue to pay for the building at no cost to the taxpayers.

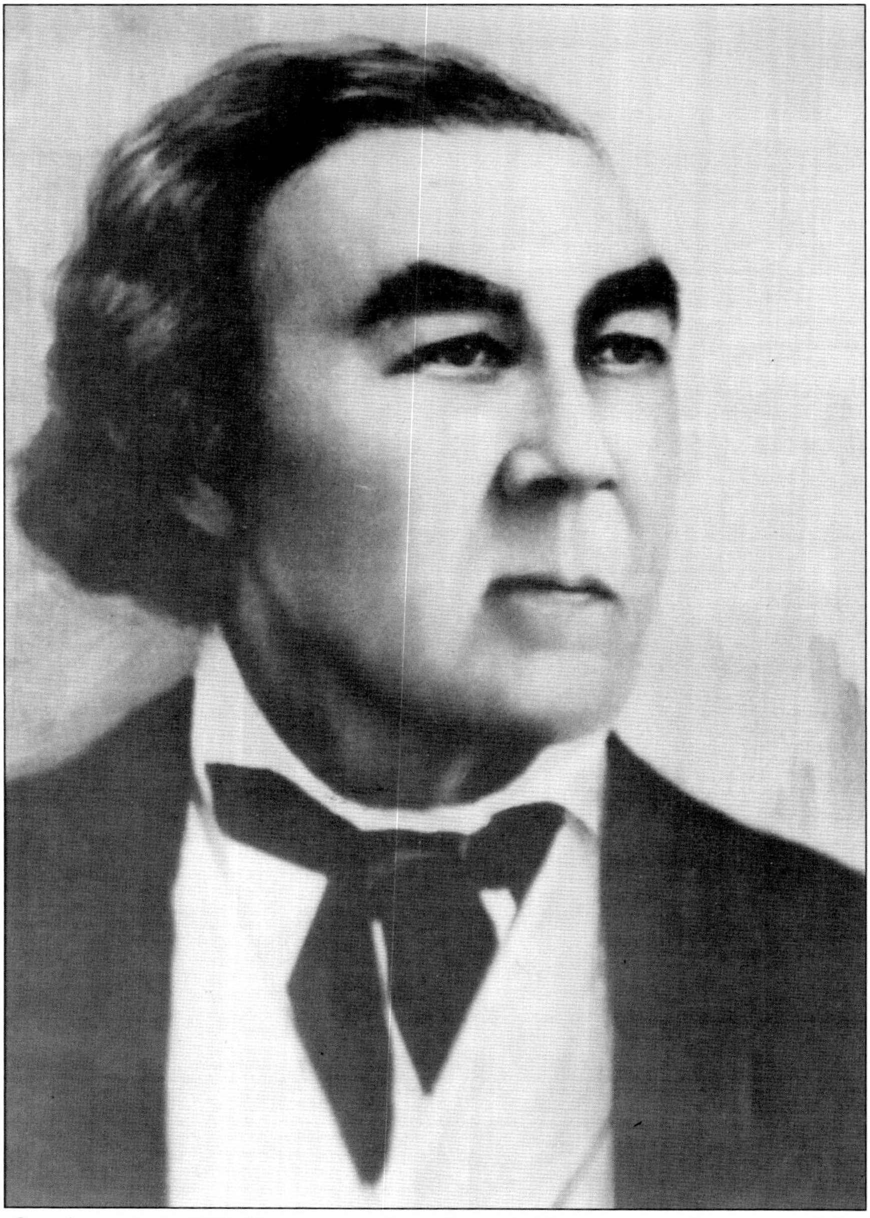

Born in San Antonio in 1795, Texas patriot Jose Antonio Navarro actively supported the Texans in their fight for independence from Mexico. He signed the Texas Declaration of Independence and served in the Congress of the Republic of Texas. He also participated in the failed Santa Fe Expedition and was imprisoned by Santa Anna. Following his release, he returned to San Antonio and supported Texas annexation into the Union. To acknowledge his contributions to Texas, the first state legislature named a newly created county in his honor in 1846. There is no evidence that he ever visited Navarro County. When asked to name the seat of government for his namesake county, Navarro replied, "Call it Corsicana for the island of Corsica, the birthplace of my father." Navarro died in 1871. A bronze statue of Navarro was erected at the south entrance of the courthouse.

Clinton Winkler is said to have delivered the petition to the Texas Legislature requesting the creation of Navarro County in 1846 and was involved in selecting the town site of Corsicana as the county seat. After serving in Hood's Texas Brigade during the Civil War, Winkler returned to Navarro County and was elected to the Texas Legislature. He served as an associate judge of the Texas Court of Appeals from 1876 until his death in 1882. The community of Winkler in southern Navarro County in named in his honor.

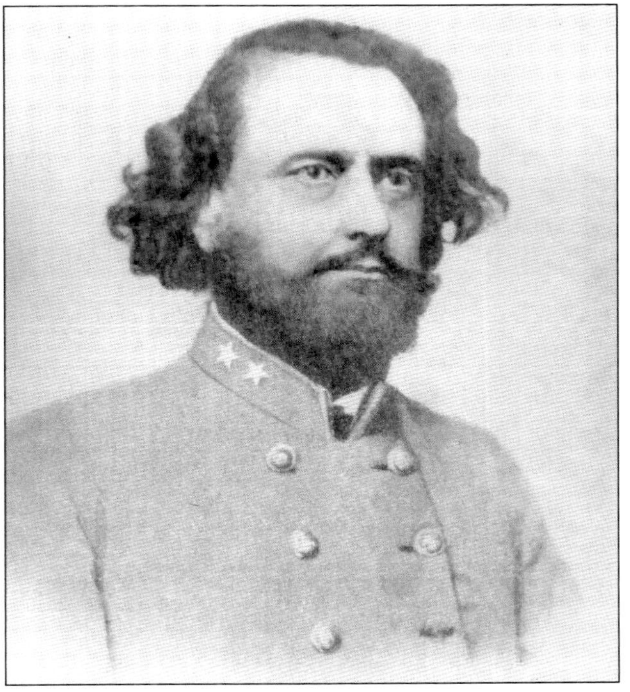

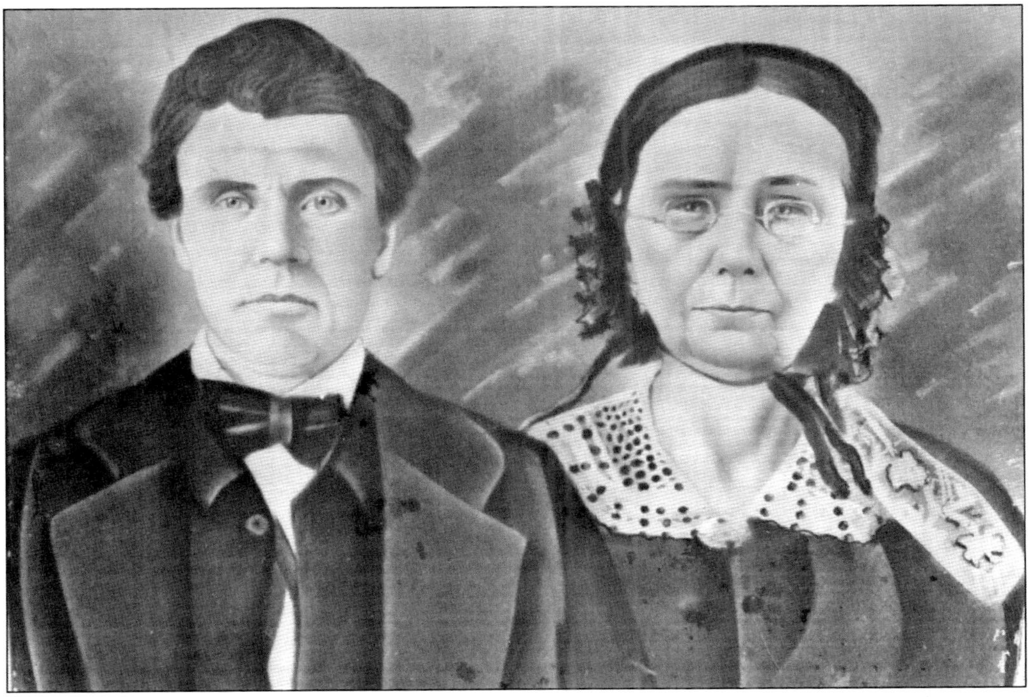

Rev. Hampton McKinney and his wife, Mary, came to Navarro County in 1846 from Illinois. He constructed a log house at what later became the Roger Mills's homesite. McKinney later moved to the courthouse square and brought in two log cabins for a hotel, a post office, and offices for county officials. McKinney, a Methodist minister, and his wife, Mary, had 12 children.

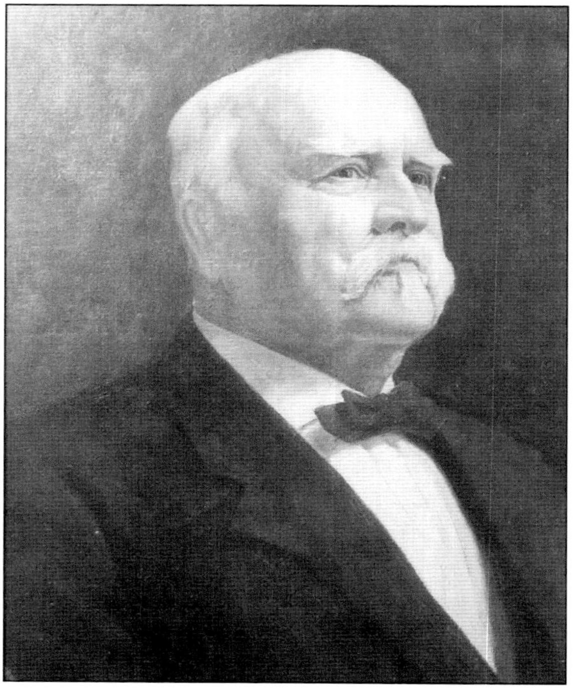

Roger Q. Mills's political career began with his election to the Texas Legislature in 1859, but his term was interrupted by the outbreak of the Civil War. Following his service in the Confederate army, Mills returned to Corsicana to resume his law practice. He was elected to the U.S. Congress in 1872, a position he held for 20 years. He was elected to the U.S. Senate in 1892 and retired in 1899. He died in 1911.

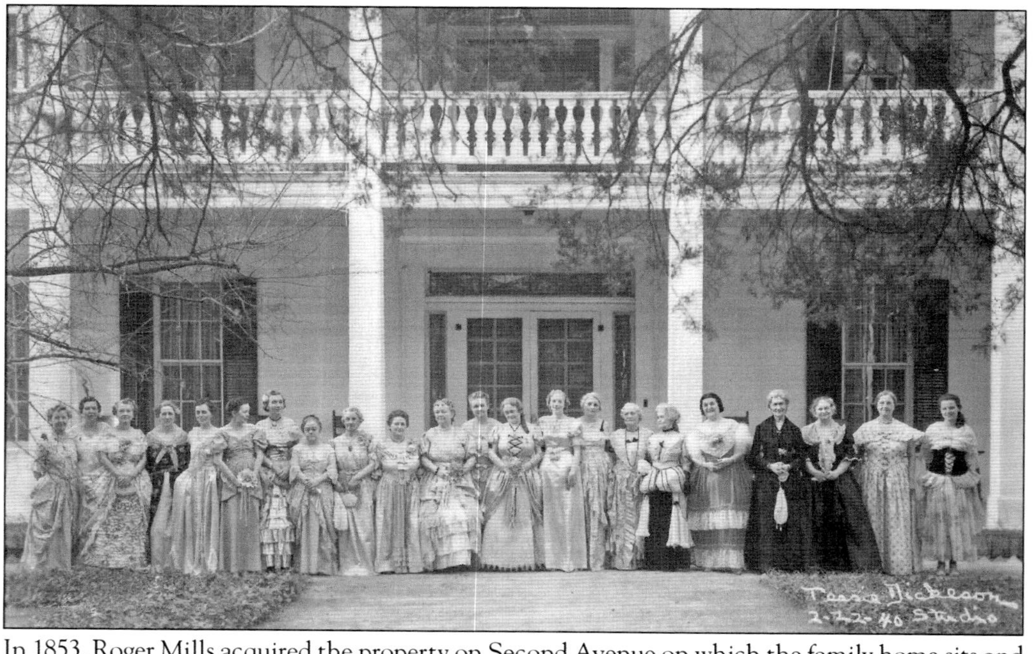

In 1853, Roger Mills acquired the property on Second Avenue on which the family home sits and began construction of the house shortly thereafter. He made several additions and expansions to the original one-story structure. The property was inherited by Mills's son Charles in 1911 and was sold to Eliot and Laura Johnston in 1944. Currently, it houses the law office of Moe and Dunn. Pictured here are members of the Daughters of the American Revolution (DAR) at a meeting at the Mills home in the 1940s.

Ethan Melton came to Texas in 1836 to settle the estate of his brother, who was killed in the Alamo. He served on the committee to select Corsicana as the county seat of Navarro County. Melton's home on Richland Creek functioned as the first post office in Navarro County. He also donated land for a church in the community of Dresden, west of Corsicana.

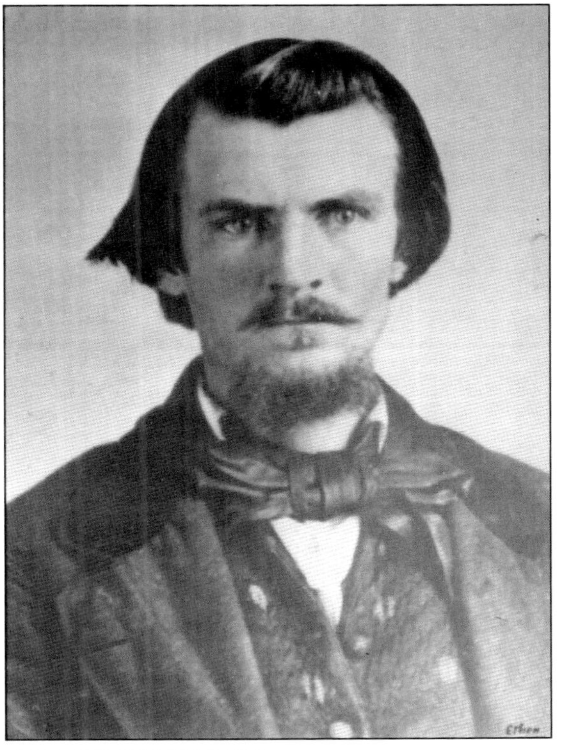

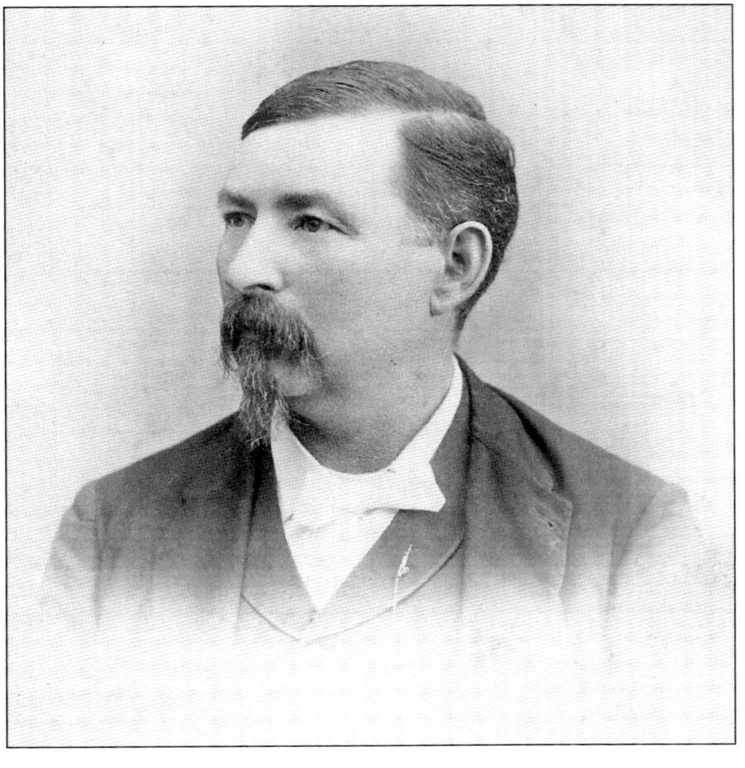

George T. Jester came to Corsicana by covered wagon with his widowed mother and five siblings in 1858. Following his service in the Confederate army during the Civil War, Jester returned to Corsicana, where he eventually founded the Corsicana National Bank. He served one term in the Texas House of Representatives and one term in the Texas Senate before being elected lieutenant governor in 1894. Following his second term, he returned to Corsicana and engaged in various business enterprises. He died in 1922.

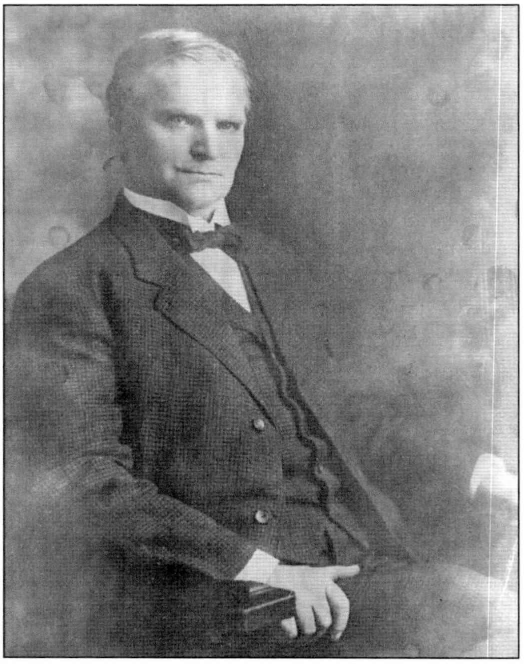

Rufus Hardy, a native of Mississippi, moved to Corsicana in 1878 to establish a private law practice. He was elected district attorney in 1884, and he served as district judge from 1888 to 1896. A staunch Democrat, Hardy was elected to eight terms in the U.S. House of Representatives, serving from 1907 to 1923. Following his retirement from Congress, Hardy resumed his law practice in Corsicana. He died in 1943 and is buried in Oakwood Cemetery.

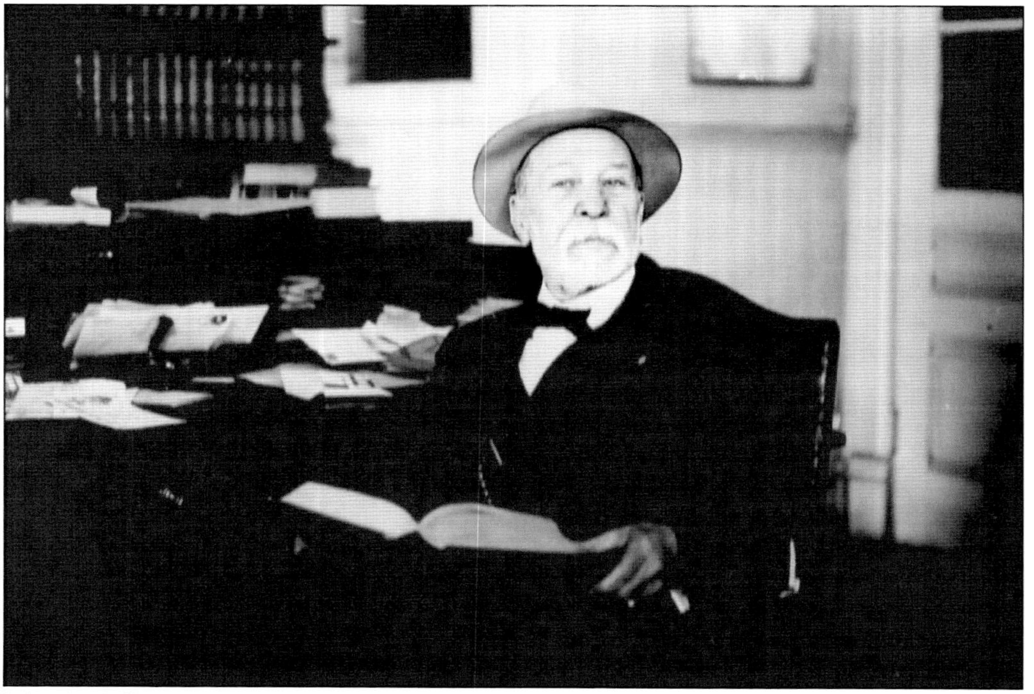

John S. Callicutt was appointed a district judge by Texas governor Miriam "Ma" Ferguson to fill the vacancy caused by the death of Hawkins Scarborough in 1935. Callicutt graduated from Southwestern University in Georgetown, and he earned a law degree from the University of Texas in 1887. He was also involved in various business interests in Corsicana, including banking and wholesale groceries. He died in 1944.

Samuel Frost came as a child with his family to Navarro County in 1846. After serving in the Confederate army during the Civil War, Frost returned to Corsicana, where he "read law" in the office of Clinton M. Winkler. He was admitted to the bar in 1870. Frost served as county attorney, county judge, district judge, and state representative in the Texas Legislature. He later served as attorney for the Cotton Belt and the Houston and Texas Central Texas Railroads. The small community of Frost in western Navarro County is named in his honor.

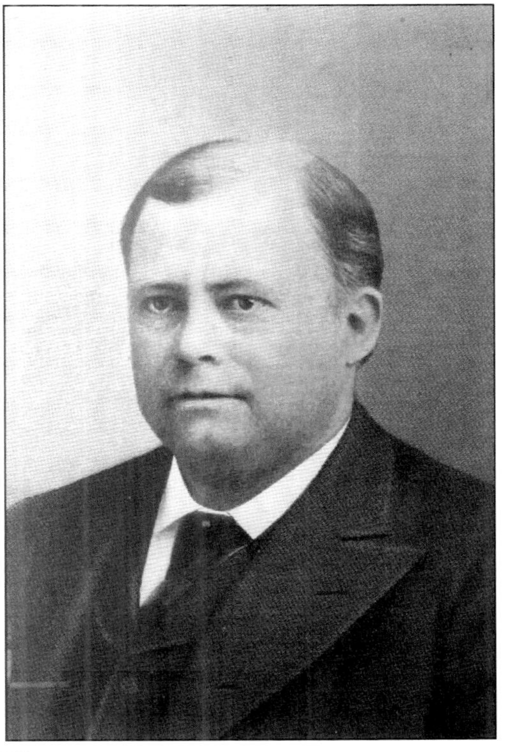

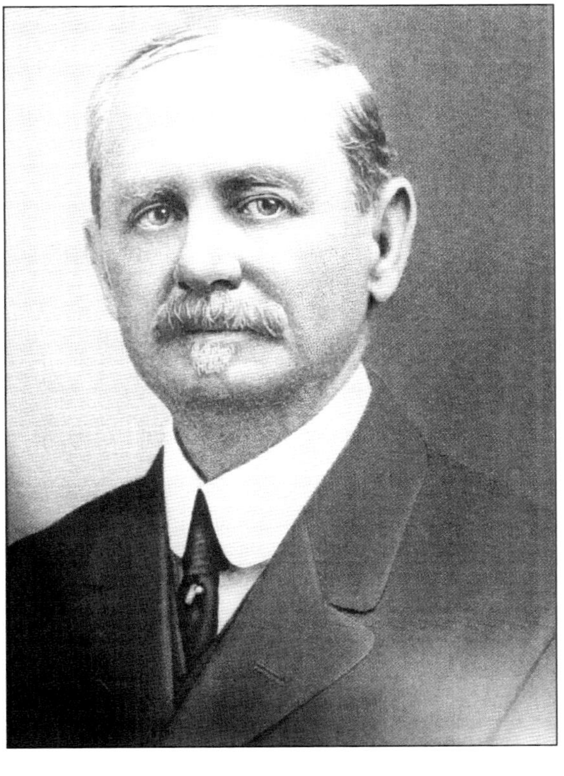

Charles Allyn, a native of New York, came to Texas after the Civil War. He opened mercantile stores along the route of the Houston and Texas Central Railroad as it expanded its line north from Houston to Dallas. Allyn came to Corsicana in 1871, the same year the railroad arrived. He was involved in various business ventures, served on the local school board, and was mayor of Corsicana. A small park at the intersection of West Seventh Avenue and South Beaton Street honors his memory.

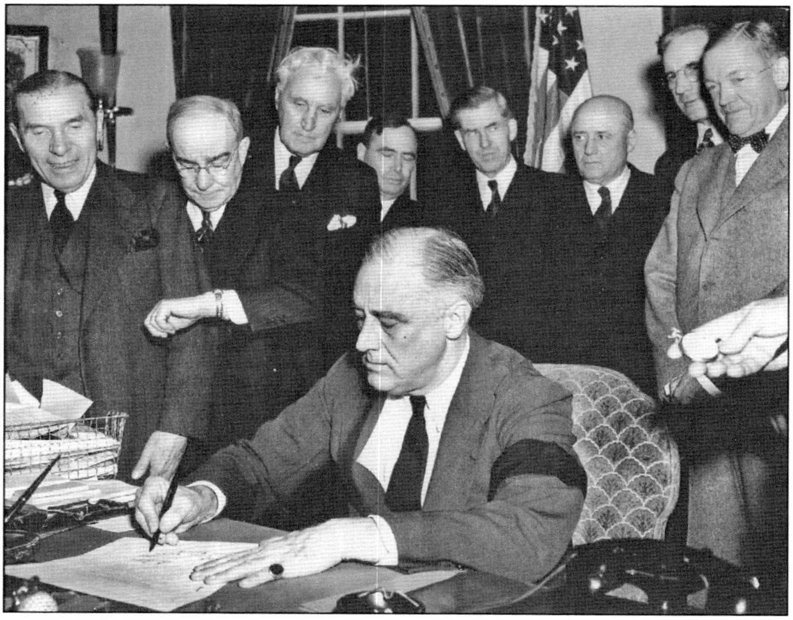

Luther Johnson was born in Corsicana in 1875. He served as county attorney and district attorney before being elected to Congress in 1922. He was the ranking member of the House Foreign Relations Committee during the perilous days of World War II, putting him in prominent roles with world leaders. The photograph above depicts him (second from left) noting the time Pres. Franklin Roosevelt is signing the Declaration of War on December 8, 1941. Pictured from left to right are Solomon Bloom of New York, Johnson, Charles Ecton of New Jersey, Joe Martin of Massachusetts, vice president Henry Wallace, House speaker Sam Rayburn of Texas, John McCormick of Massachusetts, and Charles McNary of Oregon. The black band on FDRs sleeve notes his mourning the recent death of his mother. Johnson also attended a war bond drive with British prime minister Winston Churchill (below). Johnson retired after a 25-year career in Congress. (Both, courtesy of Leonard and Seely Fuller.)

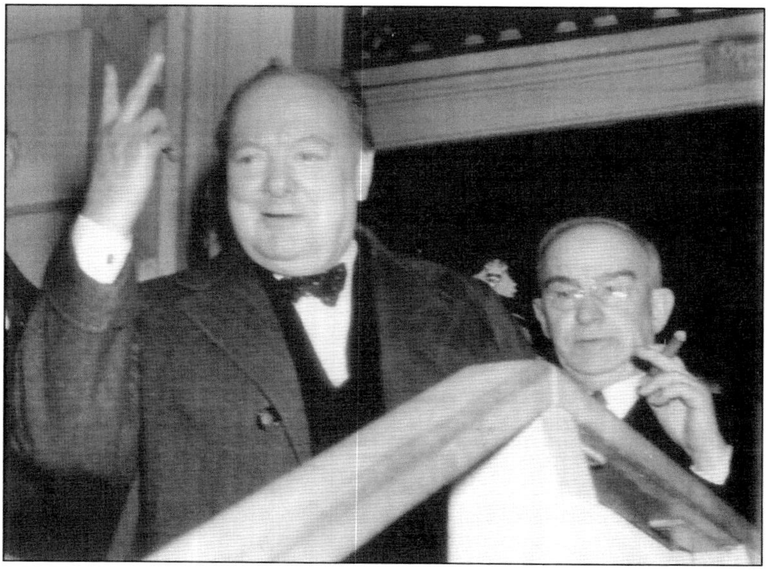

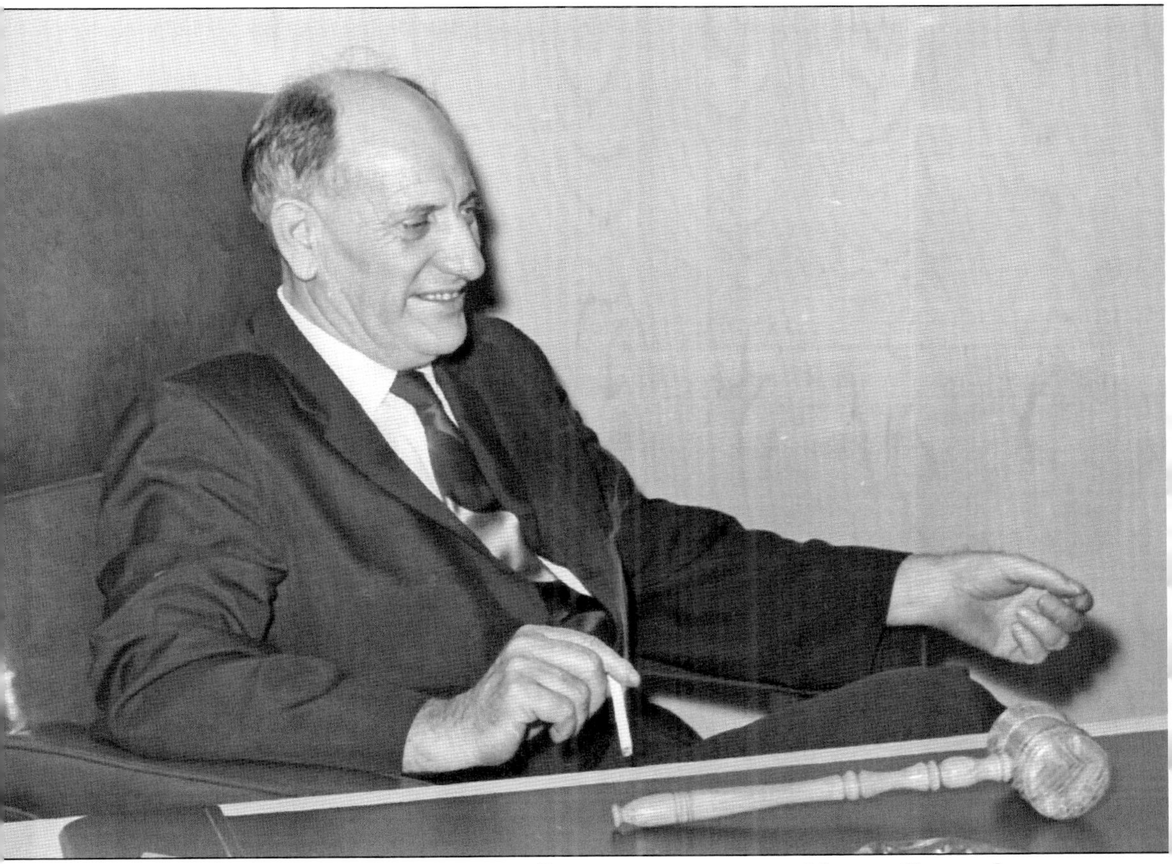

Born in 1912 in Blooming Grove, Texas, a small community in western Navarro County, James Carroll Sewell was working for the Mobil Oil Company in Indiana in 1941. On December 8, 1941, the day after the Japanese attack on Pearl Harbor, Sewell enlisted in the U.S. Navy. While serving on the *USS Hornet* in the Philippine Sea, Sewell lost his eyesight in an explosion onboard ship. Determined to fulfill a lifelong dream of becoming an attorney, Sewell enrolled at the University of Texas to pursue a law degree. While there, he married Janet Hoover, who had been his reader during his time as a law student at the university. He graduated third in his class, passed the bar, and returned to Navarro County to begin his distinguished political and judicial career. A staunch Democrat, Sewell held leadership positions in the party at the state level and developed personal friendships with powerful office holders in Washington. Sewell died in 1976. (Courtesy of Jay Sewell.)

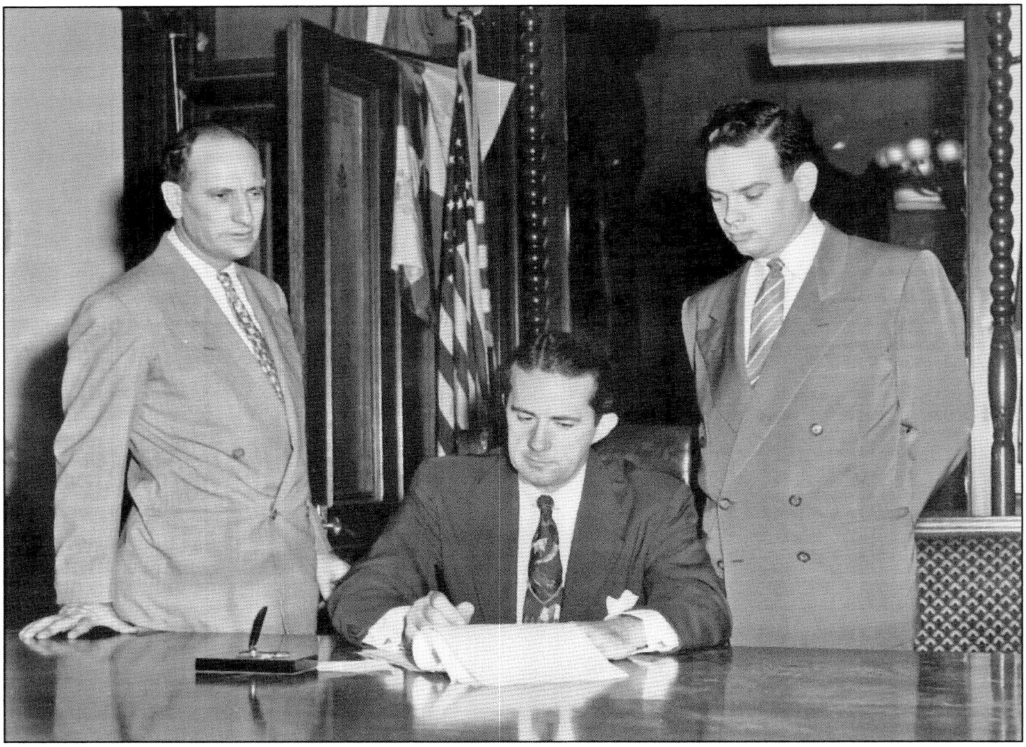

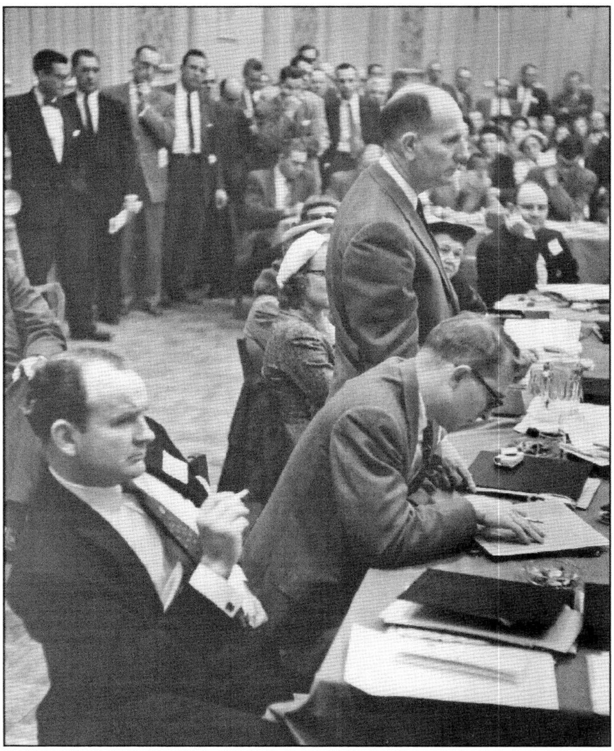

In spite of his blindness, James Sewell enjoyed a highly successful political career. In 1948, he was elected to the Texas Legislature, where he opposed passage of a sales tax and personal income tax. In 1951, he became a Navarro County judge. Five years later, he was elected district judge, a position he held for 16 years. His common greeting to friends was "I'm glad to see you." He is shown above with Gov. Allen Shivers (seated) and fellow legislator George Nokes (right). At left, Sewell is addressing the State Democratic Executive Committee in Austin. (Both, courtesy of Jay Sewell.)

Alexander Beaton, a native of Scotland, came to Texas after serving in the Mexican War. He settled in Corsicana in 1850 and became a law partner of Roger Mills. In 1852, he married Elizabeth McKinney, daughter of Rev. Hampton McKinney. Beaton was instrumental in persuading the H&TC Railroad to direct its route through Corsicana. To acknowledge his many contributions to the community, the City of Corsicana named the main street in the downtown business district in his honor.

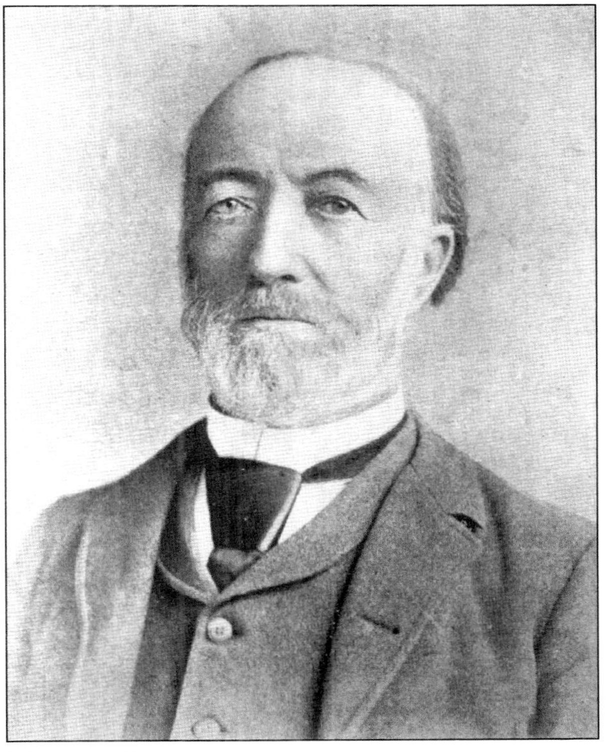

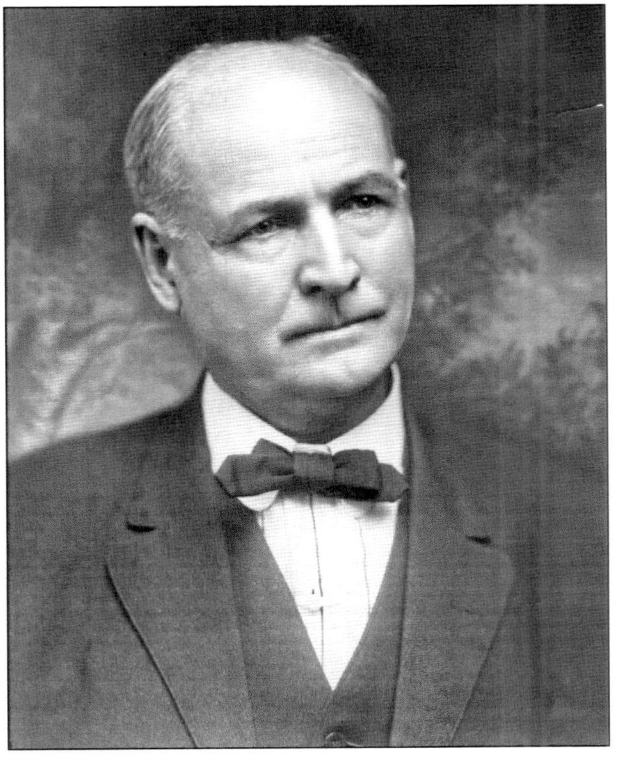

Thirty-year-old Robert Neblett was elected mayor in 1885, making him the youngest chief executive in the city's history. During his administration, he authorized the use of bois d'arc blocks to pave city streets to get downtown out of the mud. He also constructed the first brick school building. Following his term as mayor, Neblett served in the Texas Legislature.

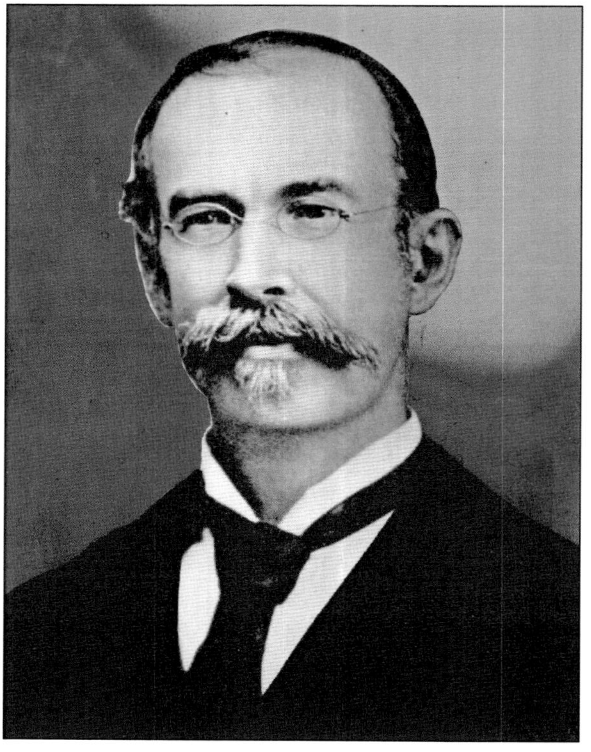

Eldred Simkins was born in South Carolina in 1839. Following his service in the Confederate army during the Civil War, he and his brother William moved to Florida, where they helped organize the Ku Klux Klan in that state. He moved to Corsicana in 1871, where he practiced law and edited a newspaper. He served as district attorney, a Texas legislator, a member of the University of Texas Board of Regents, and associate justice of the state court of criminal appeals. (Published with permission of the Tarlton Law Library, Jamal Center for Legal Research, University of Texas School of Law.)

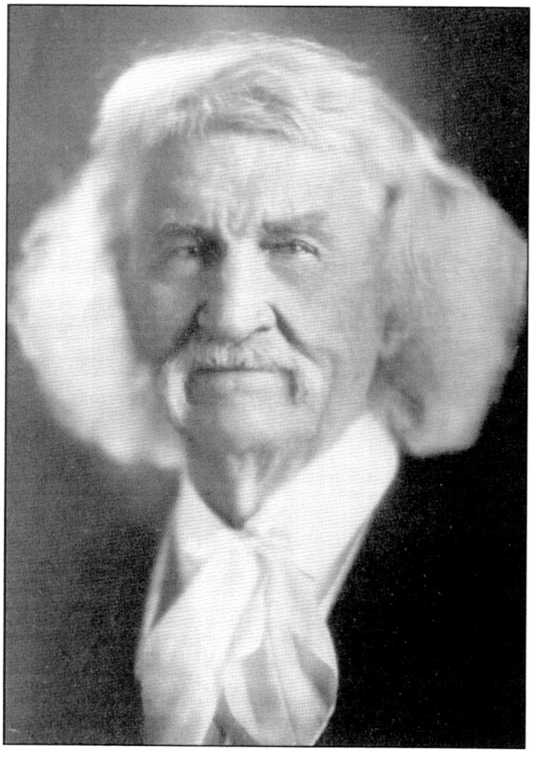

William Simkins was born in South Carolina in 1842. He joined his brother in Corsicana in 1873 to practice law. In 1899, he joined the faculty at the University of Texas Law School, and during his 30-year tenure, Simkins was one of the school's most colorful professors. He had a notable encounter with Carrie Nation, who came to Austin to rid the campus of alcohol and tobacco. (Published with permission of the Tarlton Law Library, Jamail Center for Legal Research, University of Texas School of Law.)

Corsicana's first female mayor, Sue Davis Youngblood (left), was elected to the first of her three terms in 1971 after having previously served three terms on the city council. It was during her administration that the current Corsicana Government Center was completed on North Twelfth Street. She is pictured here with community leader Fannie Mae Vernon.

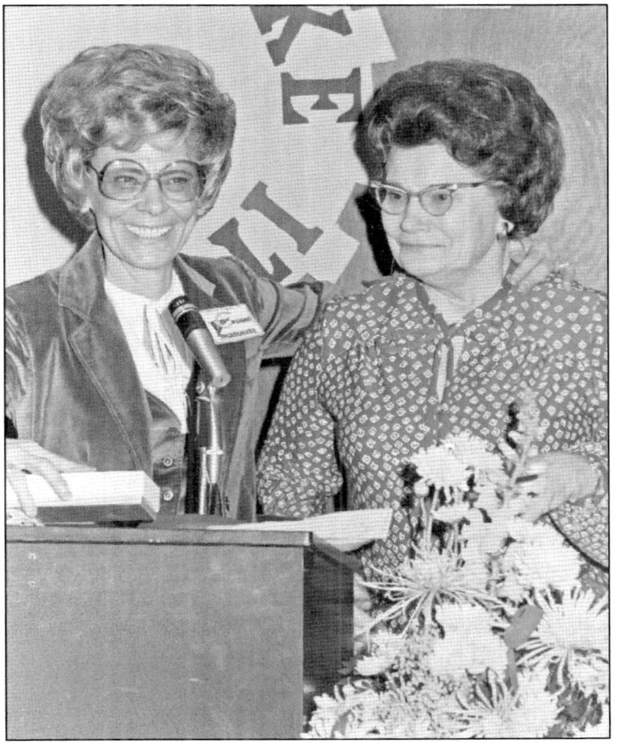

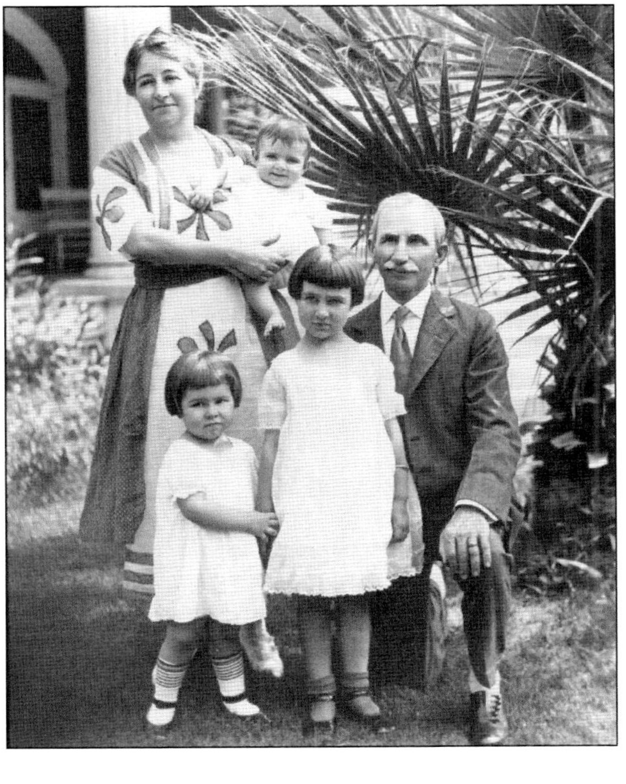

Joshua L. Halbert was born in 1869. He is pictured here with his wife, Ida Jester Halbert, who is holding son Joshusa L. Halbert Jr., along with their daughers Fannie (left) and Liza. He served five consecutive terms as mayor of Corsicana. He was instrumental in bringing the Texas Electric Railway to Corsicana, providing residents with hourly interurban service to Dallas. During his administration, Lake Halbert was constructed southeast of town as a source for city water. He died in 1929. (Courtesy of Helen Albritton.)

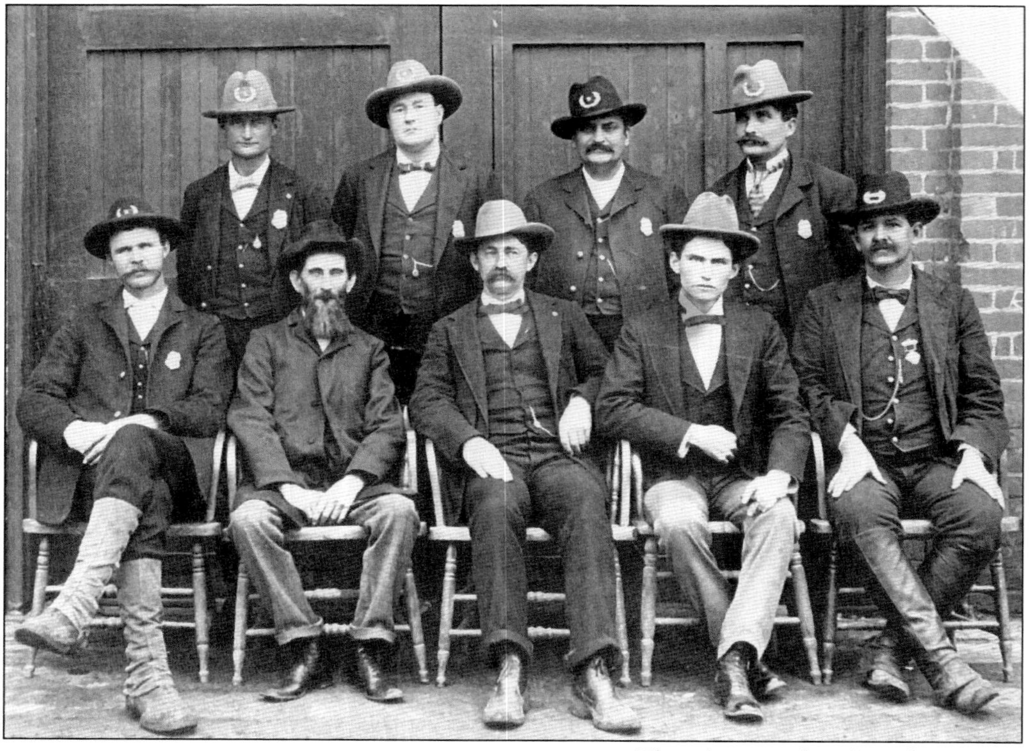

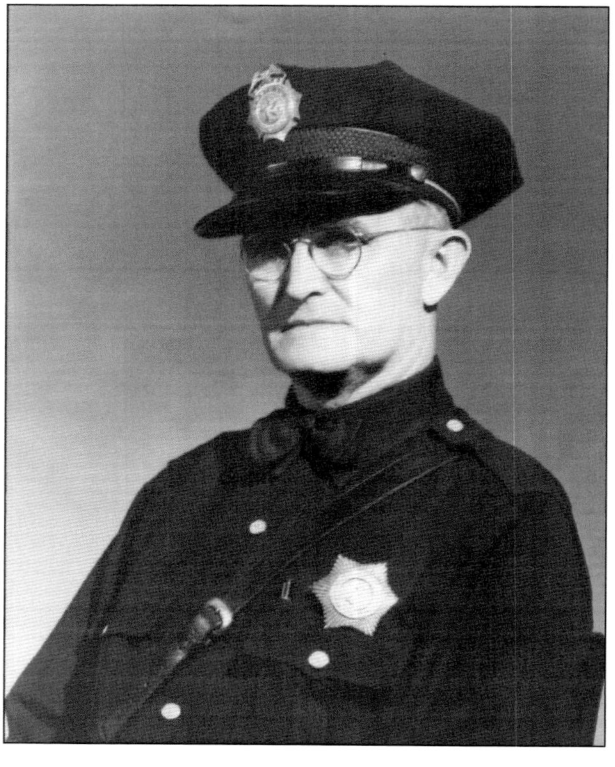

This photograph, taken about 1900, depicts the Corsicana city marshals prominently displaying their badges. From left to right are (first row) two unidentified, Z. R. Christian, city attorney L. J. Gibson, and city marshal L. W. Cole; (second row) Bob Sizemore, unidentified, Jack Parker, and Jim Stewart.

When Claude Patterson received word in 1914 that chief of police Will Knight wanted to see him, he thought it was in regard to paying his $3.50 annual street tax, an assessment required of all local men between the ages of 21 and 45. Instead, the chief offered him a position as a police officer. He received $65 a month and worked an 11-hour shift, seven nights a week. Patterson remained on the police force until 1957, a career that spanned 43 years.

Benjamin Franklin Carroll came to Texas from Mississippi, where he had served in the state legislature. He and his wife, Huldah, had 12 children. They settled in Navarro County in 1852, and five years later, he was elected to the Texas Legislature. The suits he wore while serving in the Texas House of Representatives were handmade by his wife. Carroll died in 1869. (Courtesy of Jay Sewell.)

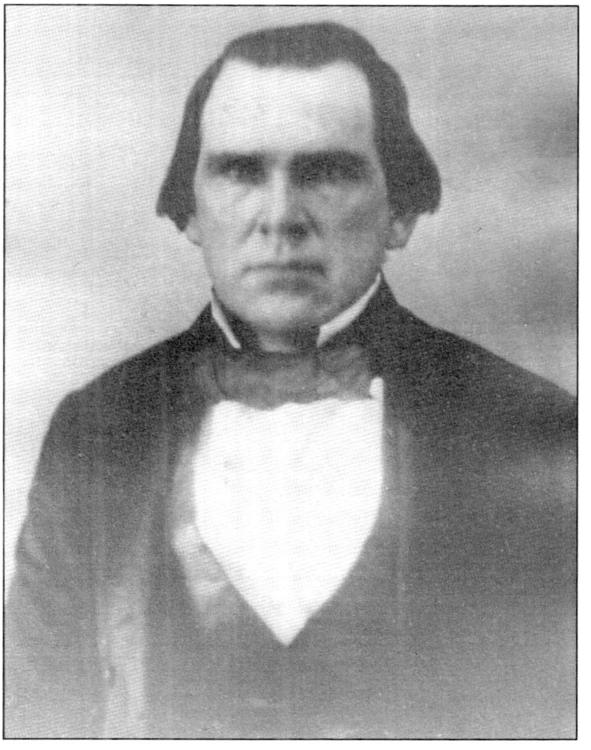

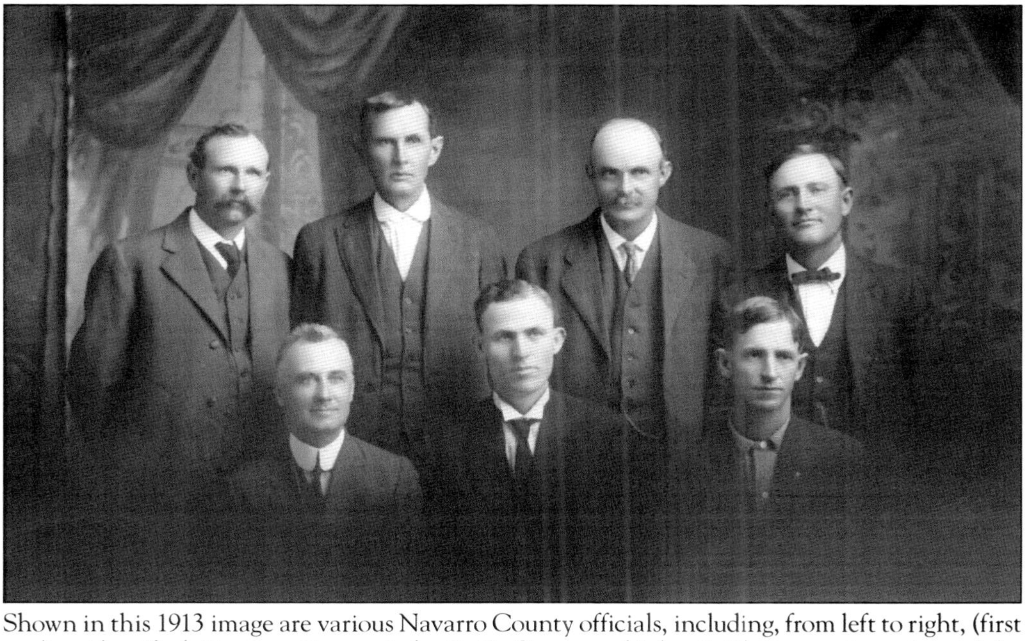

Shown in this 1913 image are various Navarro County officials, including, from left to right, (first row) unidentified, Navarro County judge R. R. Owen, and John B. Blair, superintendent of the Navarro County farm; (second row) Navarro County commissioners Tom Worthington, J. R. Slay, W. L. Medaris, and W. B. Payne. The county farm, established to house paupers and convicts, consisted of 976 acres and was located near Petty's Chapel. It operated from 1884 until 1944.

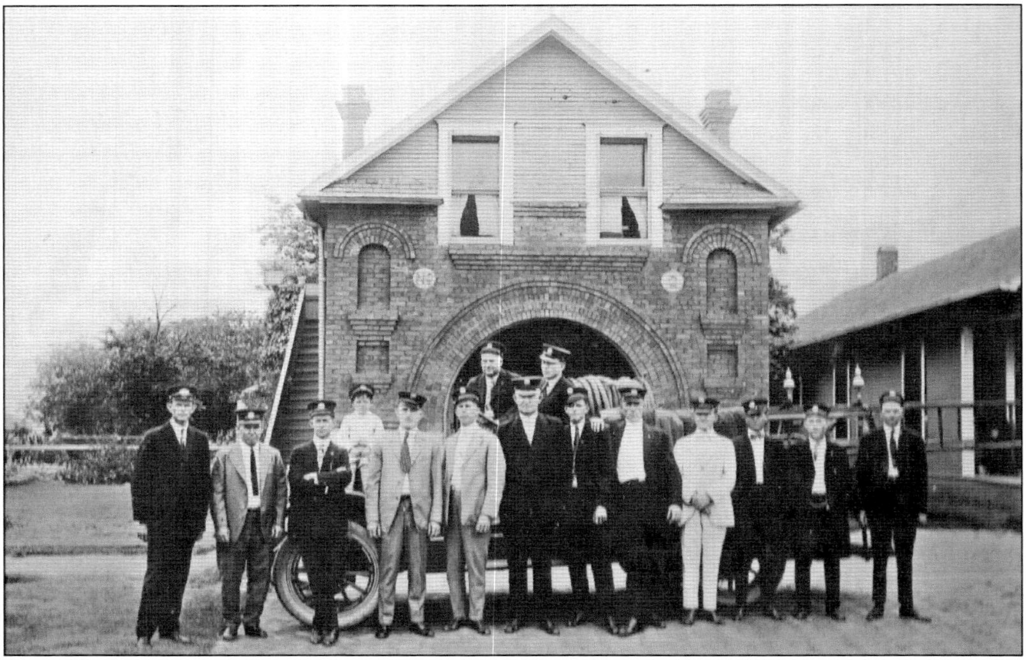

The Corsicana Volunteer Fire Department was organized in 1879 and functioned until 1924, when a paid department was established. In 1892, Frank Neal Drane served as chief and significantly upgraded the department with new equipment, an alarm bell, and additional water sources. This photograph depicts Station No. 2 at 1011 West Fifth Avenue. It was built in 1902 and was used until 1926.

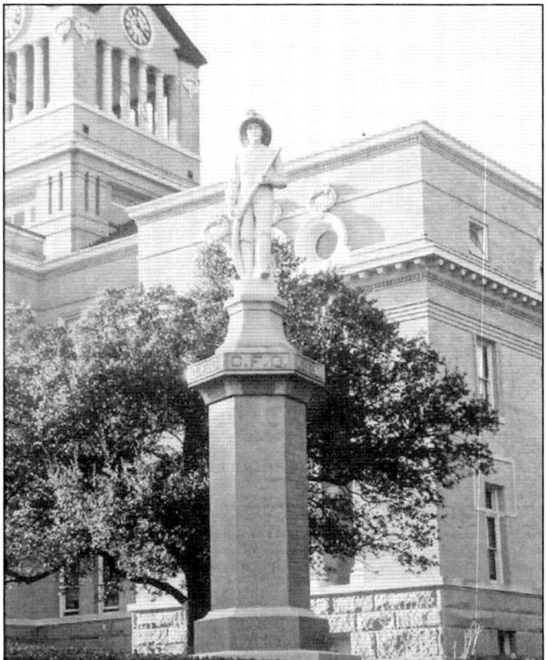

Corsicana experienced several major fires during its early years. In 1855, an arsonist burned the courthouse, hoping to destroy indictment records. To acknowledge the contributions of men who served as volunteer firefighters, a white marble monument was erected on the courthouse lawn in 1917 with the inscription CFD and the names of those who had served in various capacities over the years.

Shown here are two prominent Navarro County political figures, Judge James Sewell (left) and Sheriff Rufus Pevehouse. Beginning as a deputy sheriff in 1921, Pevehouse had two tenures as the county's chief law enforcement officer, first from 1928 to 1938 and again from 1950 to 1973, for a total of 32 years. He served as a U.S. marshal from 1939 to 1949.

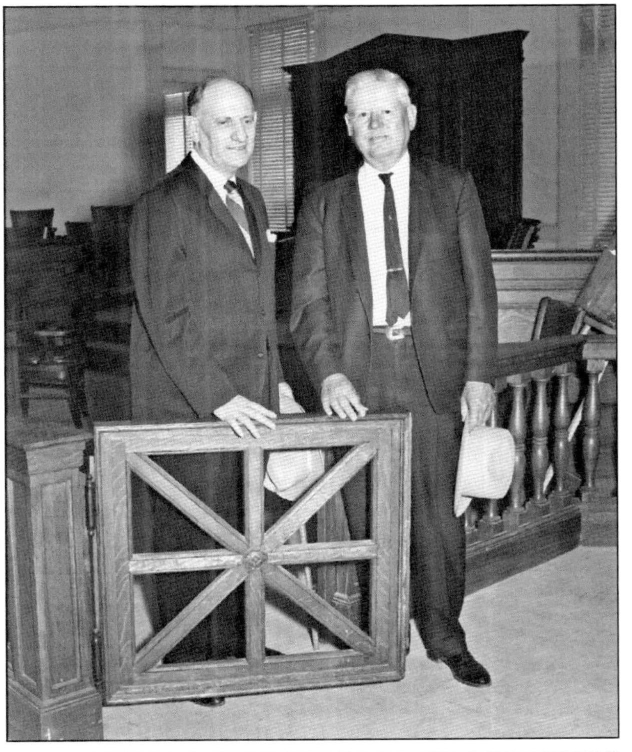

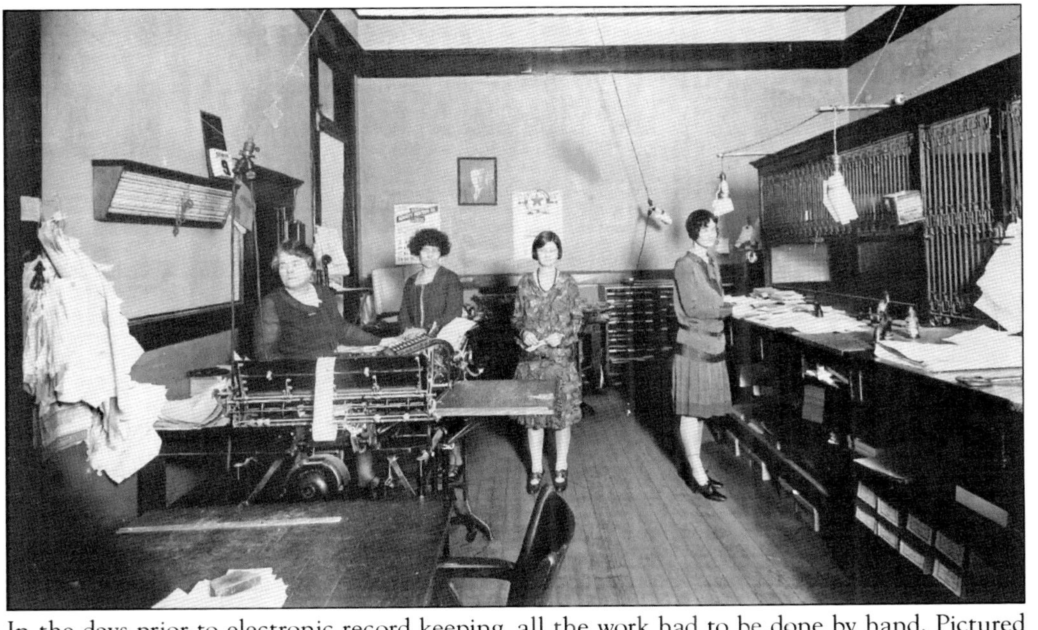

In the days prior to electronic record keeping, all the work had to be done by hand. Pictured here in the late 1920s, the staff in the office of the Navarro County tax office performs its daily duties. Pictured from left to right are Katie Woods, Minnie Green, Ethel Still, and Lottie Beth Blake. As county tax assessor and collector, Katie Wood was among the first females elected to county-wide office.

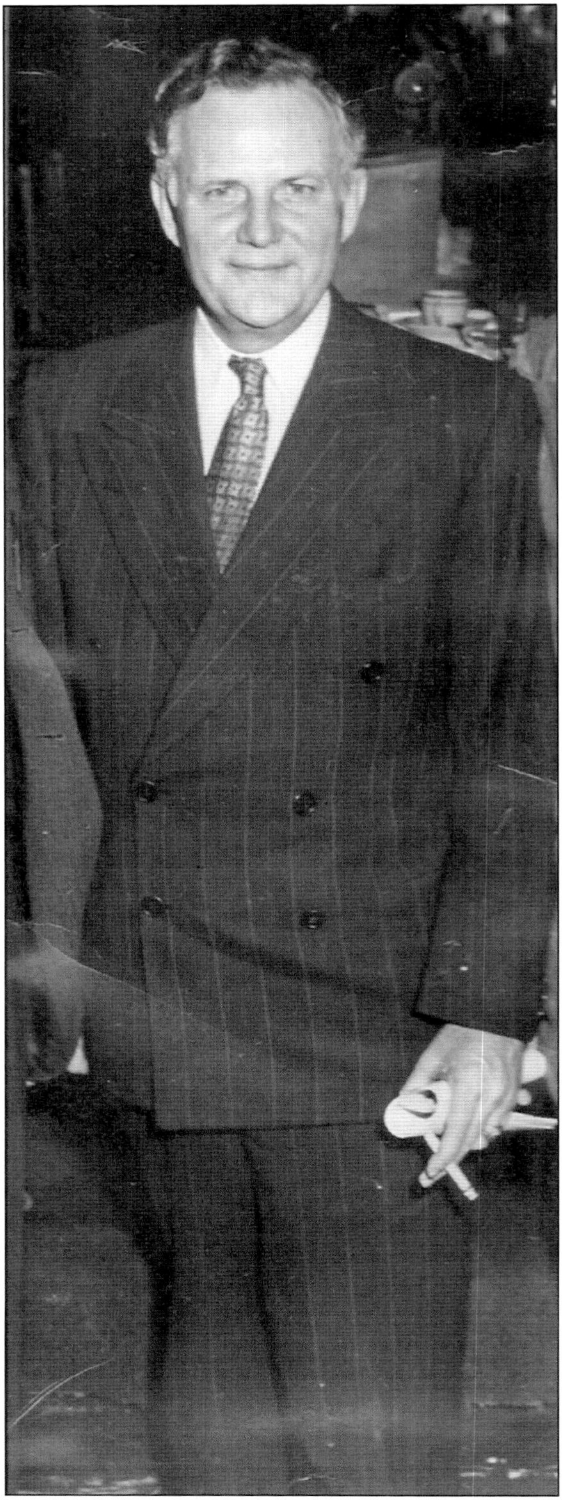

Beauford Jester was born in Corsicana in 1893. His father, George T. Jester, had served in the Texas Legislature and had been the state's lieutenant governor in the 1890s. After graduating from the University of Texas, Jester served in World War I, reaching the rank of captain. Following the war, he earned a law degree and returned to Corsicana to establish a private law practice, which primarily involved representing the oil industry. From 1929 to 1935, Jester served on the board of regents of his alma mater, the University of Texas, chairing the board during the last two years of his tenure. Several significant additions to the campus came during his term on the board, including construction of the tower on the administration building. The Jester Center, constructed on the University of Texas campus in 1968, is named in his honor. From 1942 to 1947, he served on the Texas Railroad Commission, which regulates the state's oil and gas industry. He defeated former University of Texas president Homer Rainey in the 1946 governor's race.

Gov. Beauford Jester is shown here reviewing a speech to be delivered to the Texas Legislature in 1949. A moderate Democrat, Jester's administration promoted significant reforms for public education with the Gilmer-Aiken Act and higher teacher salaries. Easily elected to a second term, Jester died on July 11, 1949, making him the only Texas governor to die in office.

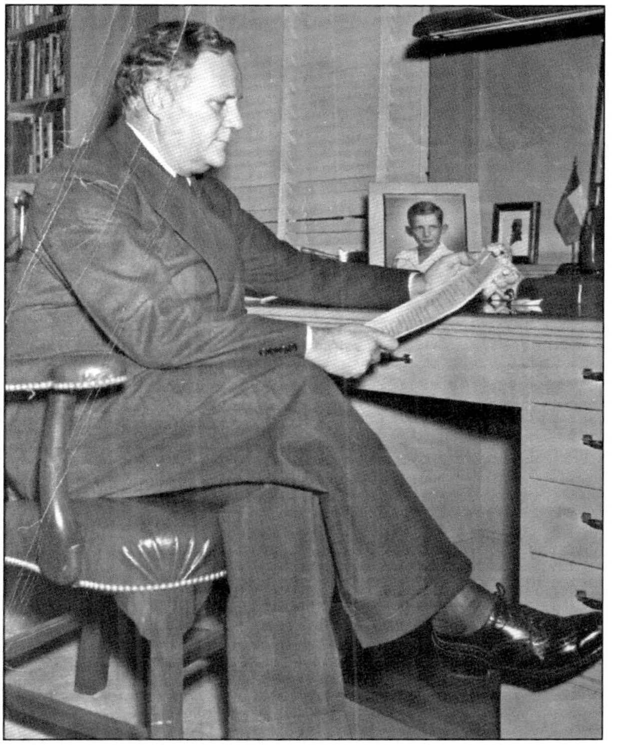

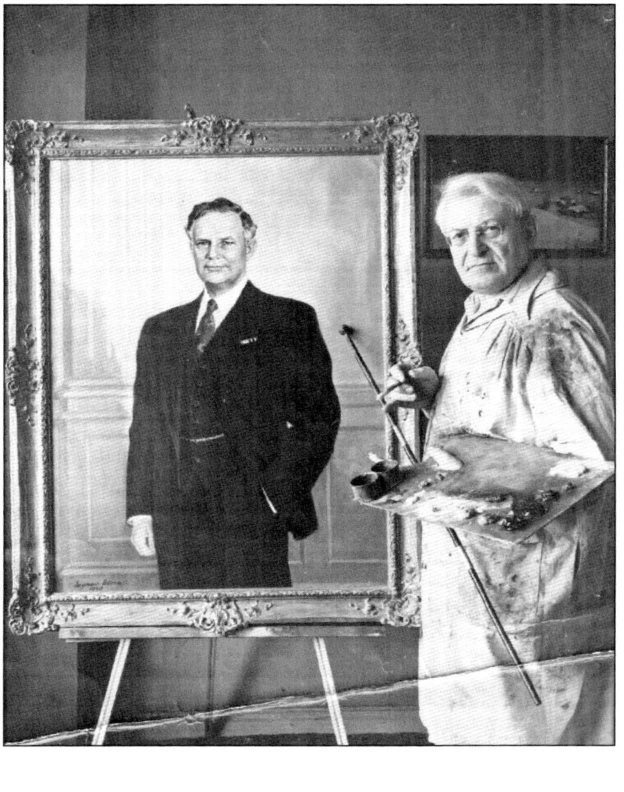

Polish-born artist Seymour Stone (1877–1957) puts the final touches on the official portrait of Gov. Beauford Jester in 1948 at the beginning of Jester's second term as the state's chief executive. The official portrait hangs in the state capitol in Austin along with the portraits of all the other governors who have served the state.

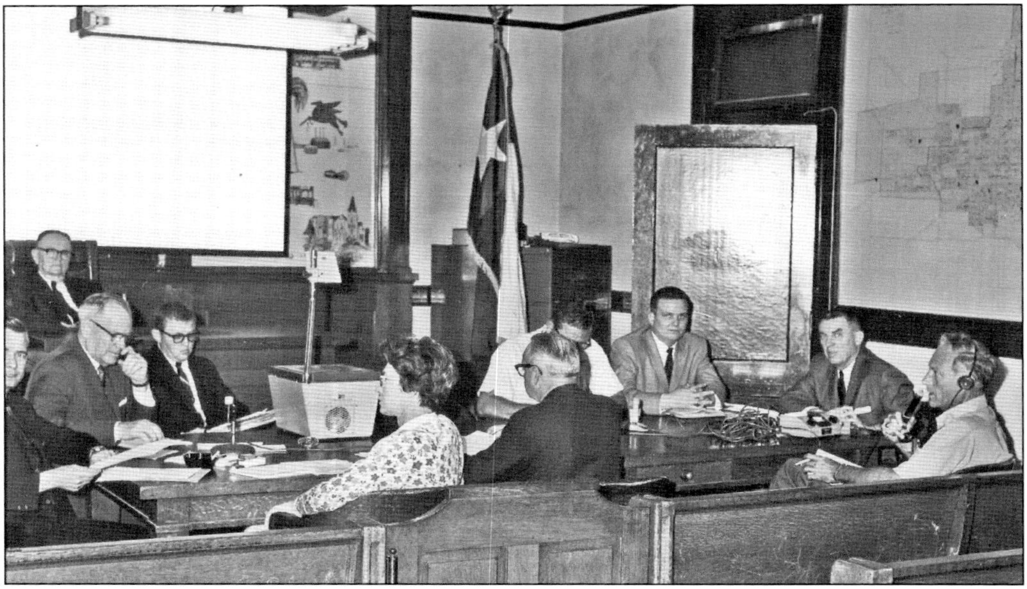

This 1963 photograph depicts the Corsicana City Council in session at the city hall on Main Street. Pictured from left to right are mayor Dr. David Campbell; city manager Rollin Snethem; city attorney Don Pevehouse; city secretary Alton Justiss; commissioners Claude Lane, Herb Johnson, and H. R. Stroube Jr.; *Corsicana Daily Sun* reporter Betty Clay; and Perry Taylor of KAND Radio. Seated on the back is commissioner Fred Prince. (Courtesy of Richard Parker.)

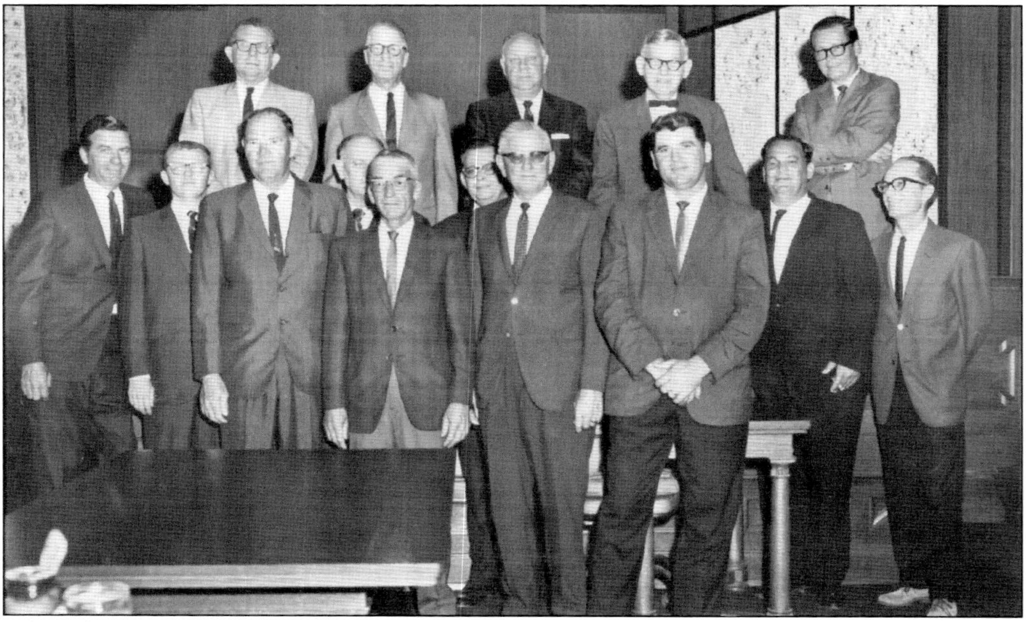

When the new county officials were sworn in on January 1, 1969, in the county courtroom, several local attorneys were present for the ceremony. Pictured from left to right are (first row) Kenneth "Buck" Douglas, Don Pevehouse, Joe Lawrence, James Sewell, Arlon Simmons, Robert Gladney, Homer McNabb, Billy Hargrove, Johnny Chirafis, and Jimmy Morris; (second row) David Ralston, Leighton Dawson, Jerry Roe, Julius Jacobs, and Bill McKie. (Courtesy of Jay Sewell.)

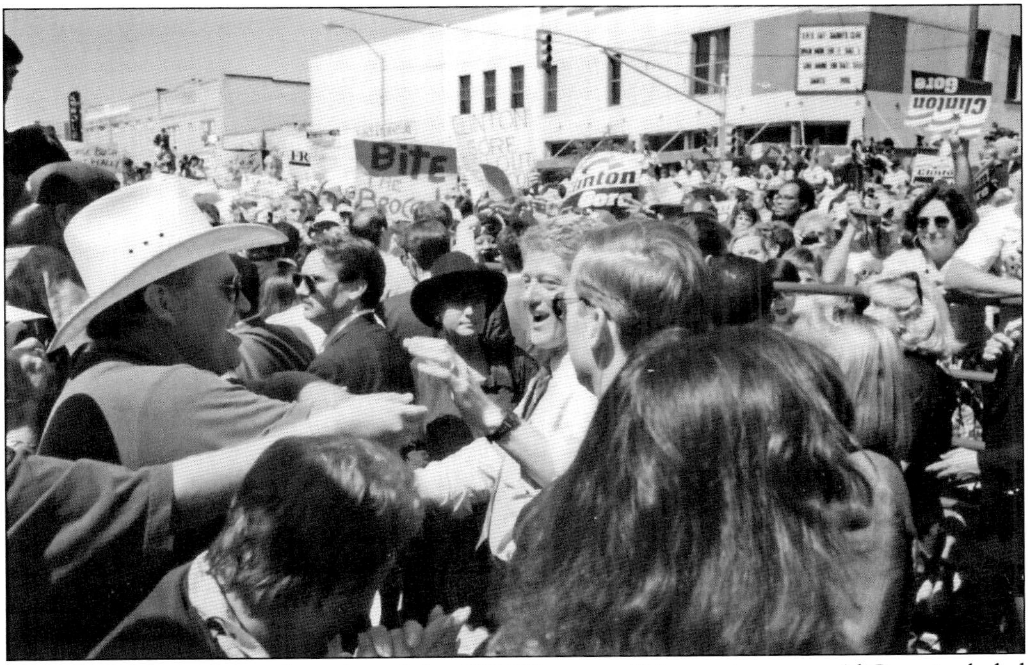

In 1992, Democratic presidential candidate Bill Clinton and his running mate, Al Gore, included Corsicana on their campaign tour through Texas. As seen in the photograph above, downtown was packed with spectators eager to see the future chief executive. Below, Eddie Pevehouse (left) and Wyvonne Putman (second from left) of the Navarro County Historical Society presented copies of Navarro County history books to Hillary Clinton (third from left) and Tipper Gore (right) during their husbands' political rally in downtown Corsicana (below). (Both, courtesy of Ines Wagoner.)

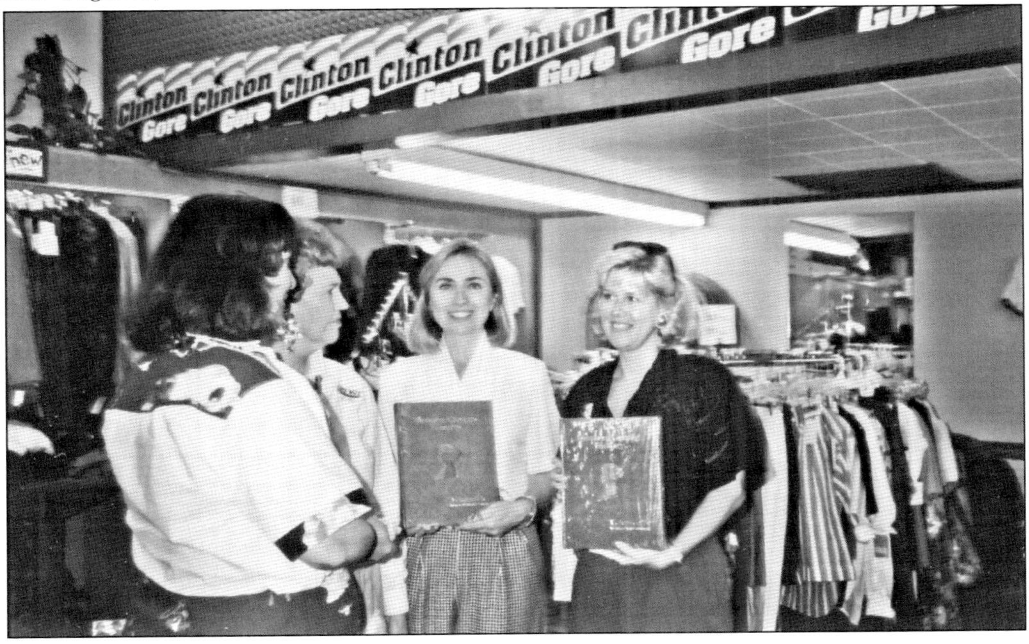

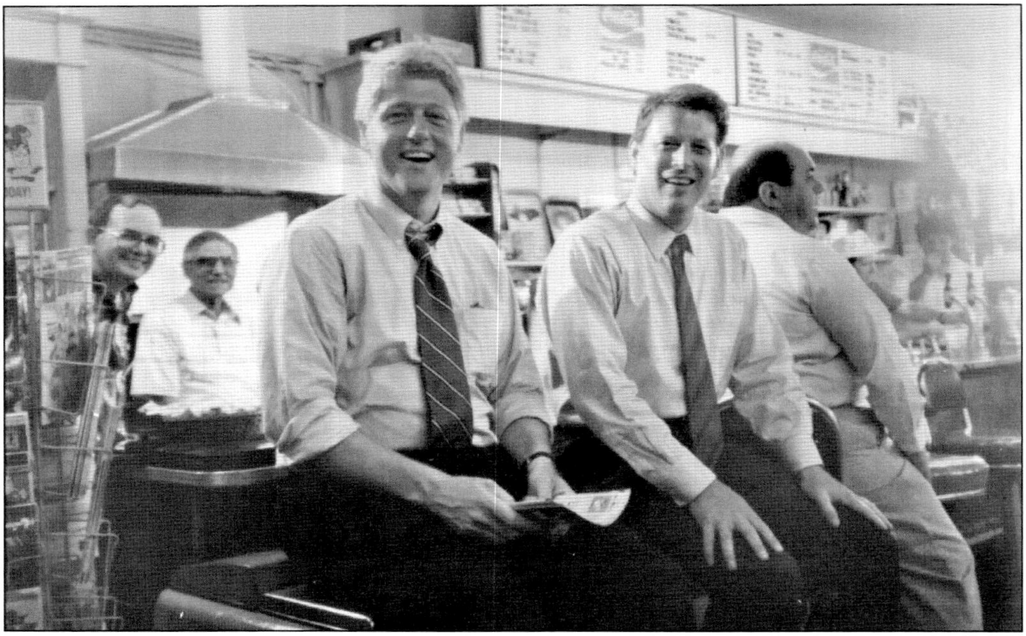

Candidates Bill Clinton (left) and Al Gore are shown seated at the soda fountain at one of Coriscana's most historic businesses, Hashop's Drugstore at 125 North Beaton Street. Hashop's has been a popular spot for coffee breaks, breakfast, and lunch for downtown shoppers and merchants for decades. Others in the photograph are congressman Martin Frost (far left), owner Joe Hashop (second from left), and Bobby Ross, grandson of the business founder Louis Hashop (far right). (Courtesy of Jordan Hollingsworth.)

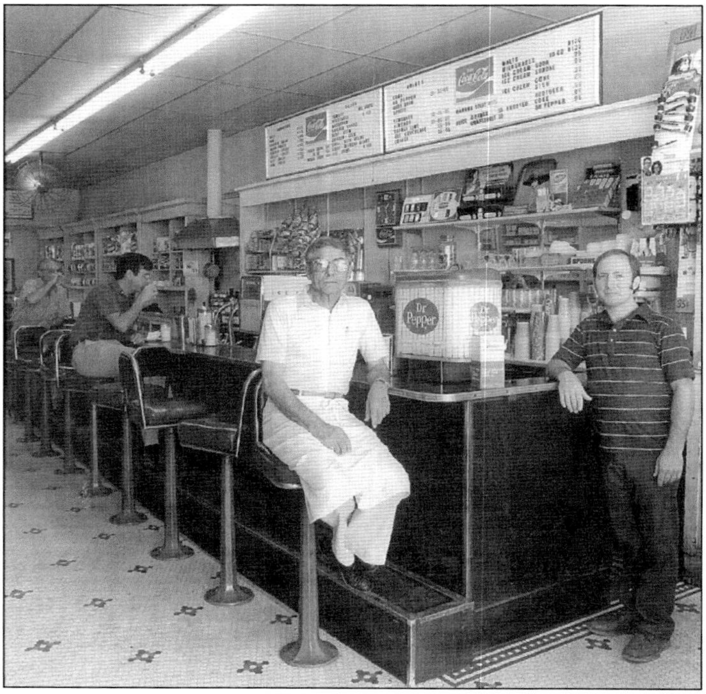

Founder Louis Hashop immigrated to the United States from his native Lebanon as a stowaway on a ship. After landing in Galveston, he made his way to Corsicana, where, in 1905, he founded a business that specialized in candies and ice cream. His son Joe (seated, wearing apron) acquired the business after his father's death in 1968 and sold it to Dee Hawkinson (standing, right) in 1989. It is currently owned by Caleb Hollingsworth and operates as Caleb's Diner. (Courtesy of Jordan Hollingsworth.)

Two

Fruitcakes, Chili, and Oil

Corsicana's Businesses and Industries

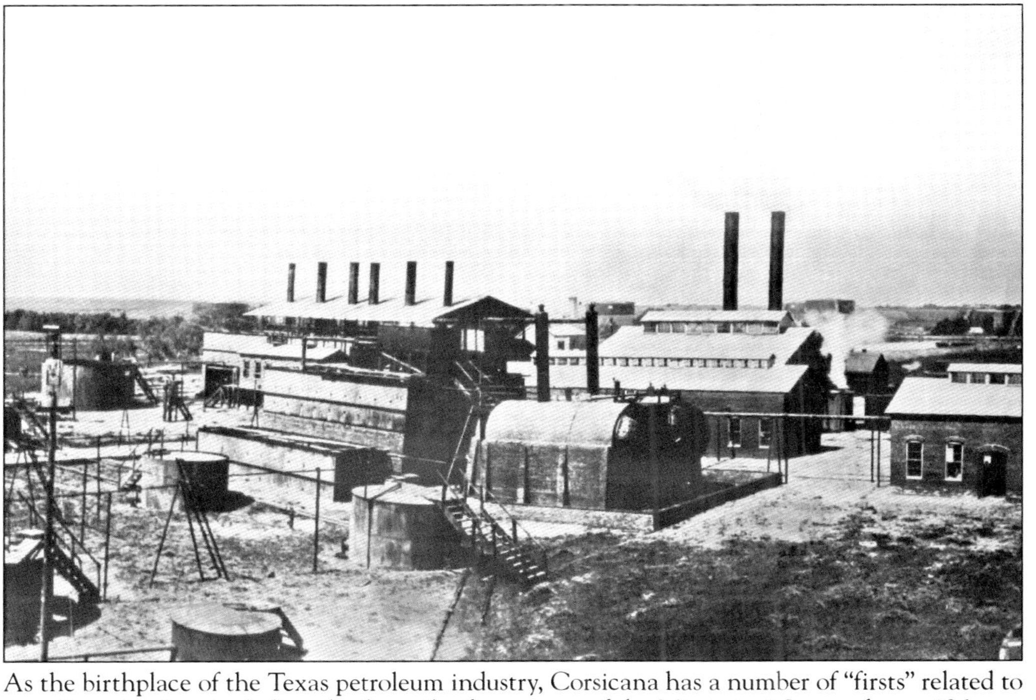

As the birthplace of the Texas petroleum industry, Corsicana has a number of "firsts" related to the oil production, including the first oil refinery west of the Mississippi. Located on a 136-acre site southeast of town and easily accessible to both the Cotton Belt and H&TC rail lines, Joseph Cullinan's refinery began operations on January 1, 1899.

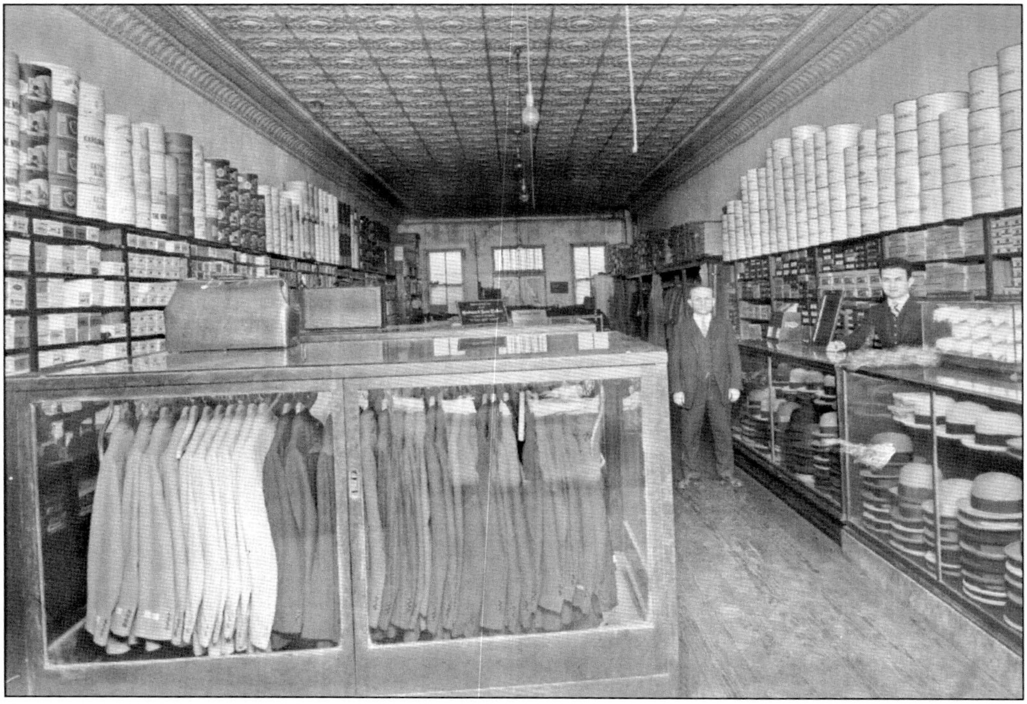

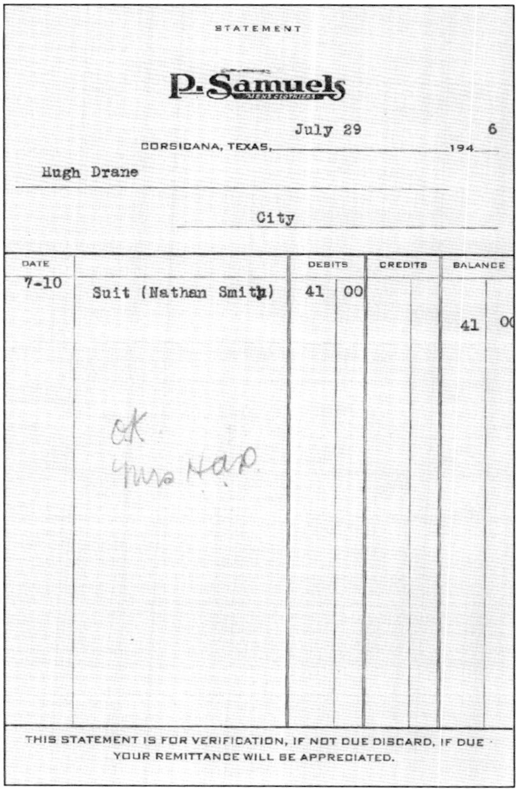

STATEMENT

P. Samuels
MEN'S CLOTHIERS

CORSICANA, TEXAS, July 29 1946

Hugh Drane

City

DATE		DEBITS	CREDITS	BALANCE
7-10	Suit (Nathan Smith)	41 00		
				41 00

THIS STATEMENT IS FOR VERIFICATION, IF NOT DUE DISCARD, IF DUE YOUR REMITTANCE WILL BE APPRECIATED.

Philip Samuels left his native Poland as a teenager, arriving at Ellis Island. He put his meager savings on the railroad agent's ticket counter, stating he wanted to go as far west as his money would take it him. His destination proved to be Corsicana, Texas, where he eventually opened a men's clothing store, P. Samuels, which operated at 213 North Beaton Street. Pictured above are Philip Samuels (left) and his son Aaron. The 1946 receipt (shown at left) was for Hugh Drane for the purchase of a suit for $41 from P. Samuels. (Above, courtesy of Babette Samuels; left, courtesy of Jon Ketcham.)

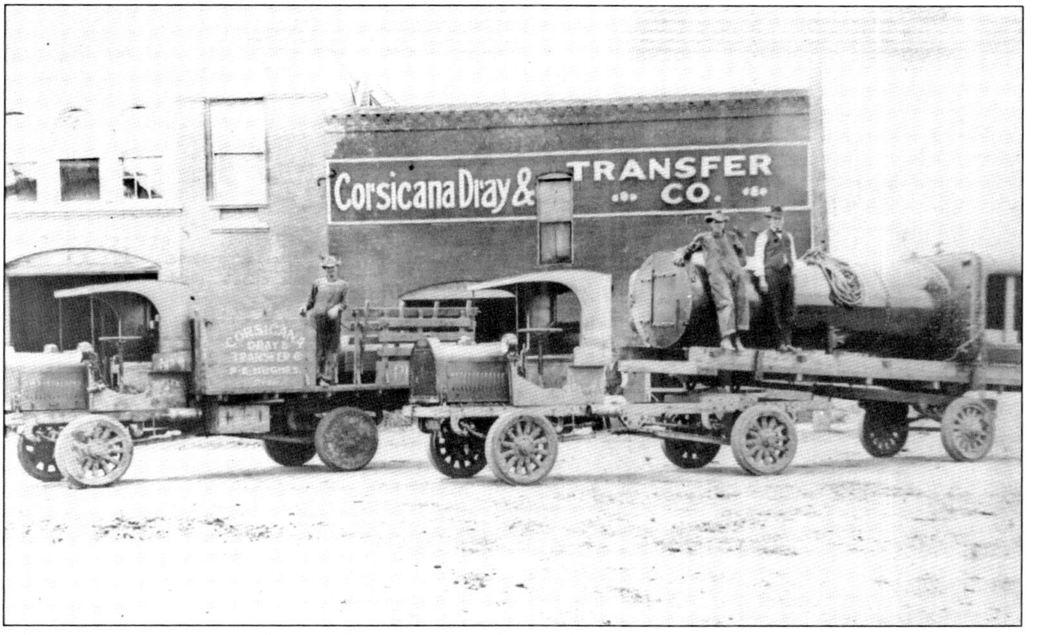

The Corsicana Dray and Transfer Company, located at the southeast corner of Sixth Avenue and Tenth Street, advertised services for heavy hauling, piano moving, fast delivery, and fine moving wagons guaranteeing the best service. In addition to packing and storing furniture, the company also dealt in wood and coal.

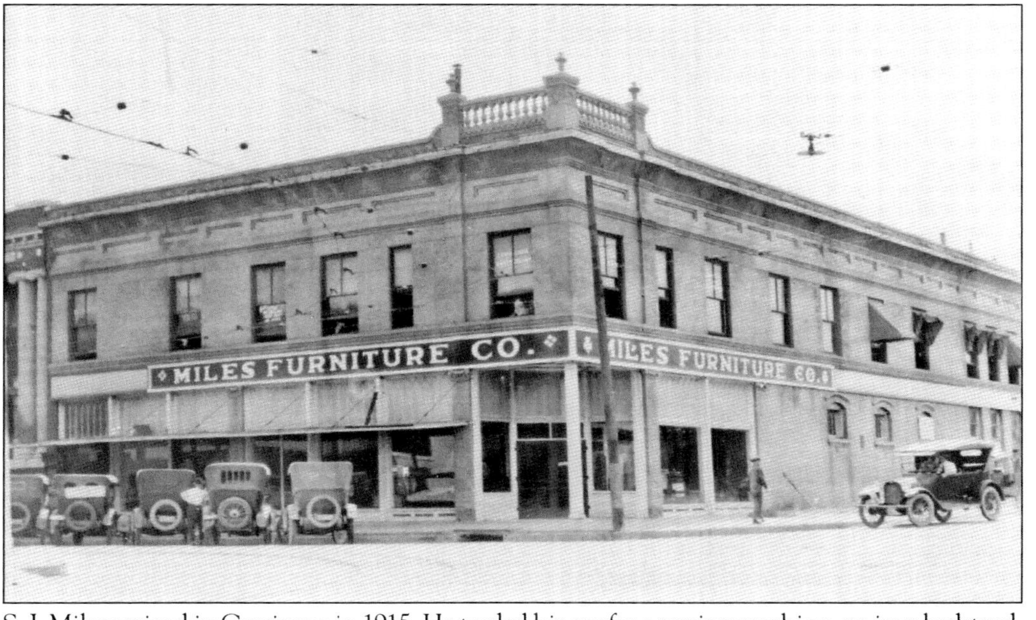

S. J. Miles arrived in Corsicana in 1915. He traded his car for a sewing machine, an iron bedstead, and cash, with which he opened a furniture store. His business was solidified when he sold cots to boardinghouse operators during the oil boom of the 1920s. Following his death in 1952, family members continued to operate the business, which is located at 300 North Beaton Street. (Courtesy of Nancy Weems.)

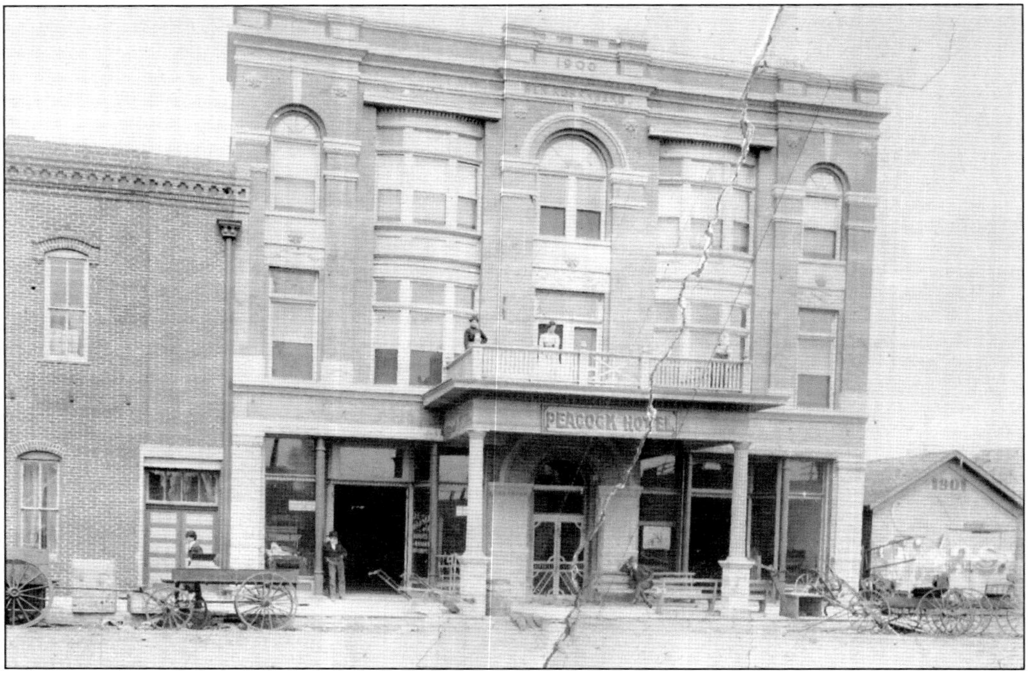

Located at 300 South Beaton Street, the Peacock Hotel was owned and operated by William J. Peacock, who was active in the Masonic lodge. According to advertisements in the *Corsicana City Directory*, guests at the Peacock could expect excellent accommodations for $1 to $1.25 per day.

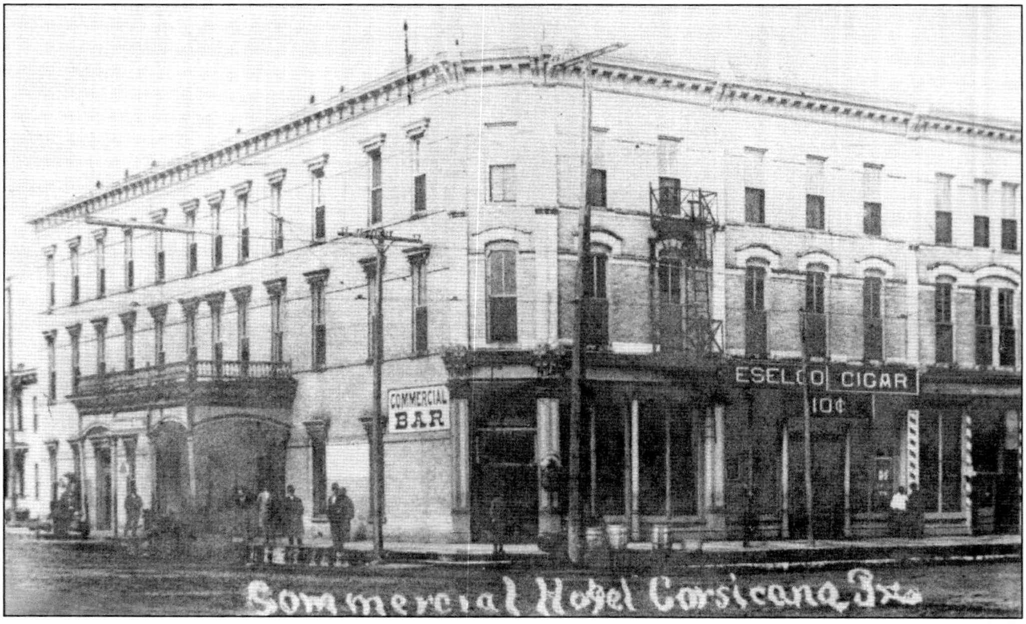

Claiming to be Corsicana's first hotel, the Commercial Hotel, located at 100 West Seventh Avenue, boasted of large, cool comfortable rooms with special accommodations for commercial men. The location was ideal, only one block from the railroad depot, with "a table unsurpassed by any hotel in the city." Rates for the rooms were $2 per day.

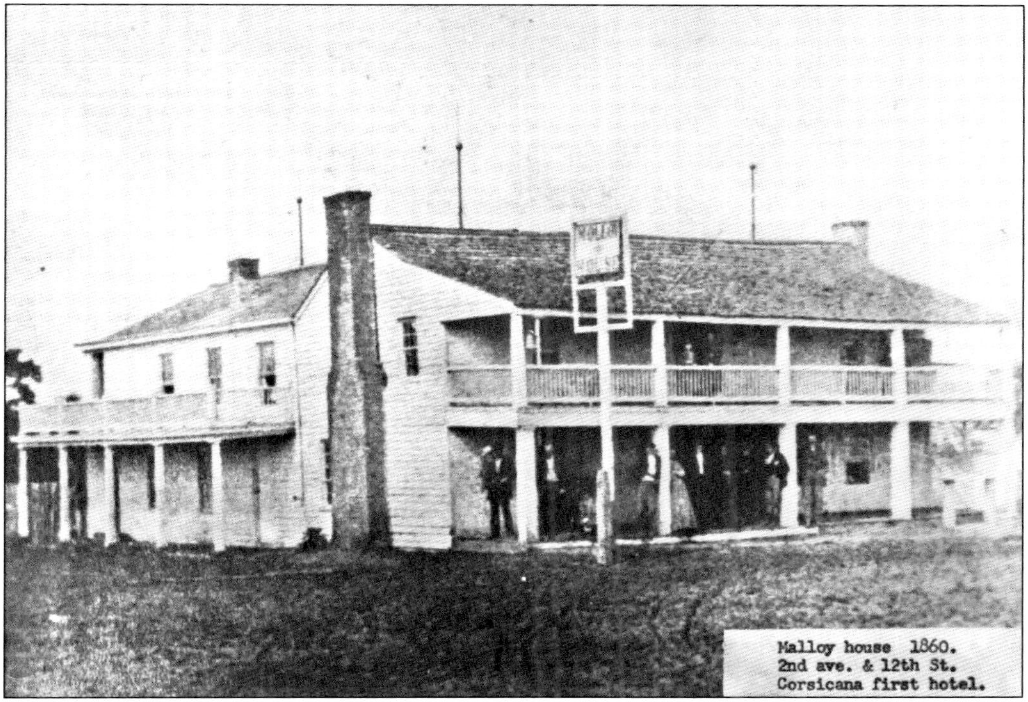

Corsicana attorney Henry Molloy opened a one-story hotel at 111 East Collin Street in 1860 and added a second floor seven years later. It passed through several owners over the years, including one-time lieutenant governor George Jester. Claims persist that the hotel is haunted by the ghost of a woman who was murdered there. It is currently occupied by Napoli's Restaurant.

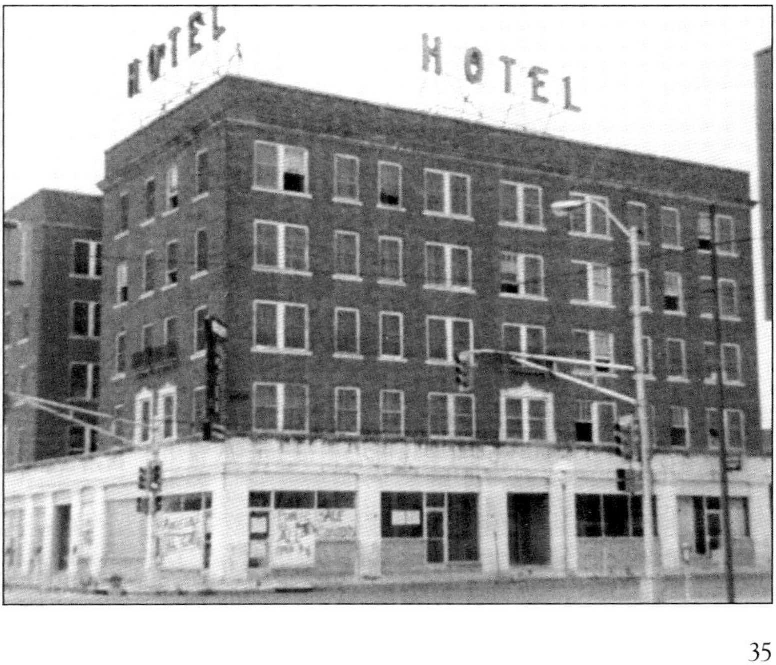

The Navarro Hotel, located at 200 West Fifth Avenue, offered 100 fireproof rooms to guests. Patrons could purchase cigars from the stand operated in the lobby by R. B. Johnson, and ladies could take advantage of all styles of hair bobbing in the beauty shop. The coffee shop was a popular gathering place for local businessmen. The building was demolished in 1980. (Courtesy of Nancy Weems.)

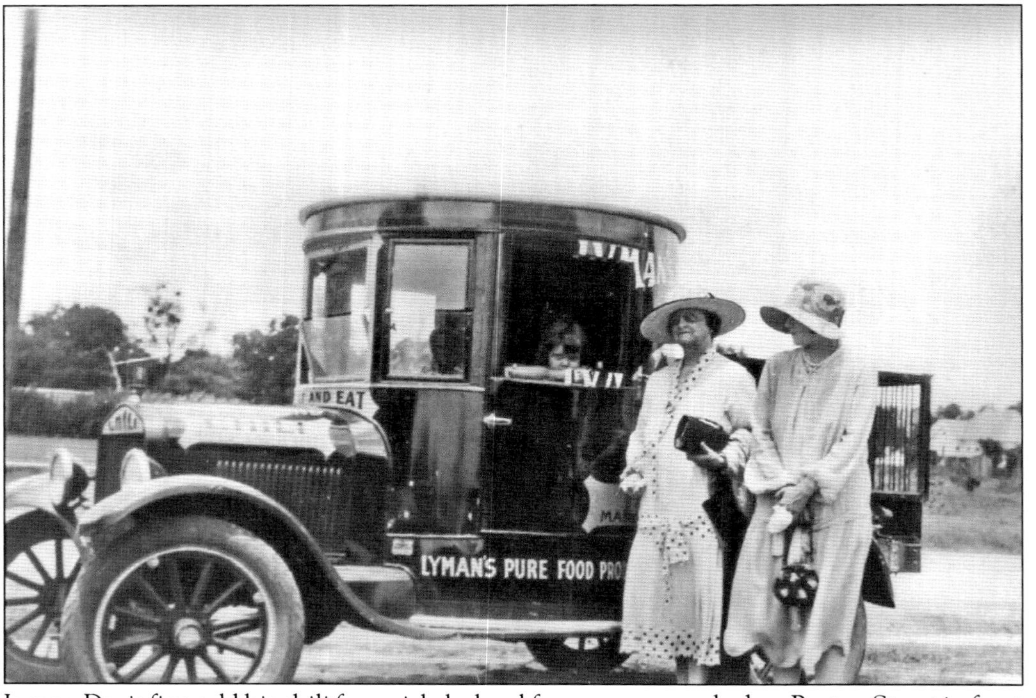

Lyman Davis first sold his chili for a nickel a bowl from a wagon parked on Beaton Street in front of the Blue Corner Saloon in 1895. He later canned it and sold it under the brand name of Wolf Brand Chili, named for his pet wolf, Kaiser Bill. Salesmen drove specially designed trucks in the shape of a can, as pictured here, as a marketing gimmick. (Courtesy of Al Hopkins.)

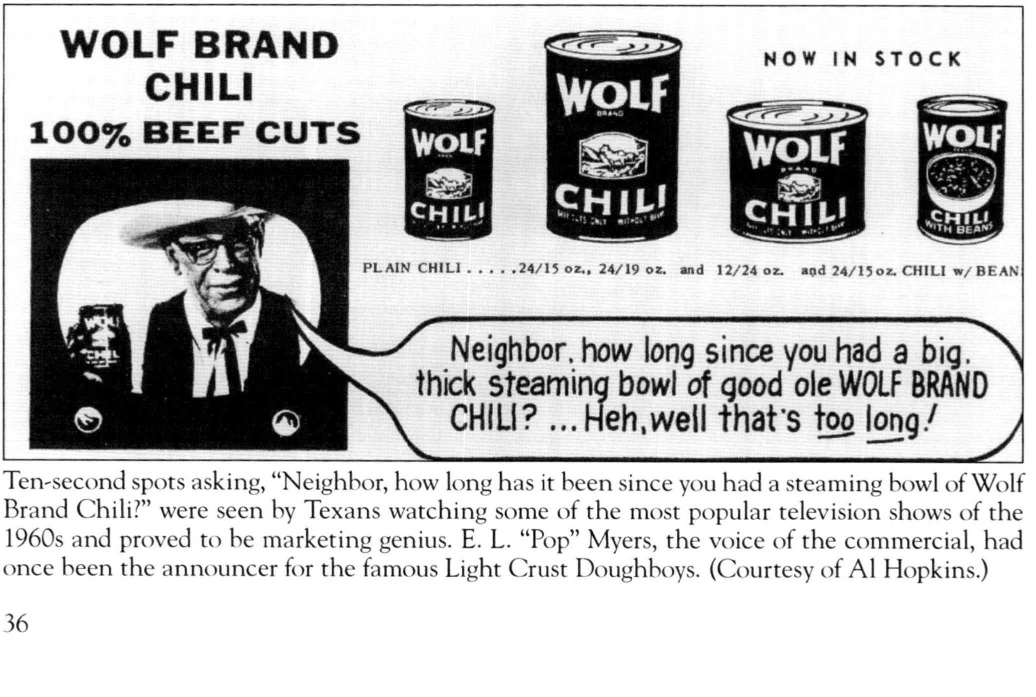

Ten-second spots asking, "Neighbor, how long has it been since you had a steaming bowl of Wolf Brand Chili?" were seen by Texans watching some of the most popular television shows of the 1960s and proved to be marketing genius. E. L. "Pop" Myers, the voice of the commercial, had once been the announcer for the famous Light Crust Doughboys. (Courtesy of Al Hopkins.)

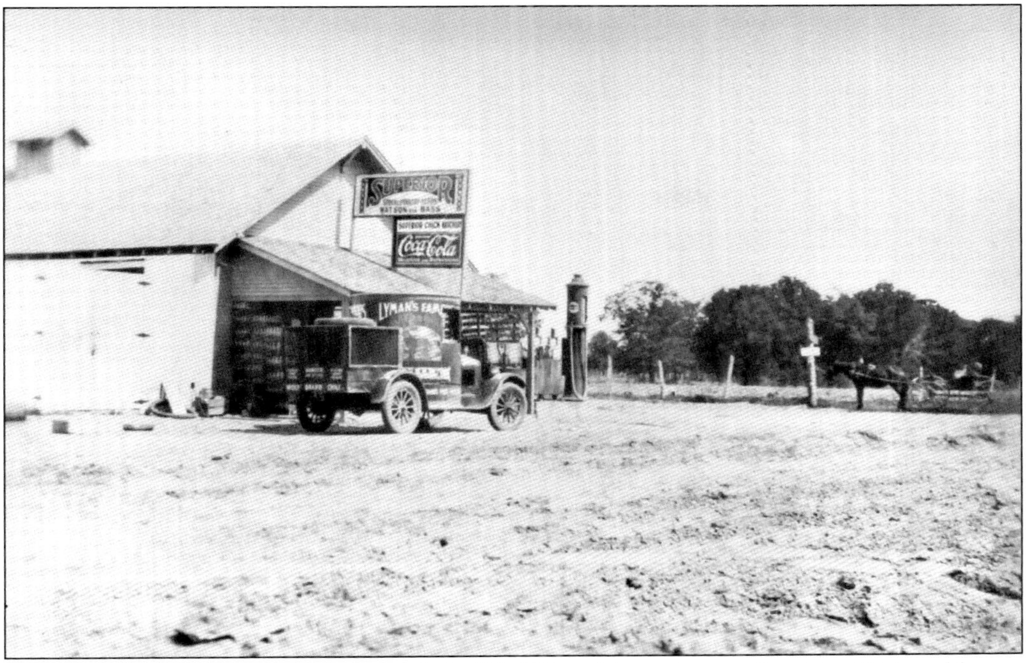

J. C. West and Fred Slauson purchased the Wolf Brand from Lyman Davis in 1924 and began to expand their market beyond the confines of Corsicana. No market was too small. In the photograph above, a Wolf Brand salesman calls on a small country store in rural Navarro County, while the image below depicts a Wolf Brand truck parked outside a supermarket in downtown Dallas. (Both, courtesy of Al Hopkins.)

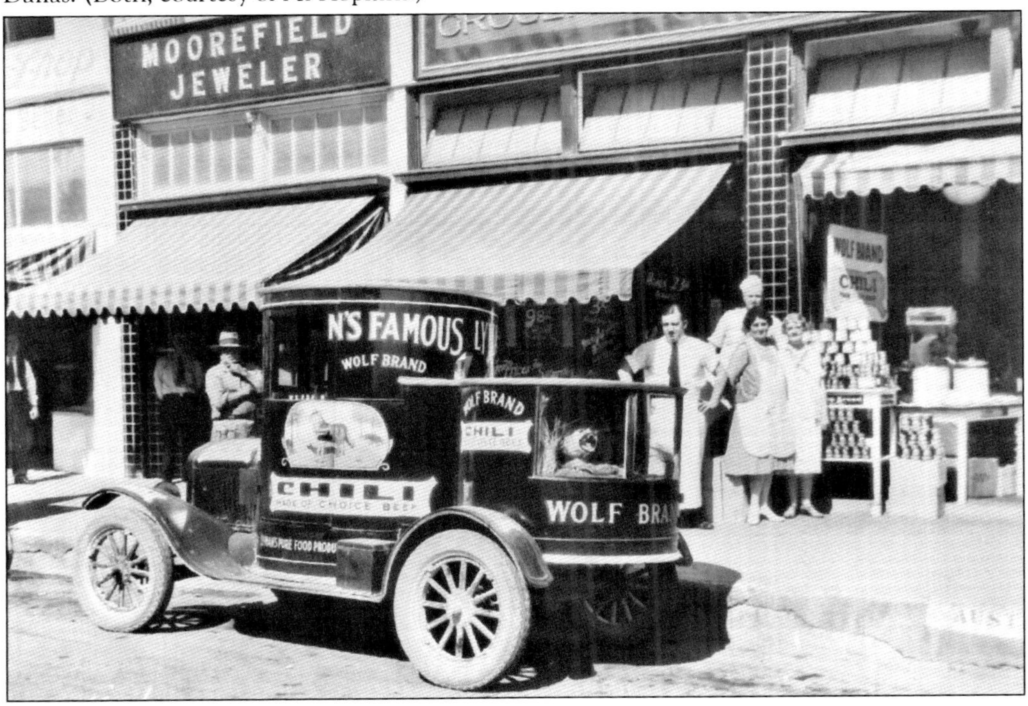

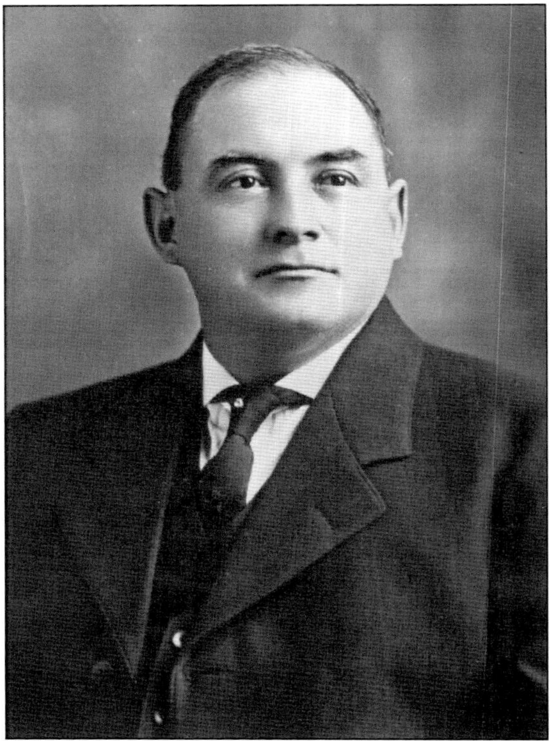

When baker Gus Weidmann (at left) was put off the train in Corsicana, he had few material possessions except a fruitcake recipe from his native Germany. Finding work in a local eatery, he established a reputation for excellent desserts. Cotton buyer Tom McElwee (below) partnered with Weidmann to establish the Collin Street Bakery. Although they moved to a new location on Sixth Avenue and later to Seventh Avenue, the business kept its original name and has become internationally famous.

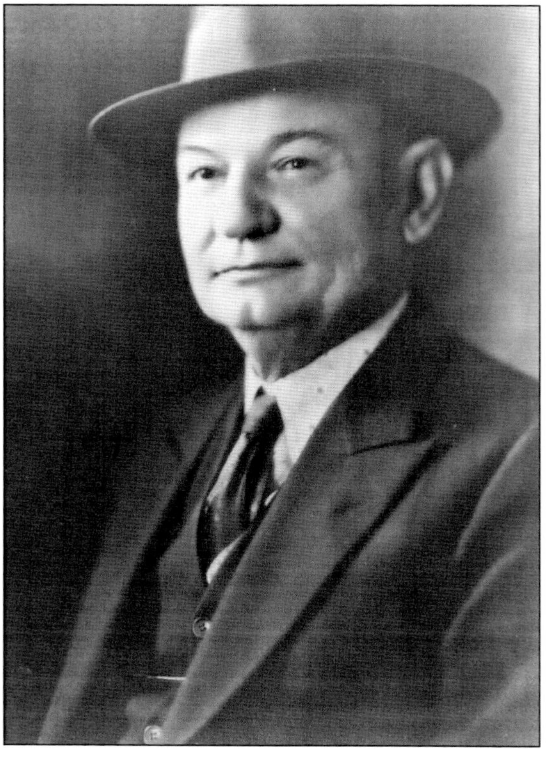

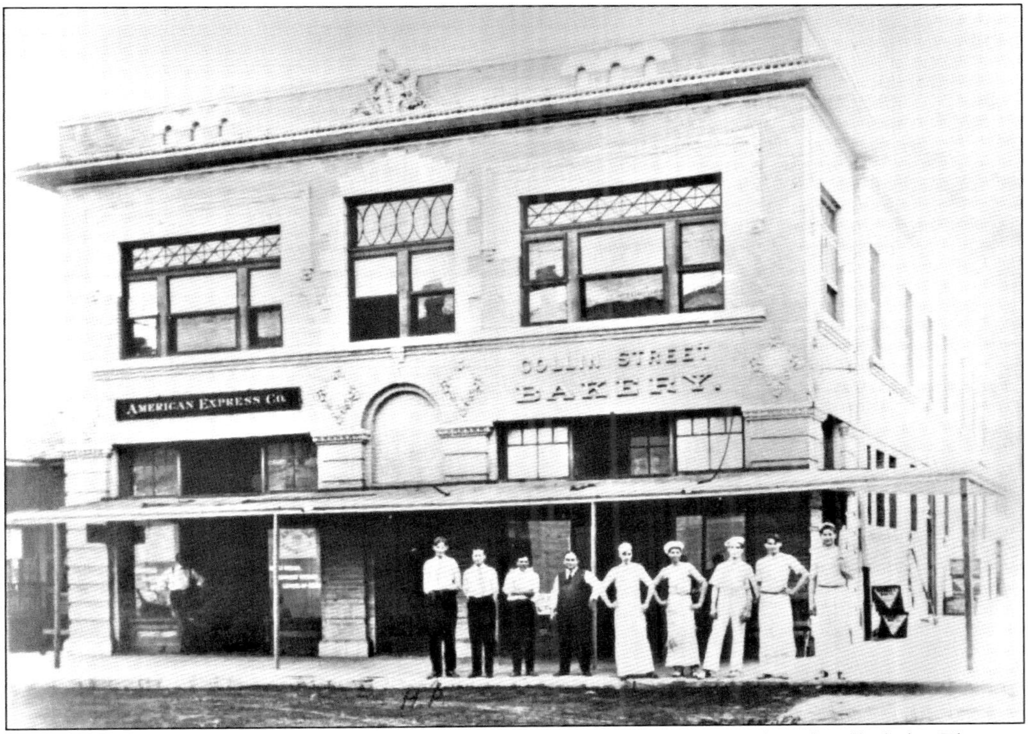

Tom McElwee, co-owner of the Collin Street Bakery, added a private hotel called the Elite on the second floor of the bakery to provide accommodations for entertainers who performed at the opera house or at the town's other vaudeville theaters, as well as other celebrities who came through Corsicana, such as Enrico Caruso, Will Rogers, and baseball legend John J. McGraw.

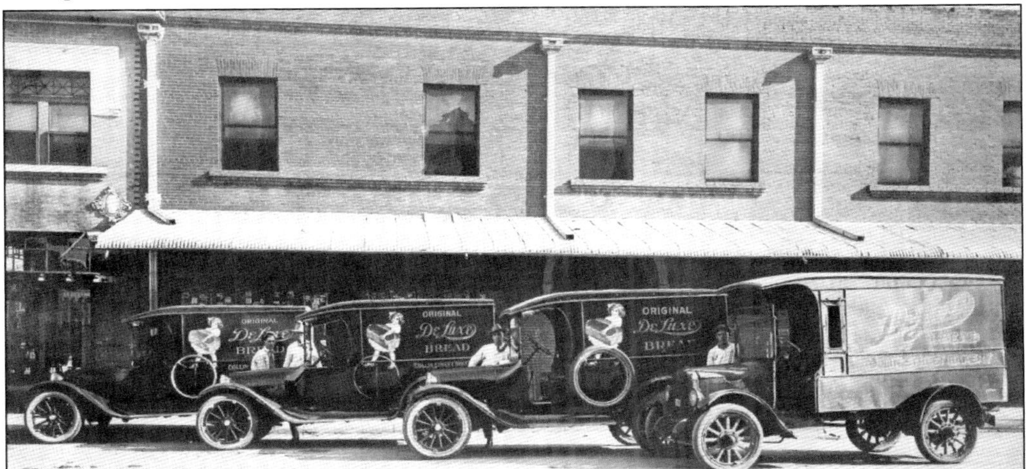

Circus performers took samples of the Deluxe fruitcake with them when they left Corsicana at the end of the 1914 season, giving the product national exposure and generating mail orders. But until the late 1940s, Collin Street's main business was delivering bread and other baked goods by truck throughout the immediate area. In 1947, new owners Lee McNutt, R. F. Rutherford, Harry Montgomery, and H. T. Cook directed the focus of the business to the Deluxe fruitcake, which customers could order by mail.

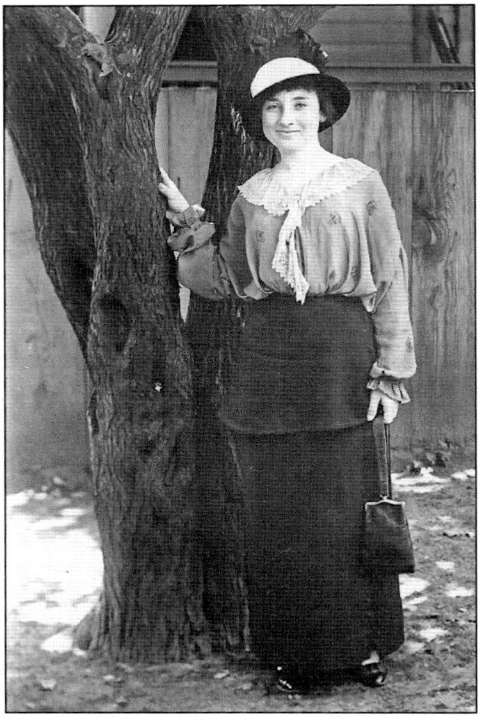

Rose Daniel Goldberg, one of 10 children of hardware store owner Simon Daniel, opened the Coffee House in 1957 at 113 West Collin Street, a location currently occupied by the Sandwich Shop. She retired at age 90 in 1990 and died at the age of 103. She is buried in the Hebrew Cemetery. (Courtesy of Sidney and Jane Miller.)

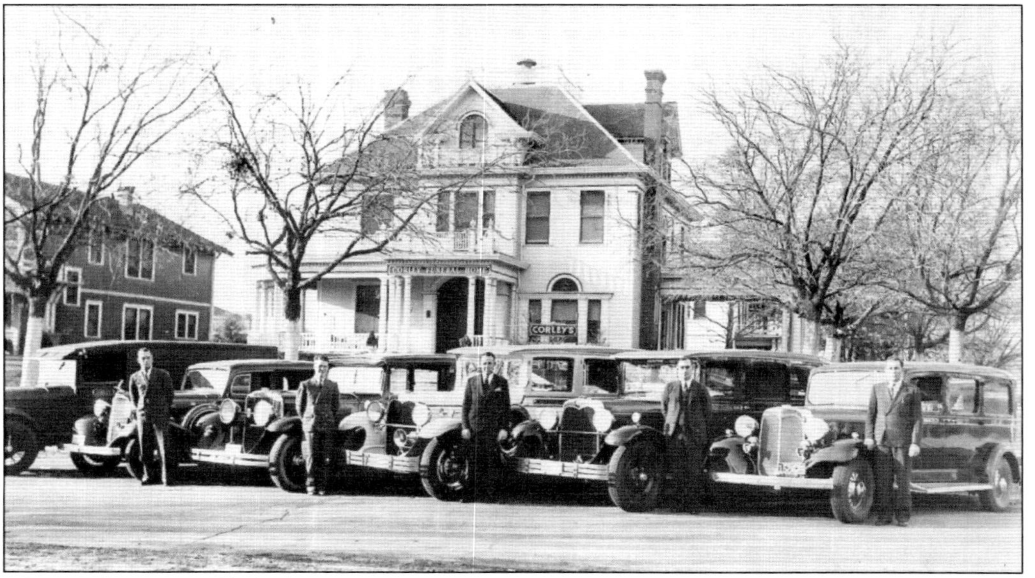

John Corley Sr. established a funeral home in Mexia in 1878. His son, John Corley Jr., opened a second facility in Corsicana in 1929. It is located in what was a private residence at 413 North Thirteenth Street immediately west of the Navarro County courthouse. Federal occupation troops were housed at this location during the Reconstruction era. John Corley Jr. was active in the community, serving as chairman of the Navarro Junior College Board of Trustees and president of the chamber of commerce and the country club. Robert Corley, John's son, operated the business until 2009, when he retired and sold it to Ron Smith. (Courtesy of Corley Funeral Home.)

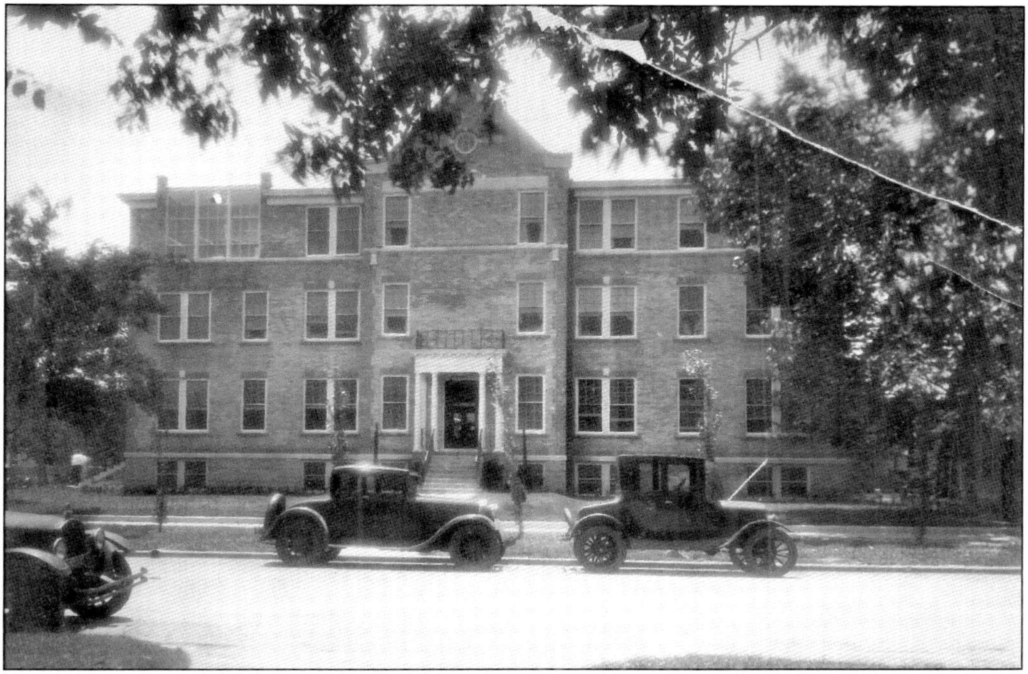

The Navarro Hospital and Clinic opened in 1928 at the corner of West Collin and Thirteenth Streets with a staff composed of Doctors E. H. Newton, T. O. Wills, Homer. T. Jester, Wilson David, and W. R. Sneed. Described in an article in the *Corsicana Daily Sun* as the latest word in modern hospital equipment, the facility was equipped with signal systems from each room to the nursing station. The four-story facility could accommodate 26 patients. Today the building has been converted into an apartment complex.

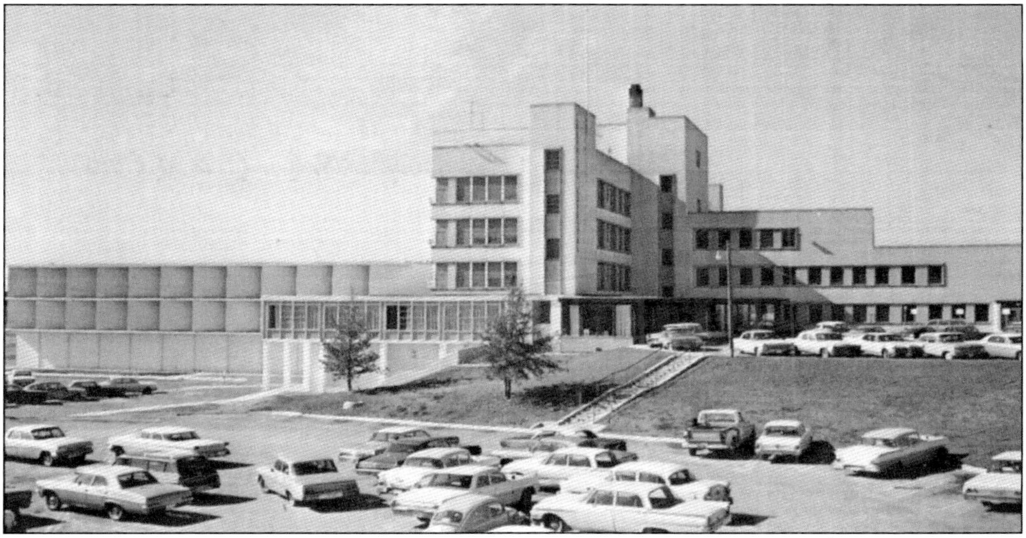

Navarro County Hospital, pictured here, was constructed in 1952 at a cost of $1.8 million. Local oilman H. R. Stroube provided leadership for the project. The original building was located on 29 acres on West Highway 22. The 100-bed facility claimed to be the most modern equipped hospital in Texas when it opened. The building was replaced by a new structure in 1983.

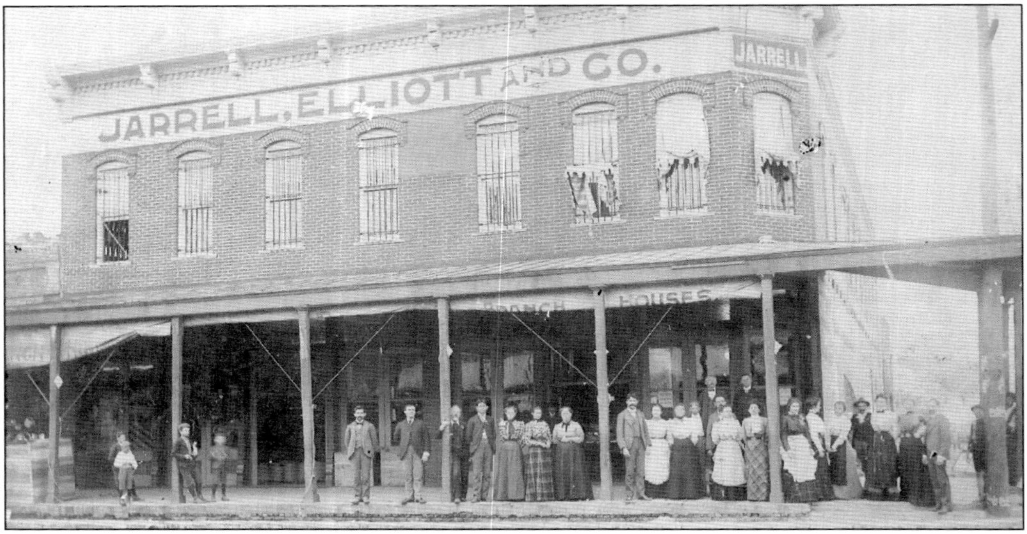

Partners Joseph Jarrell and Fount Elliott operated their business at 301 North Beaton Street, offering their customers dry goods, notions, clothing, hats, boots, shoes, millinery, and men's furnishings. It also advertised itself as a "racket store," which was similar to the "five-and-ten" store or the "dime store," in which customers could buy a wide variety of items for a nickel or dime.

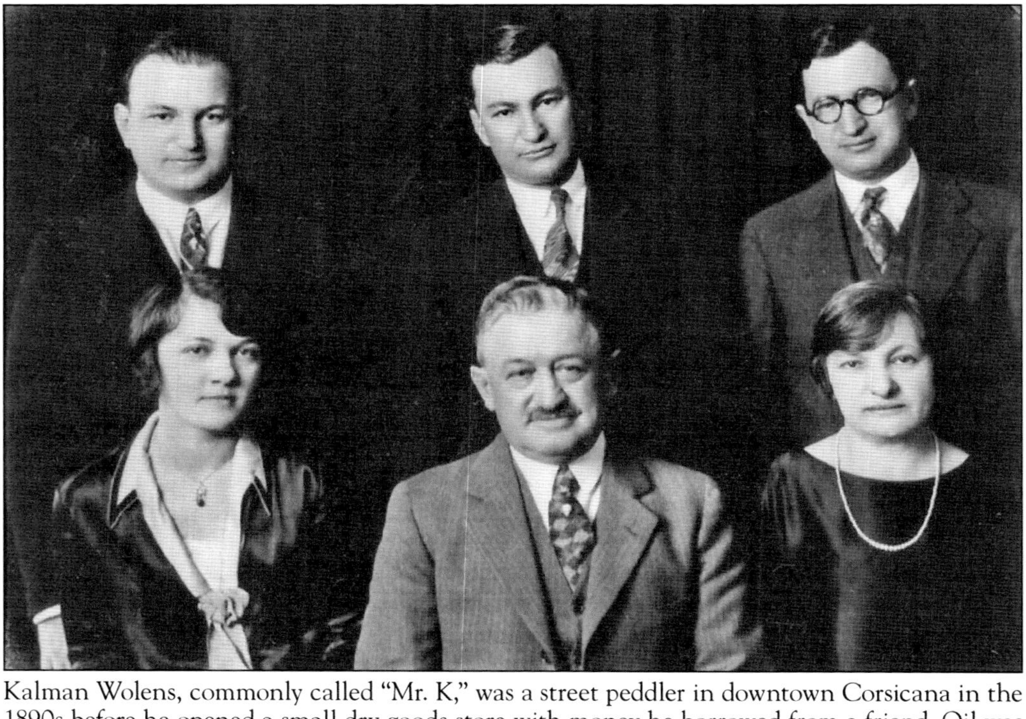

Kalman Wolens, commonly called "Mr. K," was a street peddler in downtown Corsicana in the 1890s before he opened a small dry-goods store with money he borrowed from a friend. Oil was discovered on property he owned south of town, enabling him to expand his operations to include 63 K. Wolens stores across Texas. The Wolens family, pictured here from left to right, included (first row) daughter Daisy, Mr. K, and his wife, Ida; (second row) sons Joe, Louis, and Max. The Wolens contributed to numerous charities and other worthwhile endeavors in Corsicana.

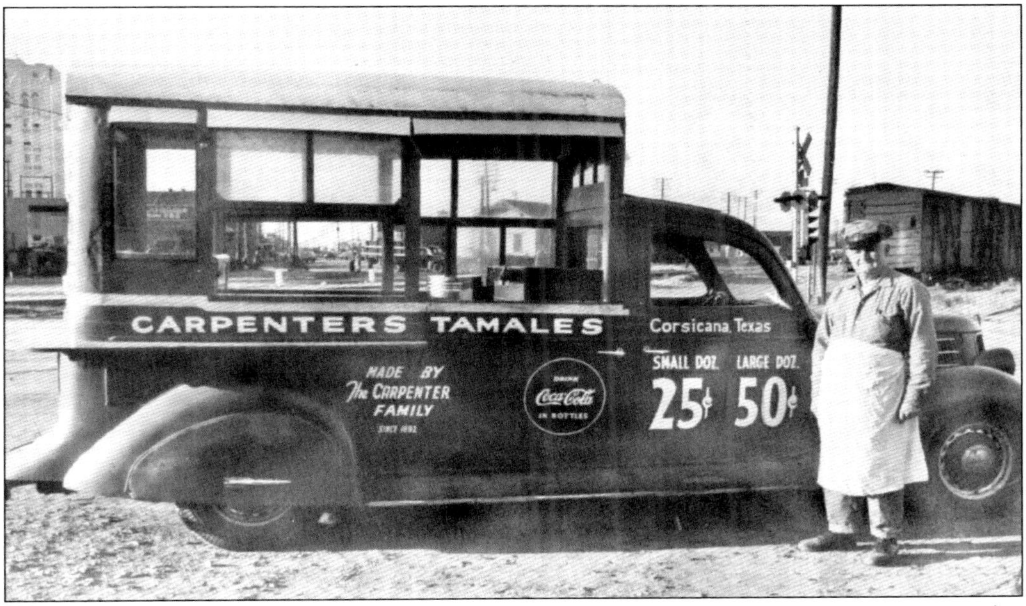

Nathan Carpenter began selling tamales from a horse-drawn wagon in 1892, announcing his arrival each day by blowing a bugle. His son, Will, shown in the photograph above, took over the business after his father's death in 1937, selling his wares from this converted 1949 Chevrolet hearse. He was open for business seven days a week up to and including the day of his death, February 1, 1967. (Courtesy of Megan Carpenter Vadasy.)

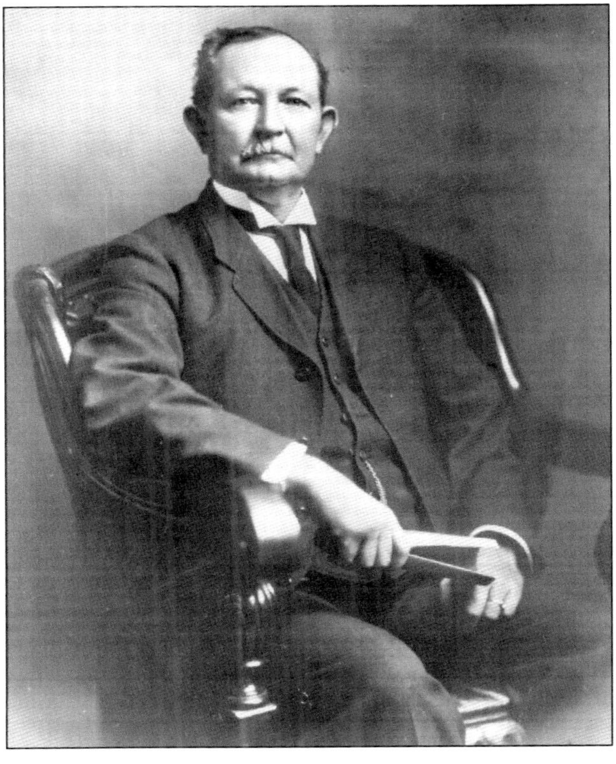

Tennessee native James Whiteselle arrived in Corsicana in 1875. In addition to Whiteselle's Brick and Lumber Company, he was involved in several other local business ventures. His cherry-red bricks were used in construction projects all over Texas. As mayor when oil was discovered in Corsicana in 1894, Whiteselle recruited experienced personnel to Corsicana to manage the newly developing oil field. He died in 1915.

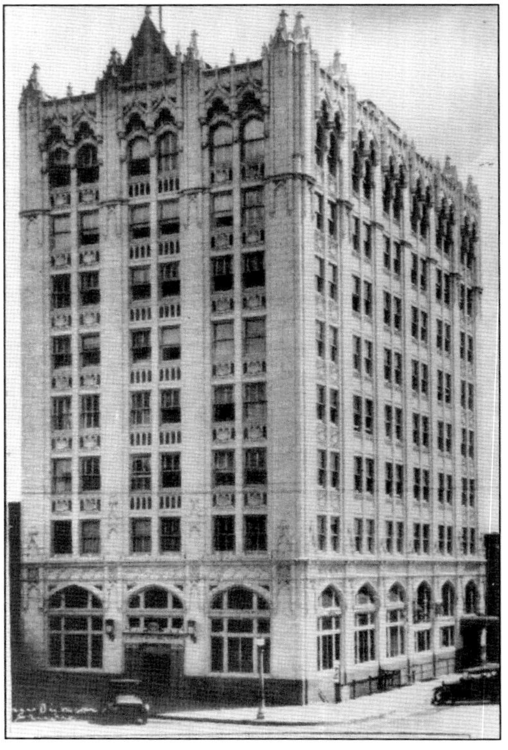

The State National Bank began operations in 1917 with B. B. Munsey as president. The eight-story structure, shown in this photograph, was completed in 1926 during the presidency of Isaac Cerf at a cost of $500,000. The bank occupied the main floor, with the remaining floors housing offices for doctors, attorneys, dentists, and other professionals. In addition, KAND Radio broadcast from studios in the bank building. Today it operates as Chase Bank.

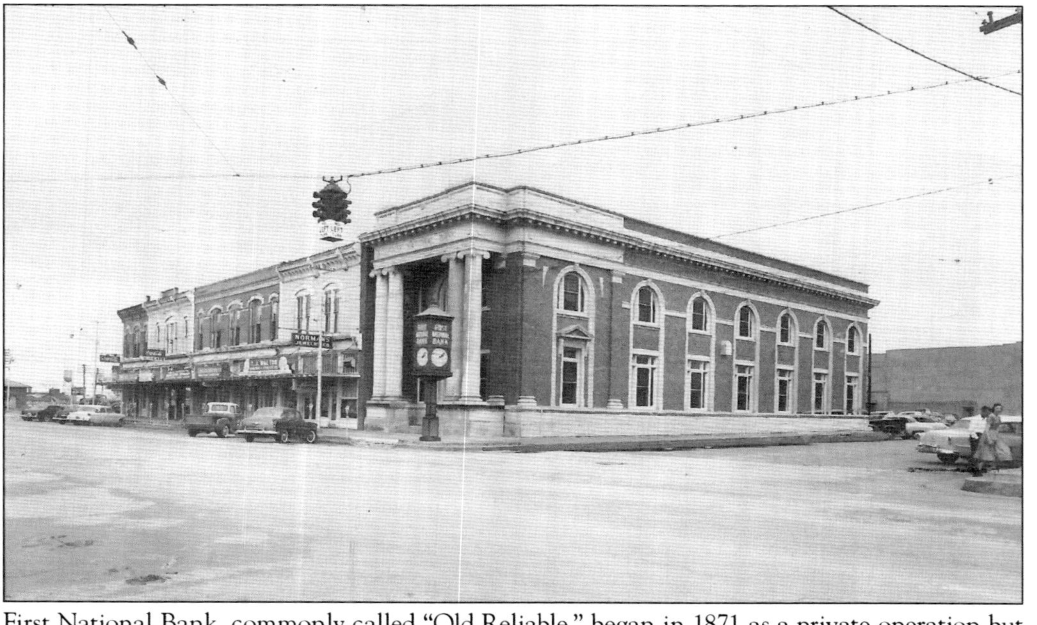

First National Bank, commonly called "Old Reliable," began in 1871 as a private operation but was incorporated and chartered in 1886. The business, which thrived under the leadership of Pres. James Garrity, was located at the corner of Beaton Street and Sixth Avenue until 1971, when it moved to a new modern facility at the corner of Main and West Collin Streets. It currently operates as a branch of Bank of America.

Corsicana National Bank purchased this clock in 1916 for $1,304.14. It originally hung on the building at the corner of Collin and Beaton Streets. It was remounted on a pedestal and moved to the corner of Sixth Avenue and Beaton Street when First National Bank and Corsicana National Bank merged. It moved again to First National's new location at 100 North Main Street, and today it is displayed at Pioneer Village.

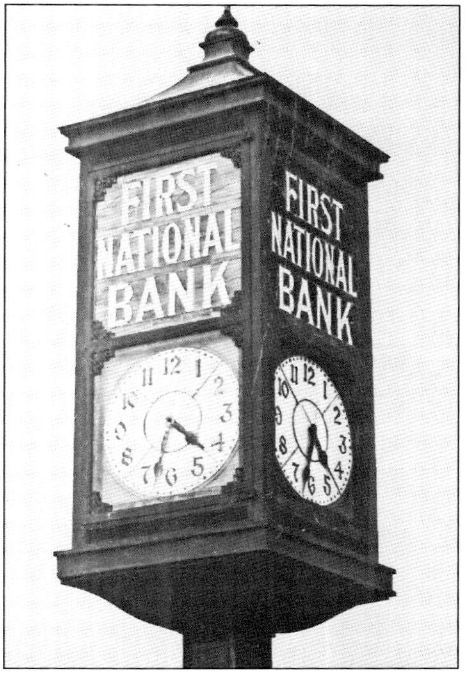

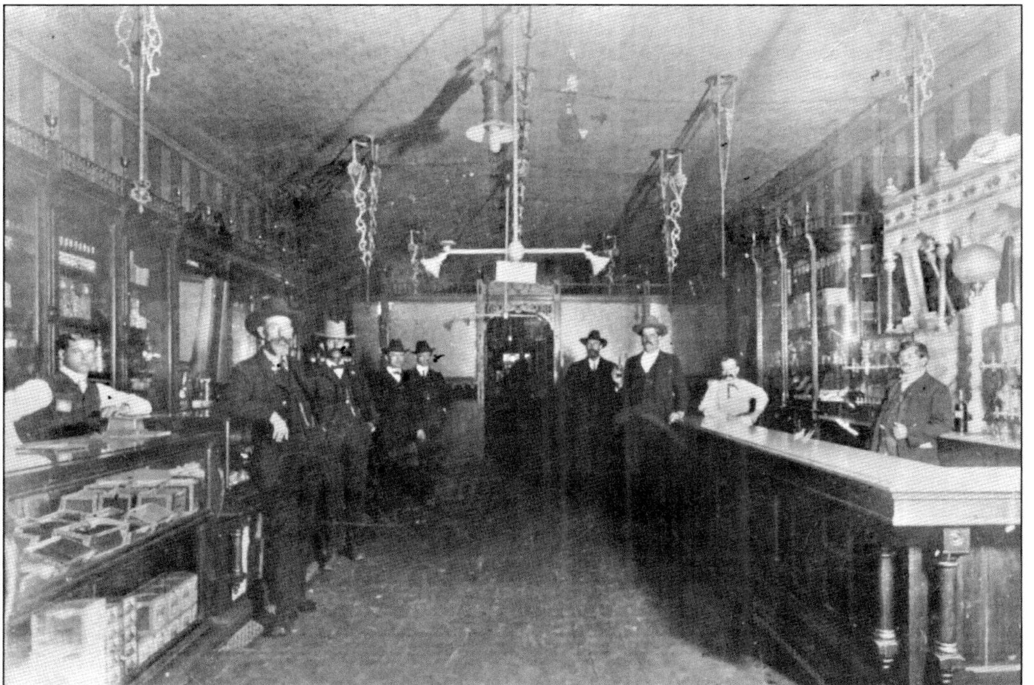

Daniel Kiber, a native of Switzerland, learned culinary skills in France prior to coming to Corsicana in 1885. He formed a partnership with Thomas Cobb. Kiber and Cobb's confectionery was located at 205 South Beaton Street. In addition to serving ice cream and a variety of candies, Kiber and Cobb also had oysters, cigars, soda water, and fruits. They also provided a catering service.

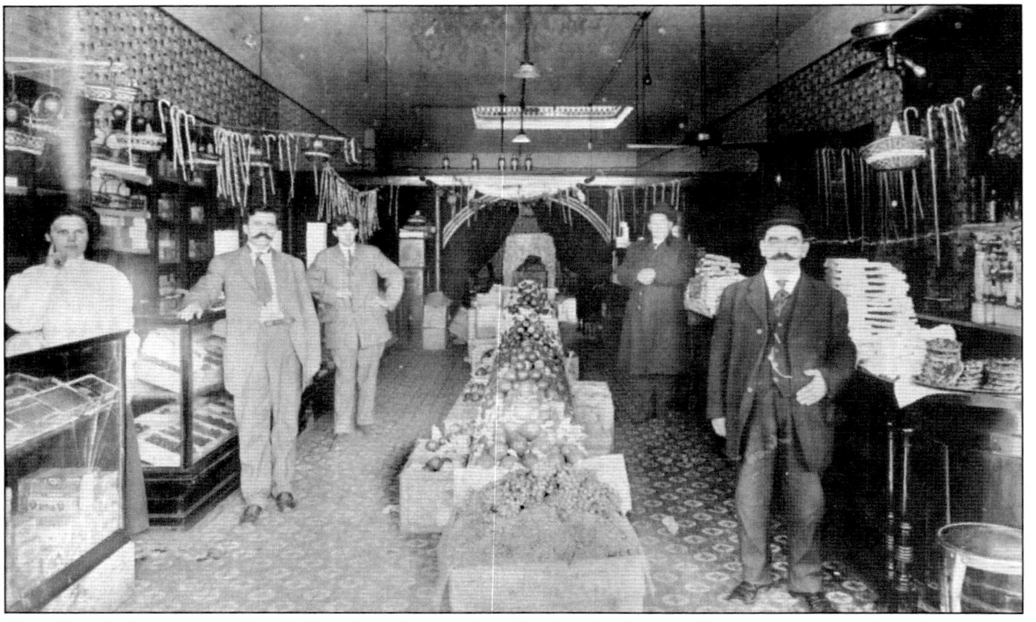

The Greek-American Candy Kitchen, located at 110 South Beaton Street, was owned and operated by John Zarafonitas and his wife, Alberta. They eventually moved the business adjacent to their home at First Avenue and Fourteenth Street. Alberta is shown on the far left, and her husband is second from the left in this 1910 photograph.

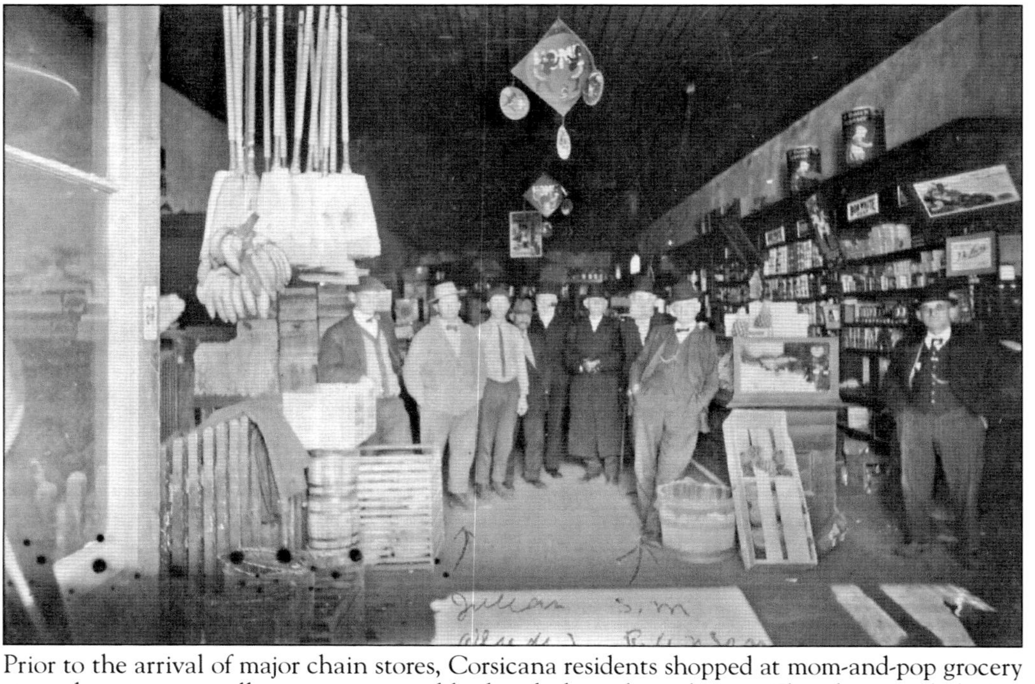

Prior to the arrival of major chain stores, Corsicana residents shopped at mom-and-pop grocery stores downtown as well as in various neighborhoods throughout the city. This photograph depicts Ransom Grocery, owned by Sam Ransom. Located at 114 East Collin Street, Ransom sold harnesses in addition to groceries and produce, and he provided his customers with delivery service.

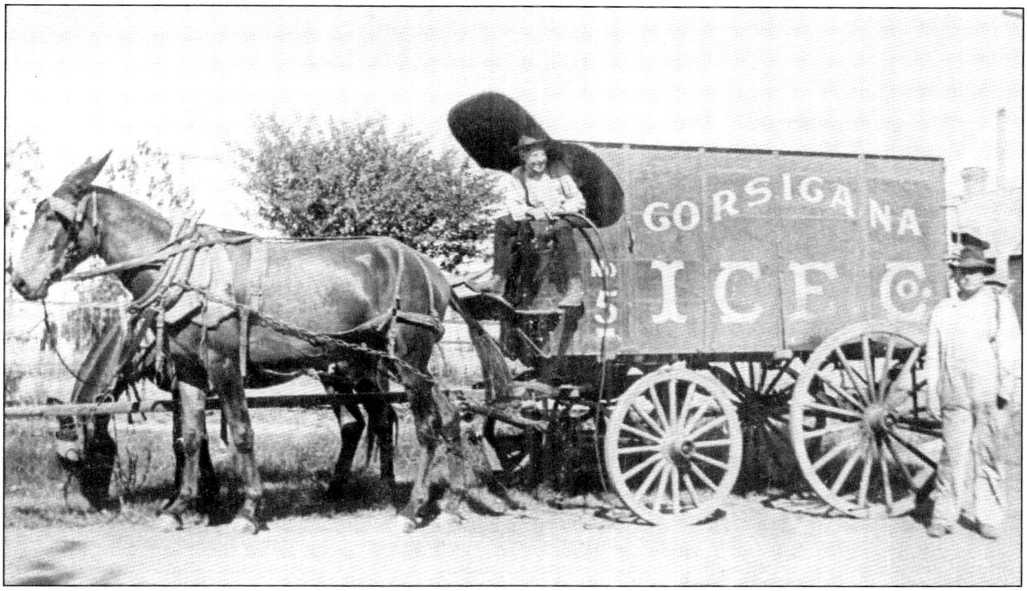

Icehouses provided important services to the community prior to refrigeration. Offices for the Corsicana Ice Company were located at 112 West Sixth Avenue, while the manufacturing operation was on South Fourteenth Street. They promised to fill orders for any quantity in any part of the state and also throughout the city of Corsicana, and boasted that Corsicana ice was more solid, lasting, and healthful than any northern lake ice.

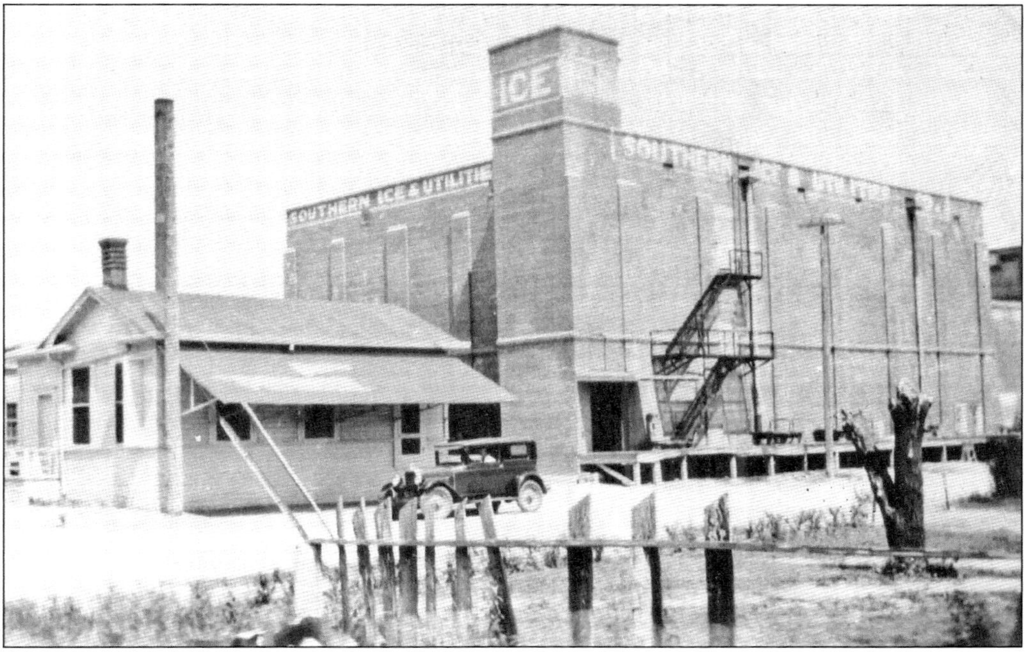

Southern Ice Utilities at 811 South Fourteenth Street delivered to all parts of the city as well as providing cold storage for perishable goods. The ice was made from pure distilled water. The company motto, published in the *Corsicana City Directory*, promised "Honest weights, good service, and satisfied customers."

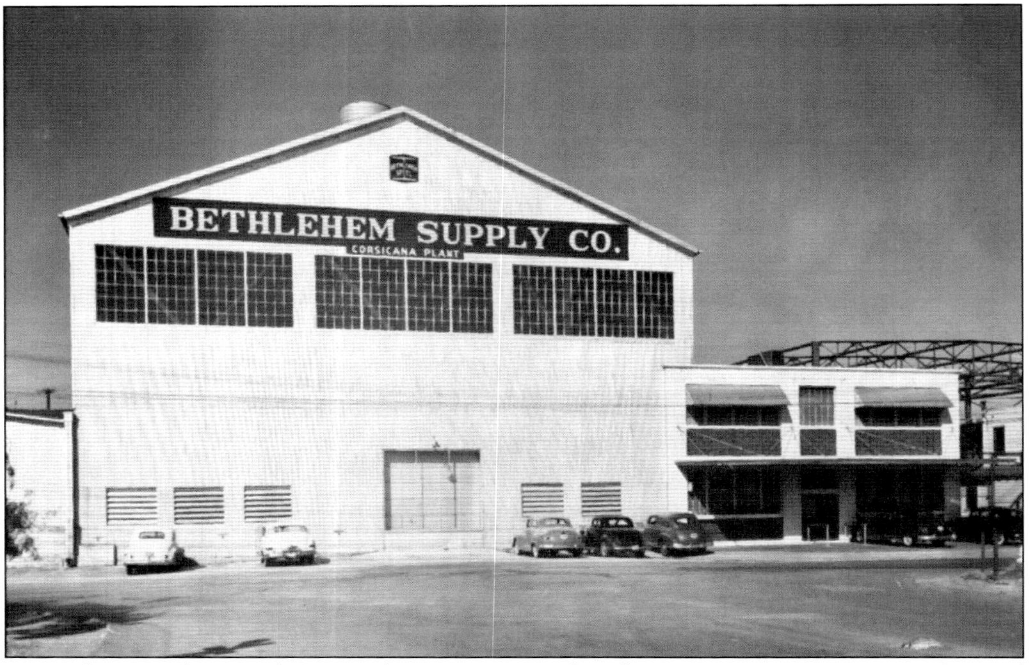

Located on North Seventh Street, the American Well and Prospecting Company manufactured oil field equipment under the trade name "Gumbo Buster." Bethlehem Steel, depicted in the photograph above, purchased the business in 1944. As shown below, during World War II, like many American industries, the plant converted to the manufacture of bombs and other war-related products. Increased competition in the oil field manufacturing equipment business and a downturn in the petroleum industry in general resulted in the plant's closing in 1959.

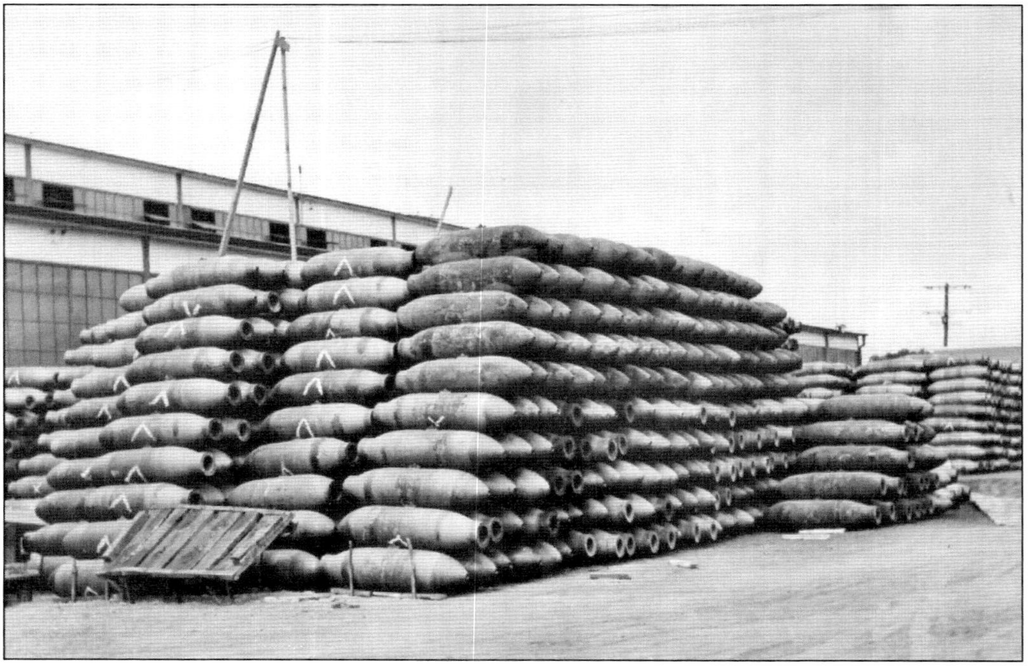

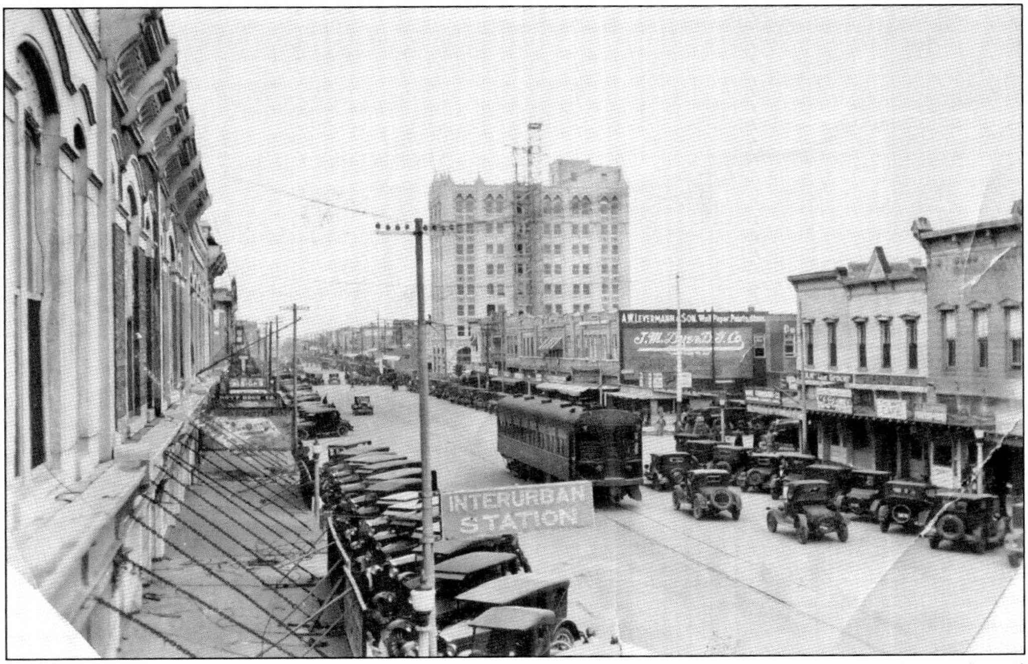

The Texas Electric Railway, commonly called the interurban, provided passenger, freight, and mail service for residents of north central Texas. Three lines operated from Dallas, including a 56-mile line to Corsicana that began operations in 1913. This 1925 photograph shows the interurban station located at the south end of Beaton Street. The interurban significantly changed rural areas, bringing new products to small towns and also providing safe and affordable transportation to metropolitan areas. As the schedule shows (below), trains generally ran on the hour, making brief stops along the route. The company abandoned the Corsicana run in 1941. (Below, courtesy of City of Corsicana, Stroube Collection.)

Dallas-Corsicana Division

TIME CARD No. 114

Subject to change without notice — Effective July 24, 1930

SOUTH BOUND—DALLAS TO CORSICANA (Read Down)

STATIONS	PASSENGER CARS													Baggage and Express Cars	
	AM	AM	AM	AM	AM	PM	PM	PM	PM	PM	PM	PM	PM	AM	AM
Lv. Dallas	*6 10	7 40	8 40	*10 10	11 40	1 10	*2 40	4 10	5 40	‡6 20	7 10	8 40	11 00	2 10	‡11 35
" Oak Cliff Jct.	6 19	7 49	8 49	10 19	11 49	1 19	2 49	4 19	5 49	6 29	7 19	8 49	11 09	......	......
" Monroe	6 28	7 59	8 59	10 29	11 59	1 29	2 59	4 29	5 59	6 40	7 29	8 59	11 19	......	11 54
" Hutchins	6 40	8 12	9 12	10 42	12 12	1 42	3 12	4 42	6 12	6 52	7 42	9 12	11 32	2 37	12 15
" Wilmer	6 48	8 20	9 20	10 50	12 20	1 50	3 20	4 50	6 20	7 00	7 50	9 20	11 40	2 45	12 30
" Ferris	6 55	8 27	9 27	10 57	12 27	1 57	3 27	4 57	6 27	7 07	7 57	9 27	11 47	3 07	12 44
" Trumbull	7 00	8 32	9 32	11 02	12 32	2 02	3 32	5 02	6 32	......	8 02	9 32	11 52	3 13	12 48
" Palmer	7 07	8 39	9 39	11 09	12 39	2 09	3 39	5 09	6 39	......	8 09	9 39	11 59	3 34	1 04
" Garrett	7 15	8 45	9 45	11 15	12 45	2 15	3 45	5 15	6 45	......	8 15	9 45	12 05	......	1 10
" Ennis	7 24	8 54	9 54	11 24	12 54	2 24	3 54	5 24	6 54	......	8 24	9 54	12 14	4 05	1 40
" Alma	7 33	9 03	10 03	11 33	1 03	2 33	4 03	5 33	7 03	......	8 33	10 03	12 23	4 14	1 52
" Rice	7 40	9 10	10 10	11 40	1 10	2 40	4 10	5 40	7 10	......	8 40	10 10	12 30	4 36	2 05
Ar. Corsicana	8 00	9 30	10 30	12 00	1 30	3 00	4 30	6 00	7 30	......	9 00	10 30	12 50	5 00	2 30
STATIONS	AM	AM	AM	M	PM	PM	PM	PM	PM	PM	PM	PM	AM	AM	PM

NORTH BOUND—CORSICANA TO DALLAS (Read Down)

STATIONS	PASSENGER CARS													Baggage and Express Cars	
	AM	AM	AM	AM	AM	AM	PM	PM	PM	PM	PM	PM	PM	AM	PM
Lv. Corsicana	......	6 00	*6 40	8 00	9 40	11 10	*12 40	2 10	3 40	*5 10	6 40	8 10	9 40	9 30	‡5 25
" Rice	......	6 19	7 00	8 20	10 00	11 30	1 00	2 30	4 00	5 30	7 00	8 30	10 00	9 53	5 53
" Alma	......	6 25	7 07	8 27	10 07	11 37	1 07	2 37	4 07	5 37	7 07	8 37	10 07	10 03	6 03
" Ennis	......	6 35	7 16	8 36	10 16	11 46	1 16	2 46	4 16	5 46	7 16	8 46	10 16	10 30	6 30
" Garrett	......	6 42	7 25	8 45	10 25	11 55	1 25	2 55	4 25	5 55	7 25	8 55	10 25	10 39	6 45
" Palmer	......	6 48	7 31	8 52	10 31	12 01	1 31	3 01	4 31	6 01	7 31	9 01	10 31	10 53	6 56
" Trumbull	......	6 53	7 37	8 59	10 37	12 07	1 37	3 07	4 37	6 07	7 37	9 07	10 37	11 02	7 01
" Ferris	‡6 40	6 59	7 43	9 06	10 43	12 13	1 43	3 13	4 43	6 13	7 43	9 13	10 43	11 13	7 13
" Wilmer	6 48	7 07	7 50	9 13	10 50	12 20	1 50	3 20	4 50	6 20	7 50	9 20	10 50	11 27	7 21
" Hutchins	6 54	7 15	7 56	9 20	10 56	12 26	1 56	3 26	4 56	6 26	7 56	9 26	10 56	11 35	7 28
" Monroe	7 07	7 30	8 10	9 30	11 10	12 40	2 10	3 40	5 10	6 40	8 10	9 40	11 10	11 50	......
" Oak Cliff Jct.	7 17	7 40	8 20	9 40	11 20	12 50	2 20	3 50	5 20	6 50	8 20	9 50	11 20	......	......
Ar. Dallas	7 25	7 50	8 30	9 50	11 30	1 00	2 30	4 00	5 30	7 00	8 30	10 00	11 30	12 10	8 00
STATIONS	AM	AM	AM	AM	AM	PM	PM	PM	PM	PM	PM	PM	PM	PM	PM

Local Trains are shown in BLACK, and make all stops.
Bluebonnet Trains are shown in RED, and may make local stops, on signal.
*Carries Baggage and Preferred Express.
‡Does not run on Sundays.
All Bluebonnet trains on this division may carry a limited amount of Preferred Express.

Route your Shipments
THE ELECTRIC WAY
Double daily service each way
See schedule on this page

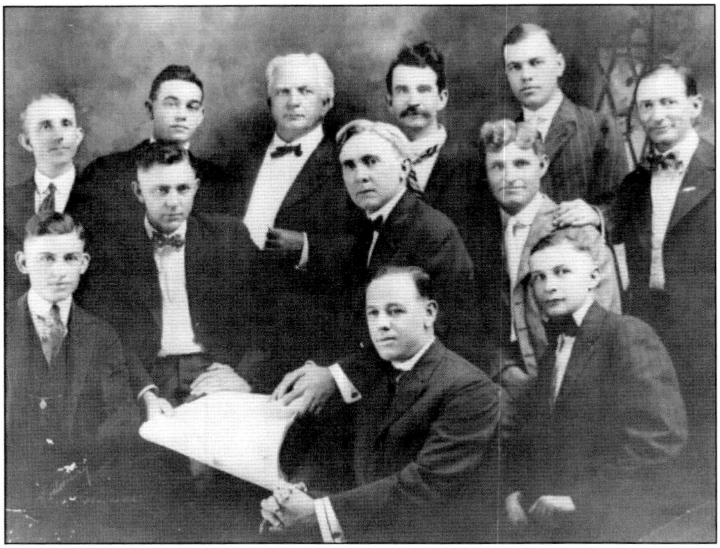

The *Corsicana Daily Sun* began publication in 1895, following a long list of earlier newspapers. Pictured here is the *Daily Sun* staff in 1916 at the time they occupied a new building on North Beaton Street. Of note in this photograph are co-owners A. A. Wortham (second row, third from left) and Lowry Martin (first row, far left). Martin was instrumental in organizing the Texas Centennial celebration in 1936.

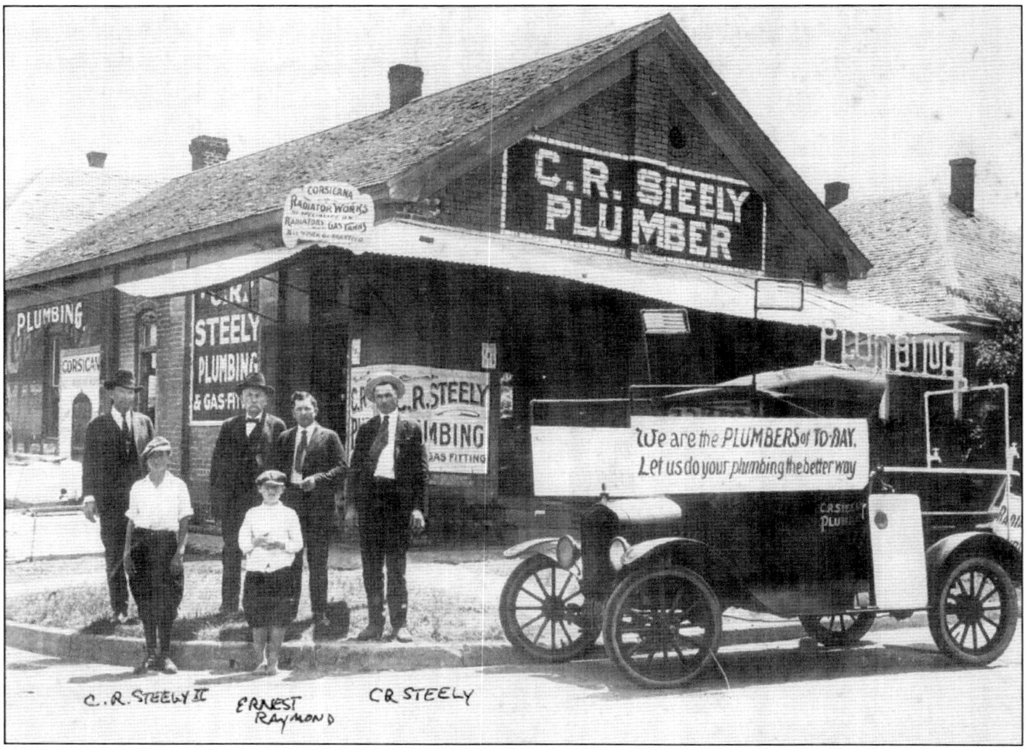

C. R. Steely Plumbing was located at Main Street and Third Avenue. Shown in this 1914 photograph from left to right are (first row) C. R. "Charlie" Steely and Ernest Raymond Steely, sons of the owner; (second row) unidentified, ? Norton, ? Peeples, and owner C. R. Steely. The business continued to operate until the 1960s.

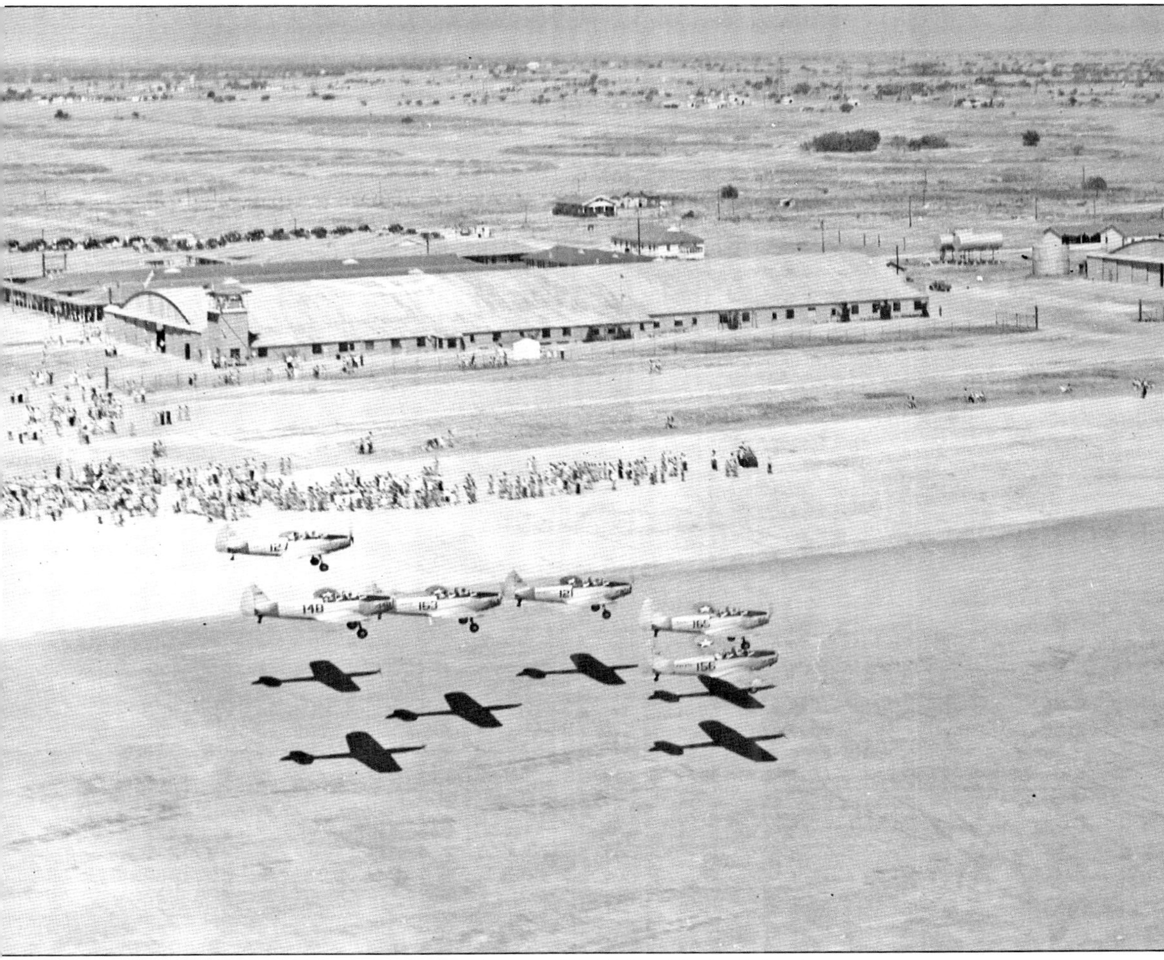

Unable to meet the high demand for pilots during World War II, the federal government contracted with civilian flying schools across the United States to train pilots for the Army Air Corps. One such facility was the Air Activities of Texas, which opened in 1941. Located 6 miles south of downtown Corsicana, Air Activities was owned by B. L. Woolley, B. W. Woolley, E. D. "Dick" Criddle, Edward "Doc" Booth, and J. O. Womack. The government furnished the airplanes, and the owners provided everything else, including civilian instructors. The local residents went to great lengths to make the cadets feel welcome in the community during their nine-week training period. More than 8,000 cadets received primary flight training at the facility, which employed 500 civilians. As the end of the war approached, the facility was closed in 1944. Navarro Junior College occupied the site as its first campus from 1946 to 1951, and today it is used as the Corsicana Municipal Airport. (Courtesy of David Criddle.)

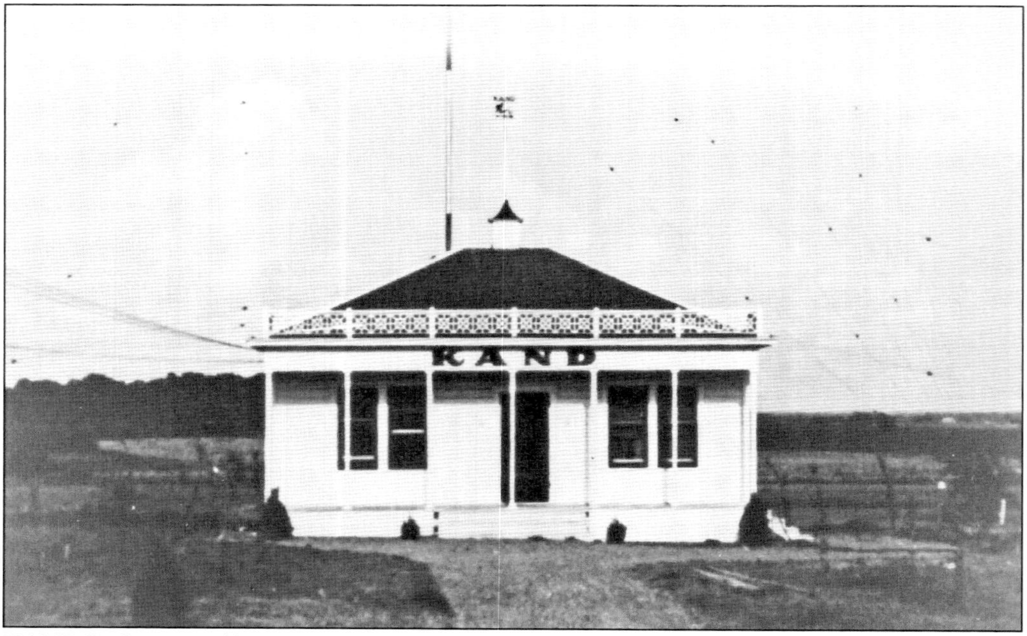

KAND Radio, owned by J. C. West, began broadcasting in 1937. As co-owner of Wolf Brand Chili, West wanted the call letters WOLF for the station, but the FCC denied his request, stating that stations east of the Mississippi began with the letter W, while those west of the Mississippi began with K. Thus the station was given the letters KAND ("canned"). Pictured below is "Ramblin" Roy Miller, a longtime KAND broadcaster who kept listeners entertained with country music and "Talk Time," and provided the latest local news and information. (Both, courtesy of Richard Parker.)

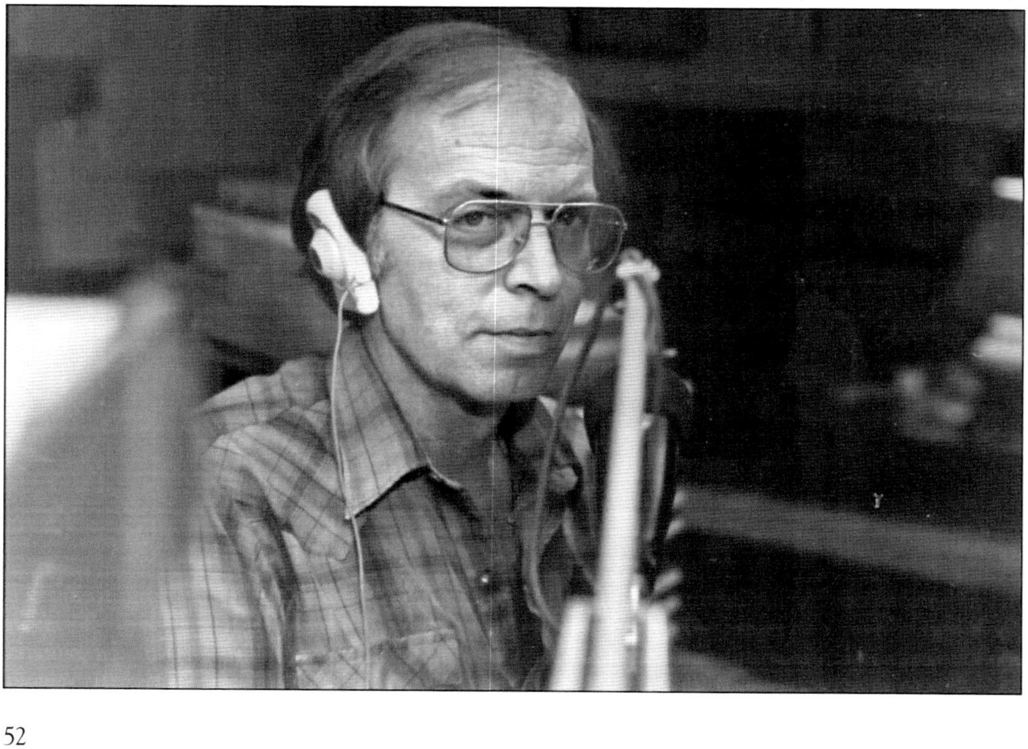

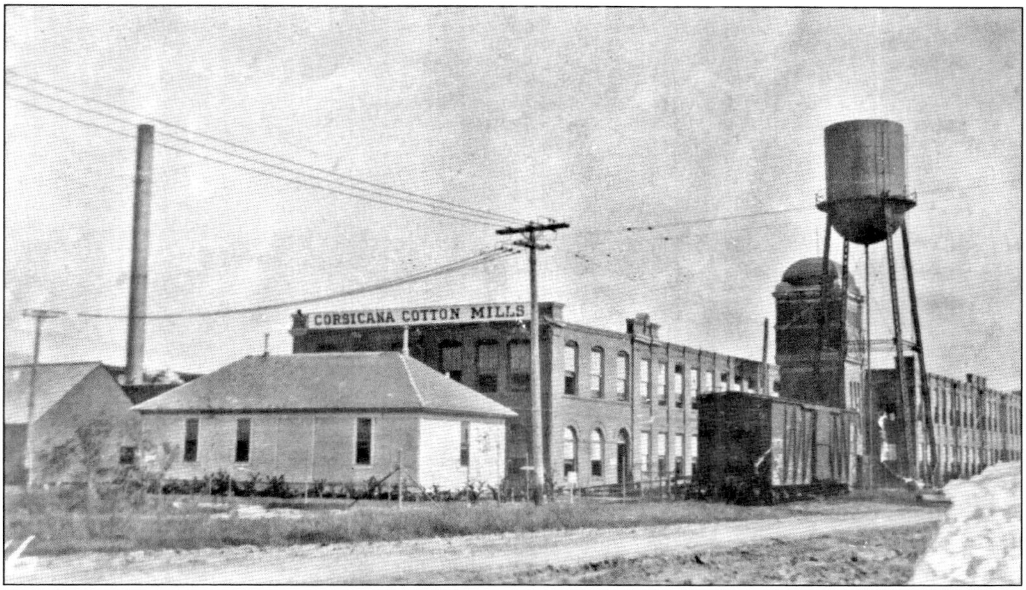

Since Navarro County was among the leading cotton-producing counties in Texas, the Corsicana Cotton Mill, established in 1900, was a natural business for the community. Employing approximately 200 workers, the mill manufactured a variety of fabrics, including cotton ducking used for tents during World War II. The facility closed in 1968. (Courtesy of John Barron.)

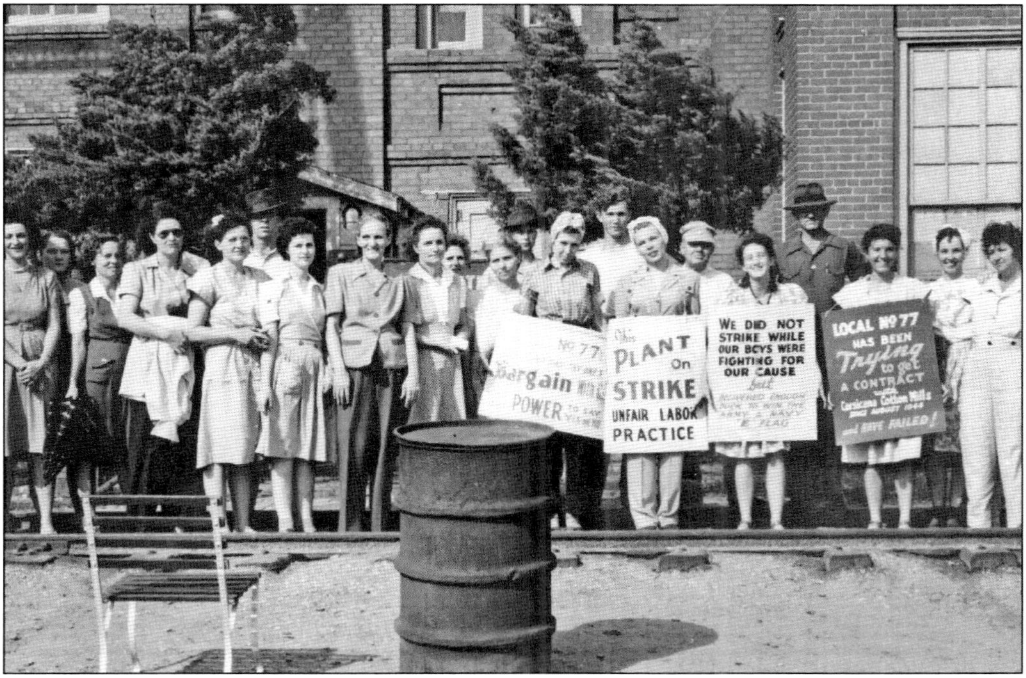

Employees at the Corsicana Cotton Mill joined the textile union in 1944 and, like many workers across the United States, pressed for higher wages and other concessions from management. This photograph was taken at the Main Street entrance of the cotton mill as workers went on strike on May 23, 1946. (Courtesy of John Barron.)

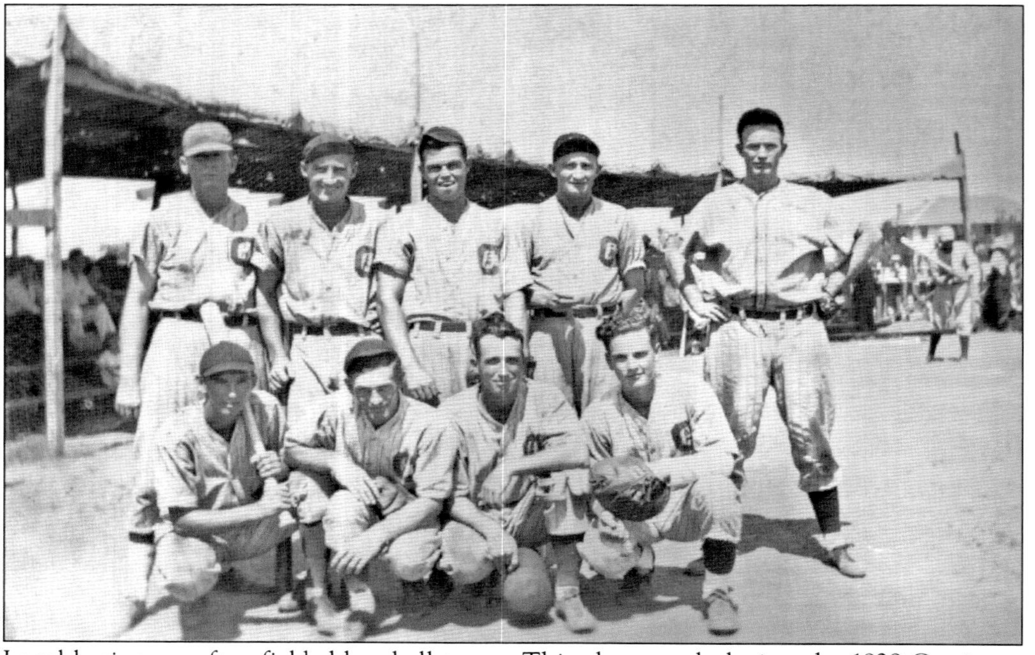

Local businesses often fielded baseball teams. This photograph depicts the 1938 Corsicana Cotton Mill team, called the Millers. From left to right are (first row) Malone "Bones" Sanders, Everett Smith, James Burnett, and unidentified; (second row) unidentified, Sam Upchurch, Cecil Bondurant, Butch Upchurch, and Benny Heathcote. Team member Calvin Barron is taking the picture. (Courtesy of John Barron.)

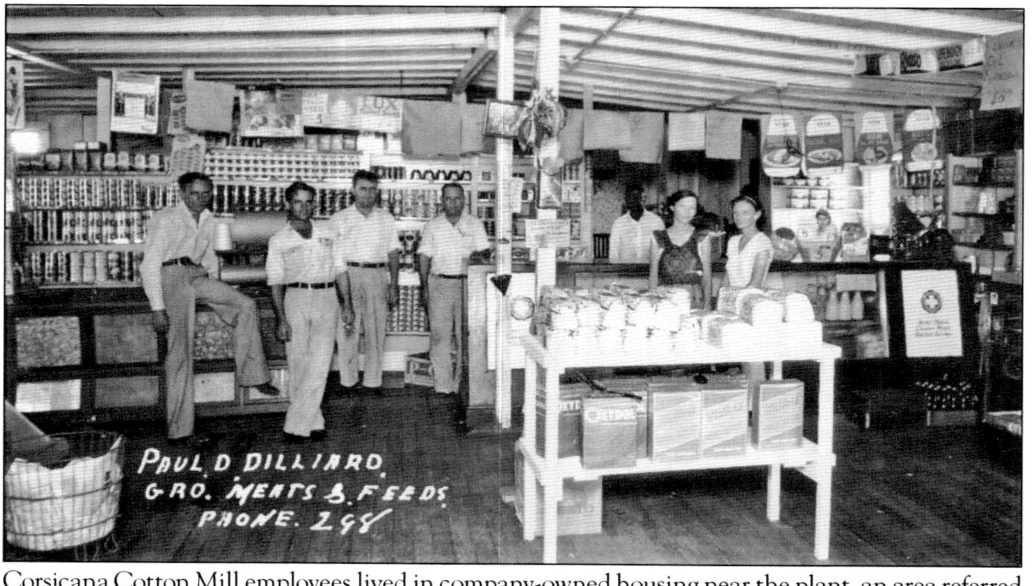

Corsicana Cotton Mill employees lived in company-owned housing near the plant, an area referred to as the Mill Block. The Paul Dilliard Grocery, shown in this 1938 photograph, was located at 901 South Beaton Street, a convenient location for cotton mill families to shop. Pictured from left to right are Perry Allred, Claude Pollock, owner Paul Dilliard, Arthur McCleary, unidentified clerk, Betty Dilliard, and Lucile Gibbs. (Courtesy of John Barron.)

S. A. Pace came with his brothers to Corsicana from Alabama by covered wagon in 1868. In 1872, he established a wholesale grocery operation on South Beaton Street. He eventually built a large warehouse on Seventh Avenue. Pace was an original member of the Corsicana Commercial Club, a forerunner of the chamber of commerce, and he also served on the library board. He advertised the "largest stock of groceries and unexcelled facilities for handling your business."

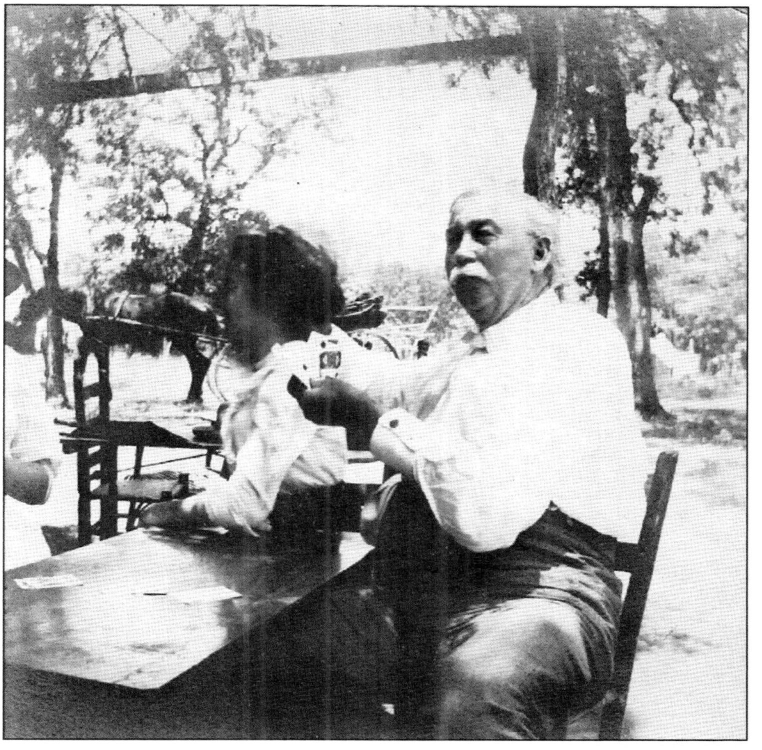

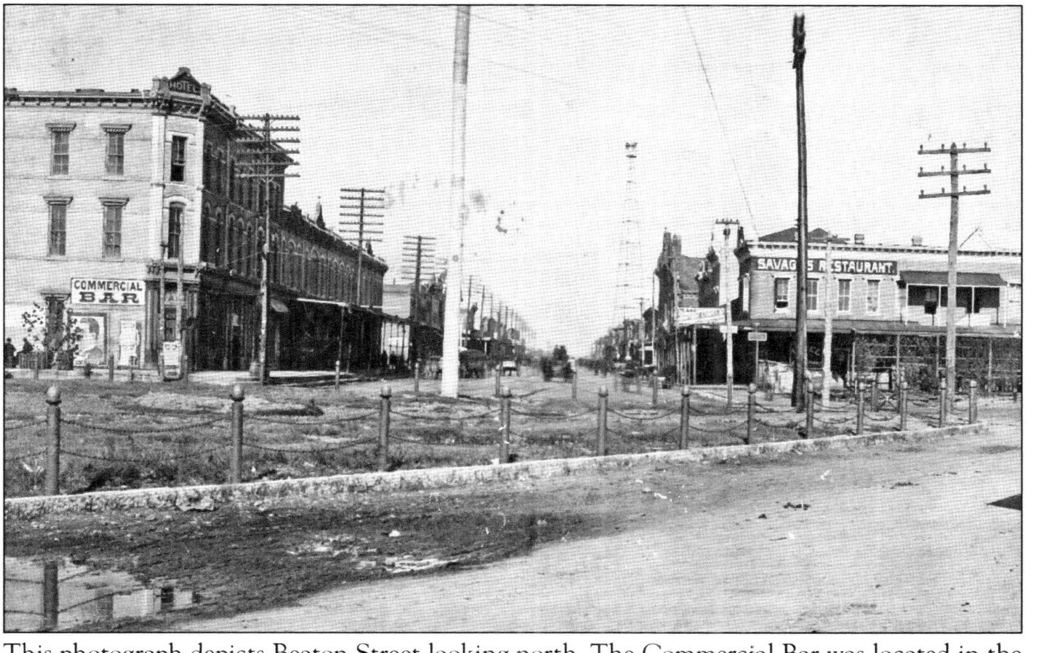

This photograph depicts Beaton Street looking north. The Commercial Bar was located in the hotel of the same name. Savage Restaurant at 117 South Beaton Street was owned by Joseph Savage, who at one time managed the Opera House Saloon. The tall tower in the center of the picture was erected in the 1880s by Mayor Robert Neblett to light the downtown area.

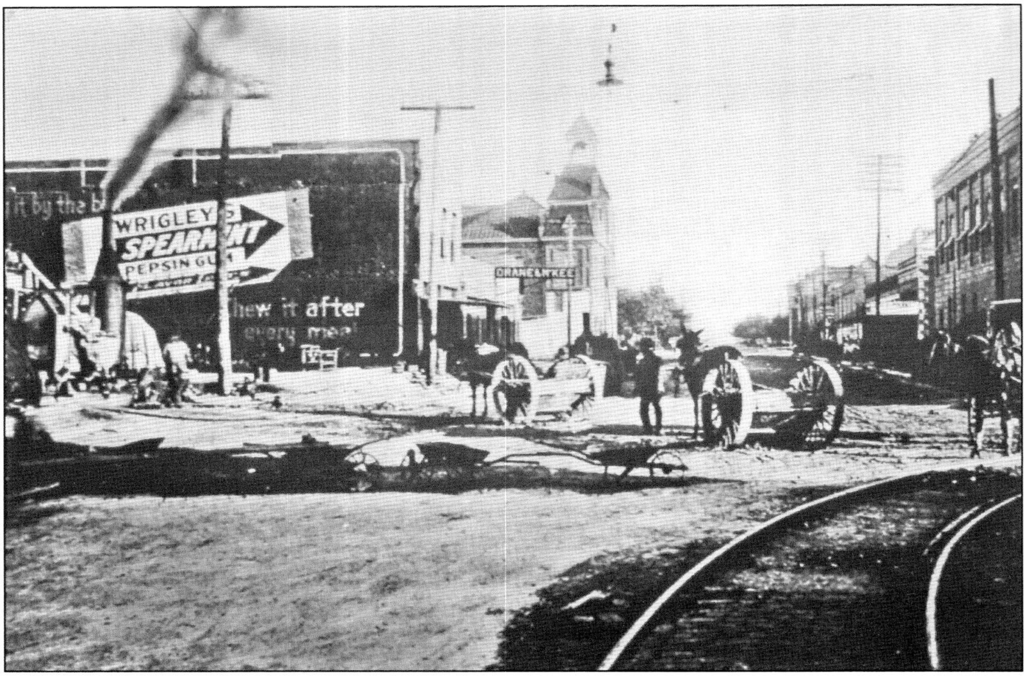

This photograph looks north on Eleventh Street (present-day Main Street) and depicts Drane-McKee at 100 North Eleventh Street, which provided auto repairs, accessories, and supplies. Moses Miller's Grocery Store at 124 West Collin Street is shown on the right, and the distinctive tower of city hall is visible in the center of the image. Note the streetcar tracks in the foreground.

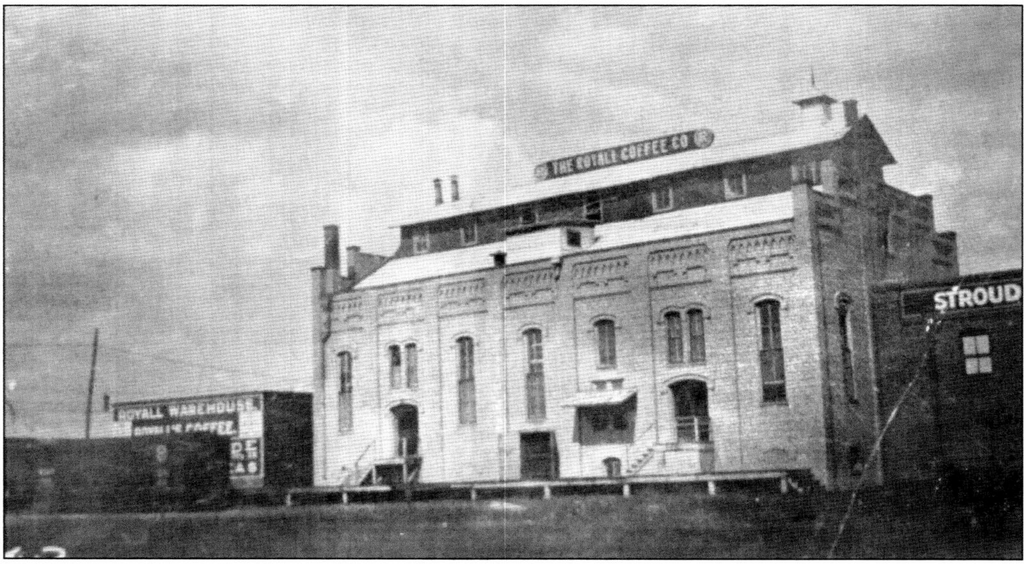

One of the more unique businesses in Corsicana in the early 20th century was the Royall Coffee Company, which billed itself as coffee roasters and importers. It claimed to be the only business of that type in Texas. John N. Royall was the president and manager of the operation, which was located at 305 South Tenth Street. John Garrity and John S. Callicutt were investors in the business. The business closed in the mid-1920s.

Simon Daniels left his native Russia at age 14. He eventually settled in Corsicana. His wife died one year after giving birth to their 10th child in 1906. Daniels first owned a saloon, but he sold the business, claiming it caused too much unhappiness. Customers could purchase almost any merchandise from his hardware store, which was located at the corner of North Beaton Street and Third Avenue. Daniels is pictured (left) with Louis Goldberg. (Courtesy of Sidney and Jane Miller.)

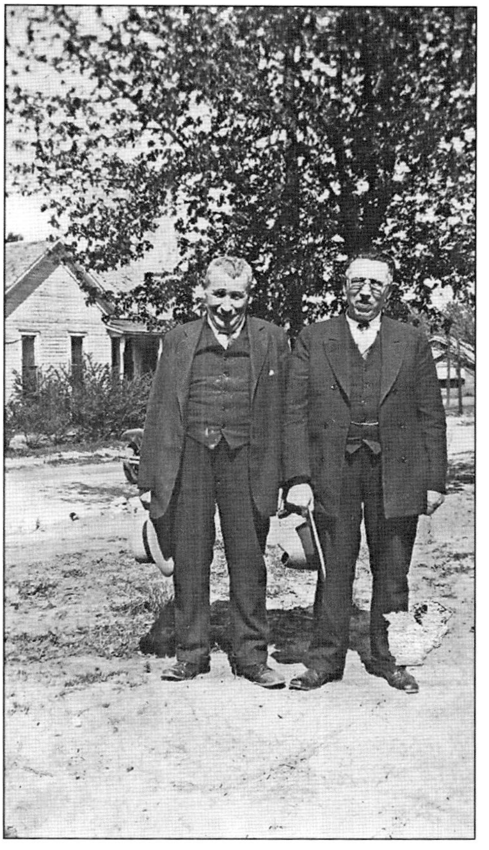

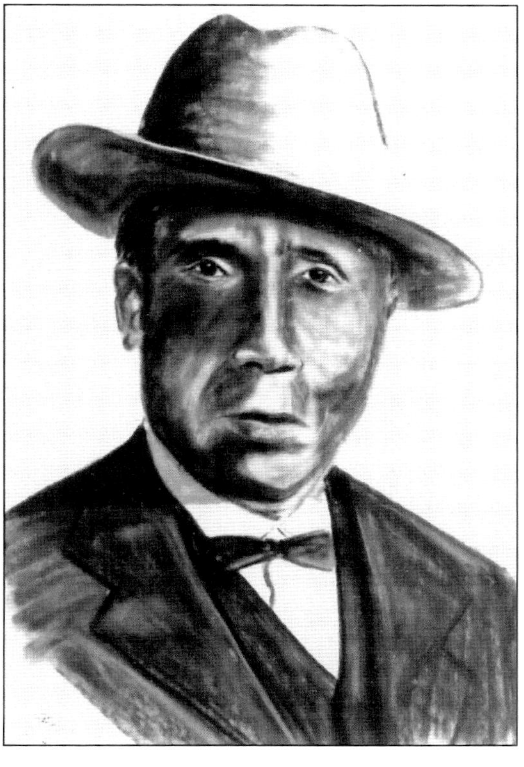

Born in the community of Chatfield in northern Navarro County, Dr. Will Coleman was among the first African American veterinarians licensed in Texas. After earning his diploma from the Veterinary Science Association in London, Ontario, Canada, and receiving his Texas certification in 1911, Dr. Coleman returned to his native Navarro County to establish his practice. From his office at 219 North Beaton Street, Dr. Coleman first traveled throughout the county by horse and buggy before he purchased a Ford Model T to make his rounds to area farms. Dr. Coleman's practice spanned 43 years.

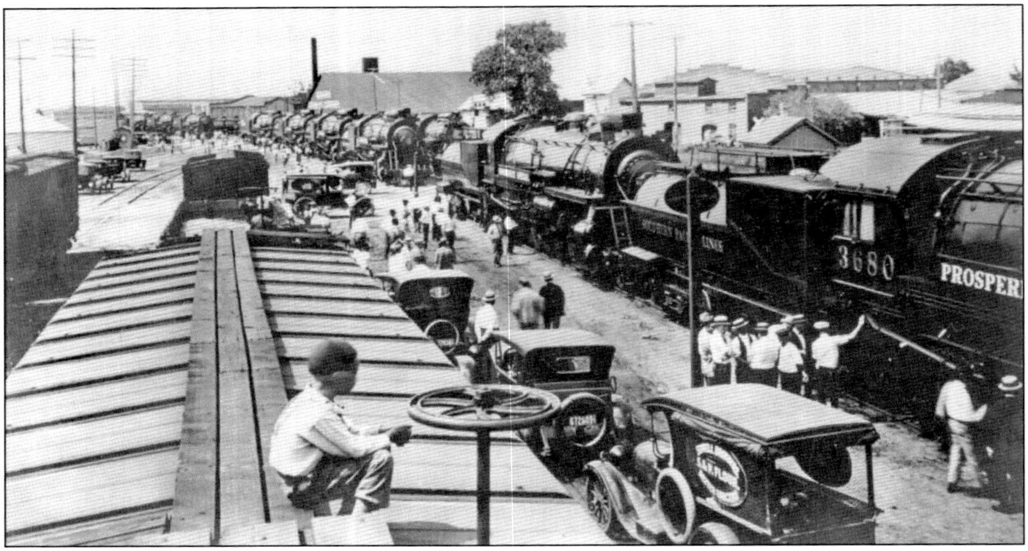

The railroad played a vital role in the growth and development of Corsicana. According to records of the Cotton Belt, in 1922, twenty freight locomotives, each weighing 441,900 pounds, were moved in a solid train from east St. Louis, Missouri, to Corsicana, Texas. Built by the Baldwin Locomotive Works for Southern Pacific, the train was named the *Prosperity Special* as a symbol of the prosperous times that were ahead for the railroad and for the country in general. An unidentified youngster watches as the train arrives in Corsicana. (Courtesy of City of Corsicana, Stroube Collection.)

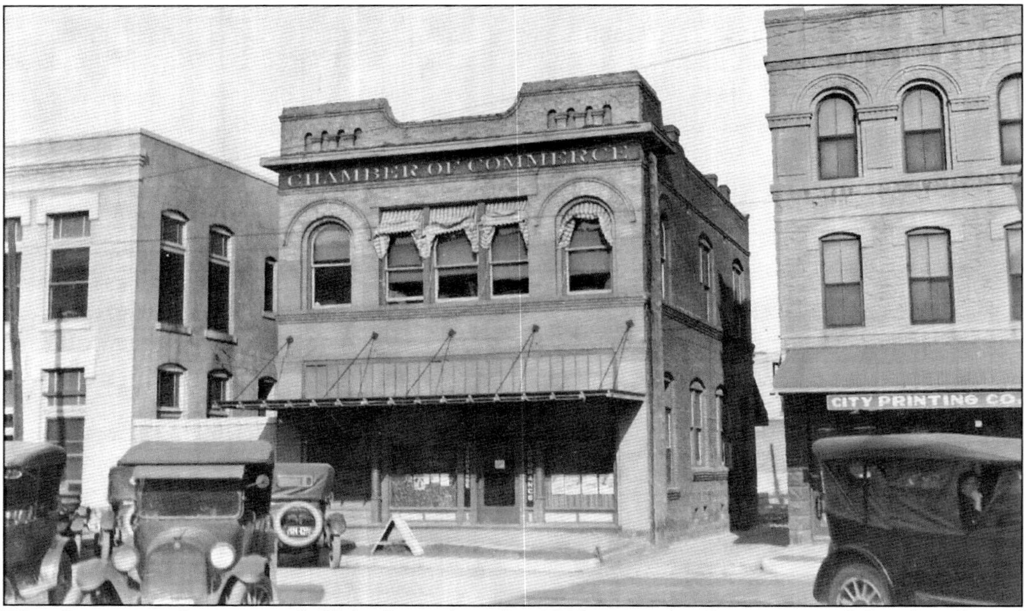

The Corsicana Commercial Club, formed in the 1890s, was the forerunner of the chamber of commerce. In 1917, the club merged with a similar group called the Corsicana Business League to form the Corsicana Chamber of Commerce to promote the growth of the community and improve residents' quality of life. The chamber of commerce office depicted here was at 109 South Main Street.

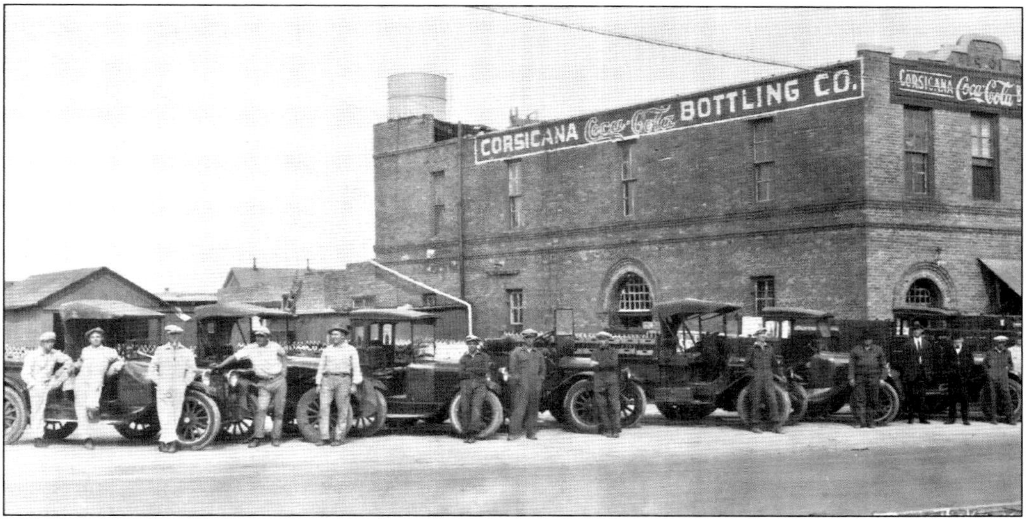

Harris Kinsloe managed the Corsicana Bottling Company, located at 407 South Ninth Street. The company manufactured and bottled soda water, sarsaparilla, ginger ale, and various types of mineral water. By 1922, when this photograph was taken, the plant was bottling Coca-Cola. John B. Miller and John Echols were plant managers at that time.

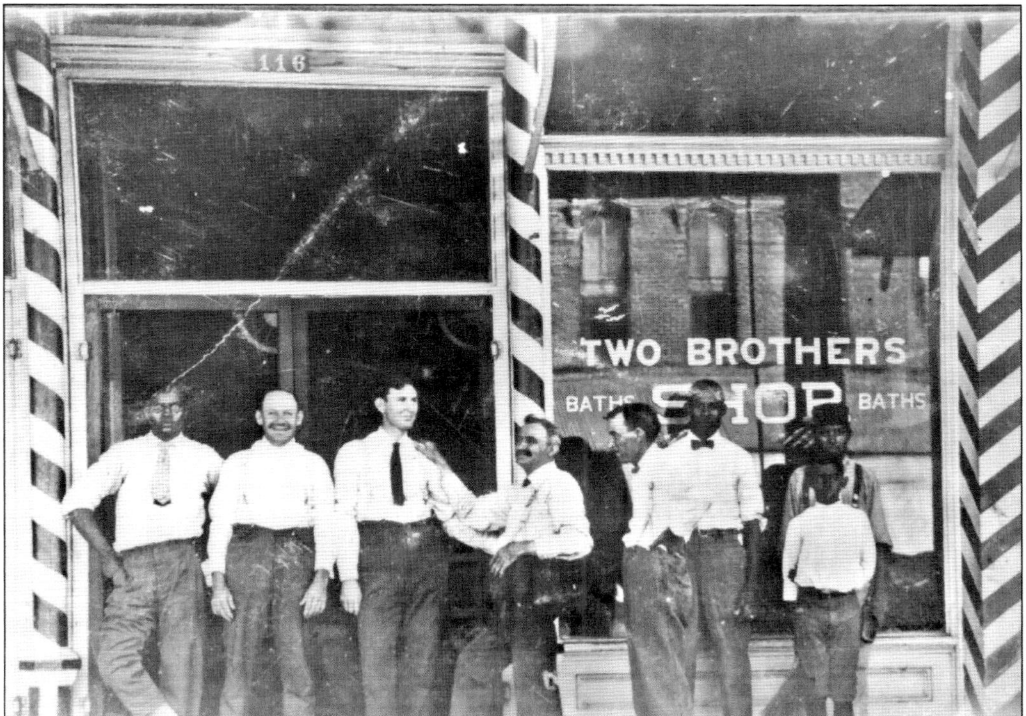

Barbershops were an exclusive male-only haven. Men came not only for a shave and haircut, but also to "talk shop" and share information about a variety of topics. Each customer had his own personal shaving mug. The photograph depicts unidentified men in front of the Two Brothers Barber Shop, which was owned by A. S. Vandiver and located at 116 North Beaton Street.

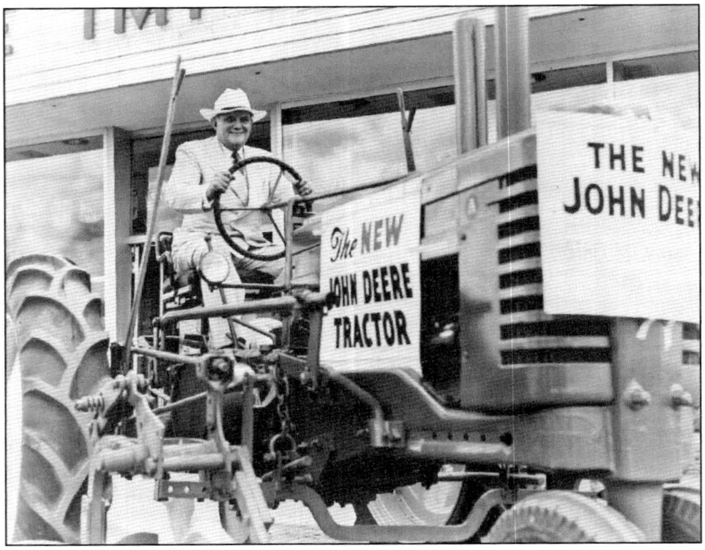

Stroube Implements opened at 1506 South Seventh Street on July 24, 1948, as the local dealership for John Deere tractors and farm equipment. Large numbers of townspeople came to celebrate the grand opening. Among the special guests was Texas governor Beauford Jester, shown here on a new John Deere tractor. (Courtesy of Steve Stroube.)

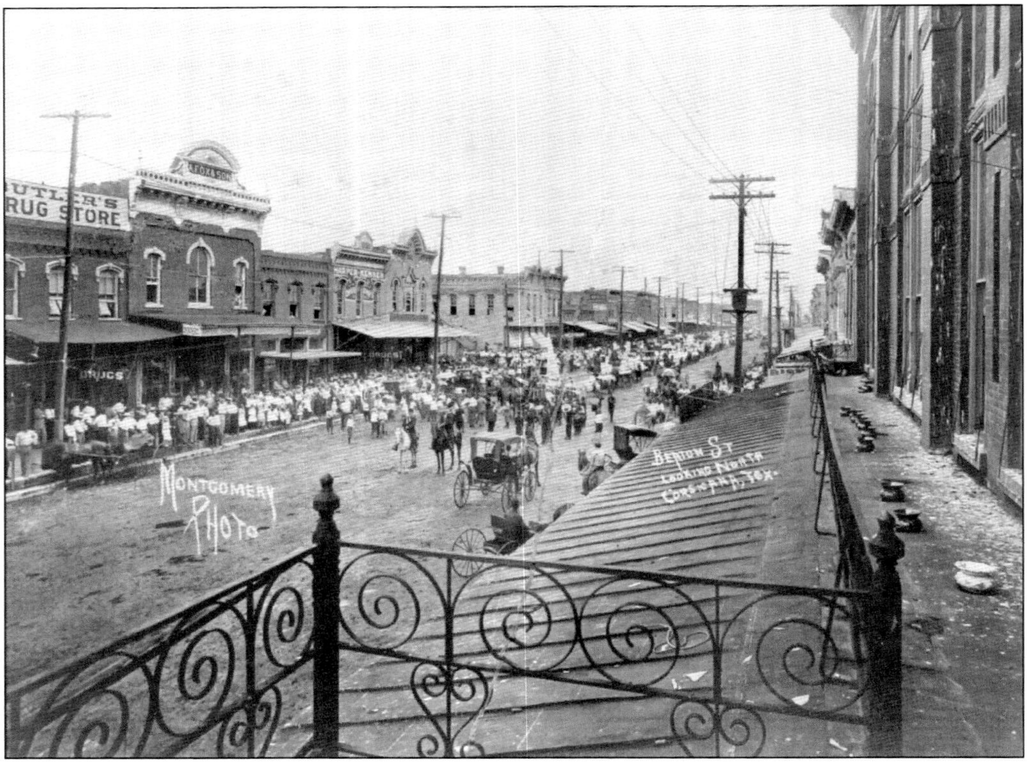

This photograph of the stock show parade on Beaton Street was taken about 1910 by Joseph Montgomery, whose studio was at 118 North Beaton Street. Butler's Drug Store (left), at 108 South Beaton Street, was owned by James E. Butler. A. (Alexander) Fox and Son (Eli), next door at 106 South Beaton, sold dry goods, notions, carpets, and gentlemen's furnishings. This photograph was taken from the balcony of the Merchant's Opera House. Note the spitoons on the balcony.

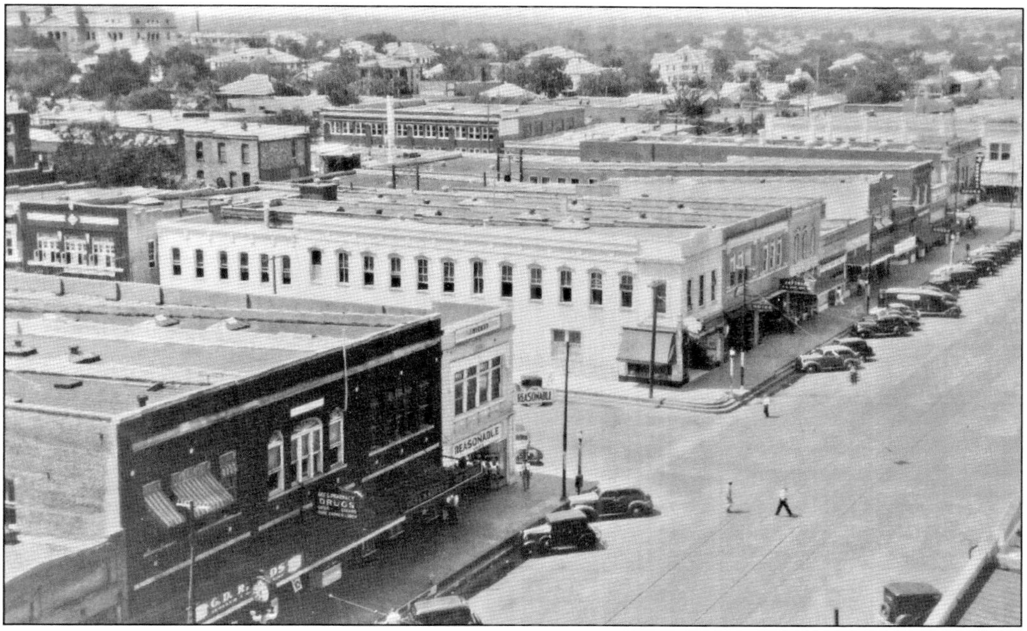

This 1936 photograph of Beaton Street depicts G. D. Rhodes Jewelers (lower left) at 118 North Beaton Street, Gee's Pharmacy at 120 North Beaton, and Reasonable Millinery Shop at 124 North Beaton. The millinery shop was owned by Julia Redden, whose husband, Charles, was a salesman at Harris and Jacobs Clothing Store.

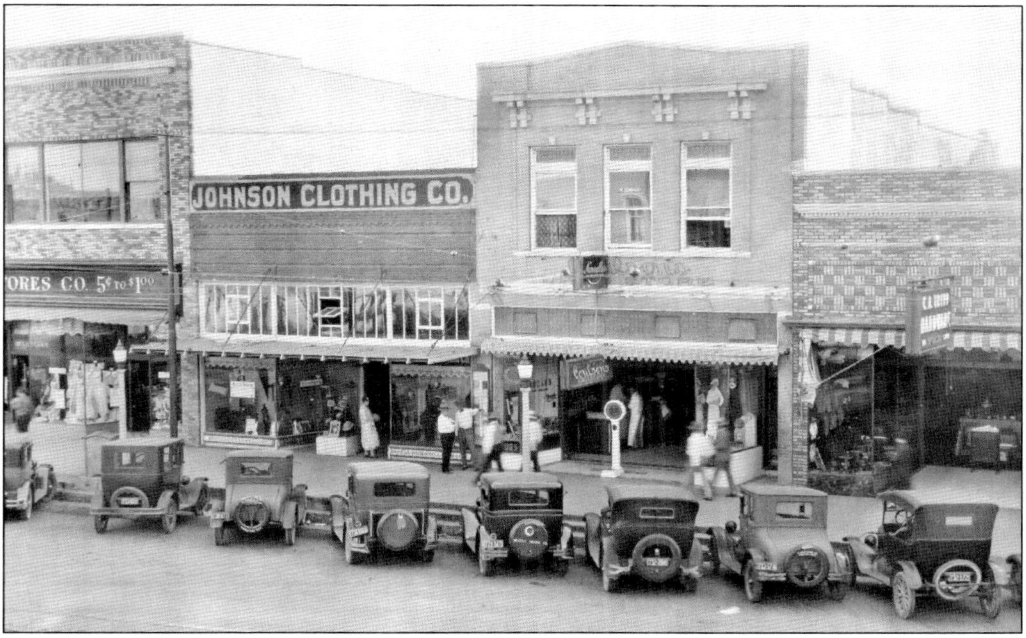

This 1931 photograph depicts F. W. Woolworth at 102 North Beaton Street, Johnson Clothing company at 108 North Beaton, Coulson's Drug Store at 110 North Beaton, and C. A. Tripp Hardware Store at 112 North Beaton. Johnson's boasted of selling society brand clothes, while Tripp's advertisements reminded customers, "the recollection of quality remains long after the price is forgotten."

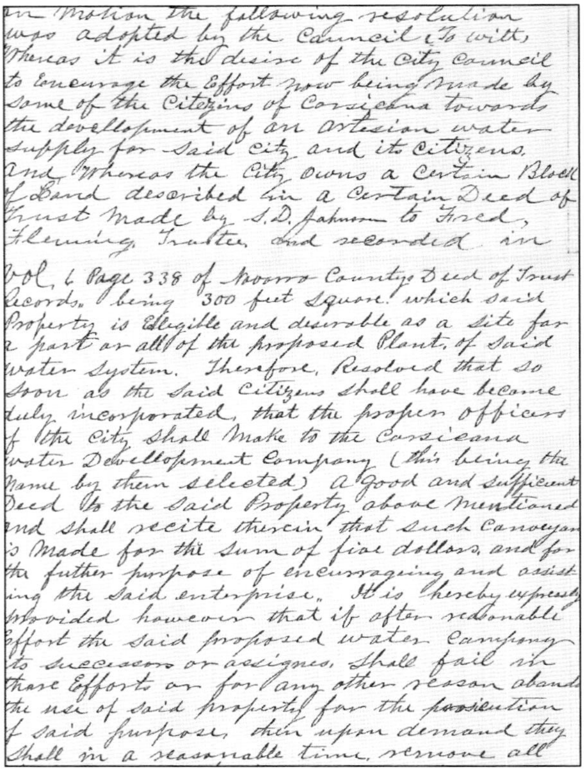

n motion the following resolution
was adopted by the Council (to wit,
Whereas it is the desire of the City Council
to encourage the effort now being made by
some of the Citizens of Corsicana towards
the devellopment of an artesian water
supply for said city and its citizens,
and Whereas the City owns a certain Block
of Land described in a certain Deed of
Trust made by S.D. Johnson to Fred,
Fleming, Trustee and recorded in
Vol. 6 Page 338 of Navarro County Deed of Trust
Records, being 300 feet square which said
Property is Elegible and desirable as a site for
a part or all of the proposed Plant, of said
water System. Therefore, Resolved that so
soon as the said Citizens shall have become
duly incorporated, that the proper officers
of the City shall make to the Corsicana
water Devellopment Company (this being the
name by them selected) a good and sufficent
Deed to the said Property above mentioned
and shall recite therein that such conveyan
is made for the sum of five dollars, and for
the futher purpose of encourraging and assist
ing the said enterprise. It is hereby expressly
provided however that if after reasonable
effort the said proposed water Company
its successors or assignees, shall fail in
their Efforts or for any other reason aband
the use of said property for the prosecution
of said purpose, then upon demand they
shall in a reasonable time, remove all

When the cotton market collapsed in the 1890s, town leaders were determined to attract new industry to diversify the economy. The resource that was lacking was an adequate water supply. The city council deeded several tracts of land in town to the Corsicana Water Development Company to sink an artesian well. On June 9, 1894, drillers discovered oil in the 300 block of South Twelfth Street while searching for water, launching the state's first commercial oil field. (Courtesy of Corsicana City Records.)

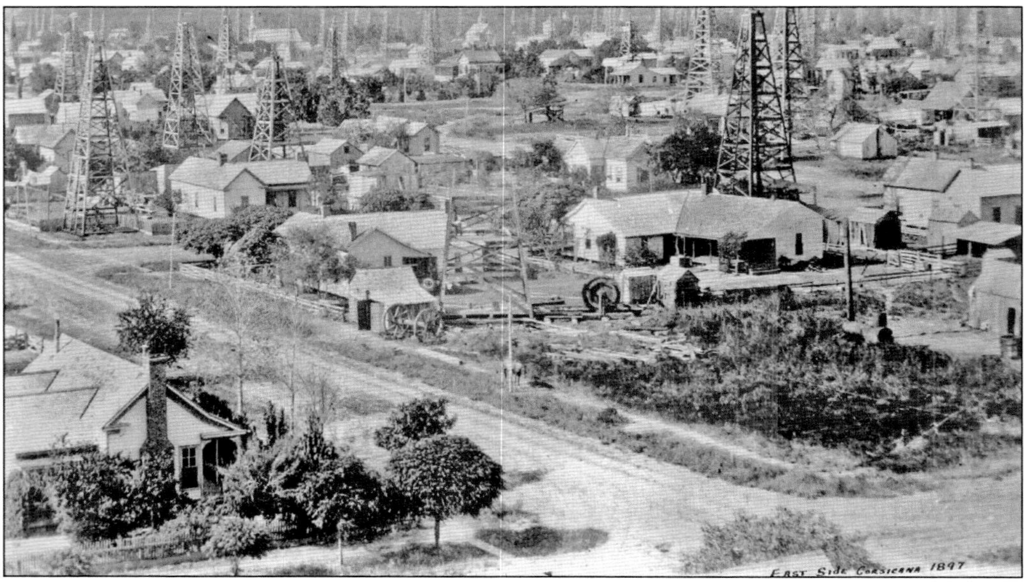

The purpose of drilling artesian wells to expand the city's limited water supply was to attract new industry to Corsicana. The inadvertent discovery of oil in the process accomplished this goal, with the 1894–1895 city directory listing more than 30 oil-related businesses. As depicted in this 1897 photograph, by the end of the 1890s, there were 1,000 oil wells within the city limits of Corsicana producing more than 800,000 barrels of oil per year.

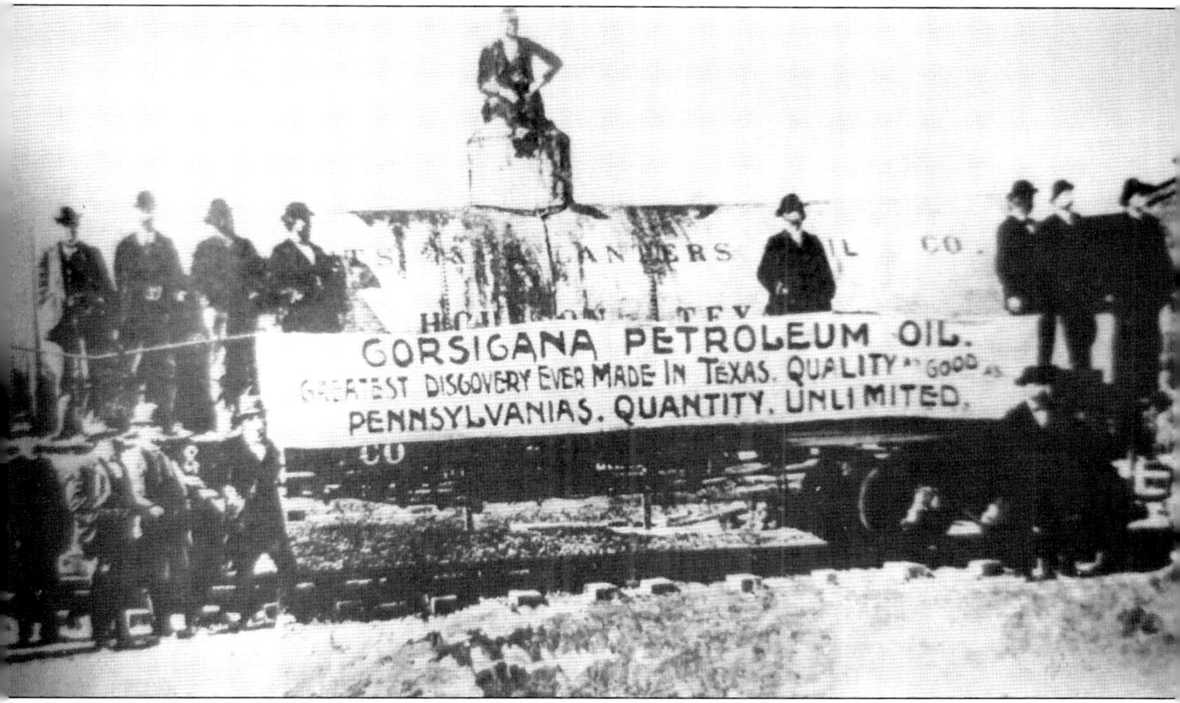

The discovery of oil and the development of the first commercial oil field in Texas not only boosted the local economy, but also raised community pride, as depicted in this photograph of a railcar filled with Corsicana petroleum. Several important developments related to the petroleum industry occurred in Corsicana. Brothers C. E. and M. C. Baker modified the rotary equipment they had used to drill water wells to be more suitable for drilling for oil. Joseph Cullinan persuaded the St. Louis, Arkansas, and Texas Railroad (commonly called the Cotton Belt Railroad) to provide a coal-burning locomotive, which was converted to petroleum fuel and made a flawless run to nearby Hillsboro. Corsicana was among the first towns in Texas to use petroleum products to pave its streets and also to use natural gas for heating and lighting. The first refinery west of the Mississippi River was constructed south of town. Some of the state's first laws related to conservation and production were initiated by leaders in the oil industry in Texas.

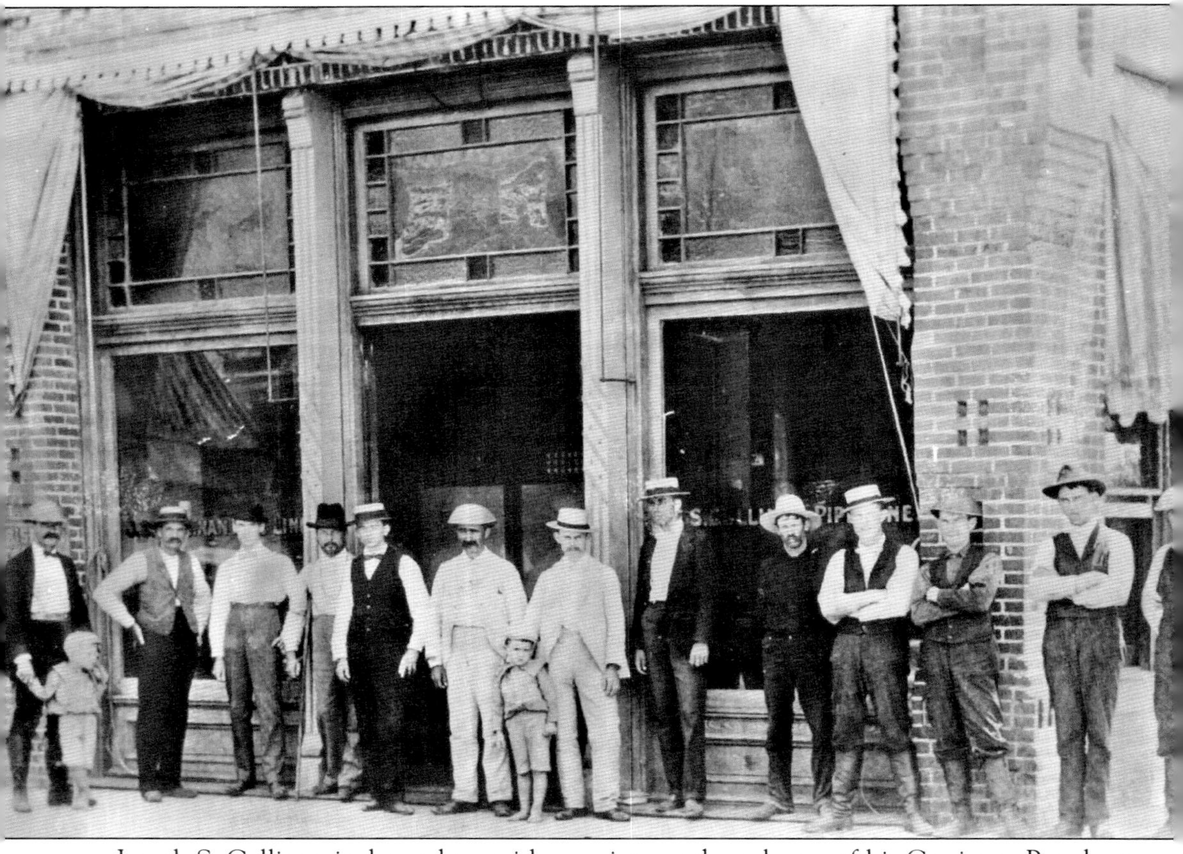

Joseph S. Cullinan is shown here with associates and employees of his Corsicana Petroleum Company office at 111 West Sixth Avenue. Corsicana oil producers realized early on they lacked the expertise needed to manage the newly developing field. Mayor James Whiteselle invited Cullinan to evaluate the situation and provide direction to the new industry. Born in Pennsylvania in 1860, Cullinan started working in the oil patch at age 14, learning the business from the ground up. He introduced a number of innovative concepts in production, transporting, and marketing petroleum through his company, which later evolved into the Magnolia Petroleum Company. Cullinan moved to Beaumont in 1901, where he helped develop the Spindletop field and founded the Texas Company, commonly called Texaco. The Texaco charter was drafted by Corsicana attorney W. J. McKie. He moved his operation to Houston, making that city the focal point of the oil industry in the southwestern United States. Pictured above from left to right are J. S. Cullinan, Craig Cullinan (boy), George Smith, F. T. Whitehill, Dr. Michael Cullinan, Willis Collier, W. H. Page, John Cullinan (boy), W. C. Procter, E. R. Brown, Danny Burk, W. T. Cushing, Frank Cullinan, Ed Wright, and Frank Perifeld.

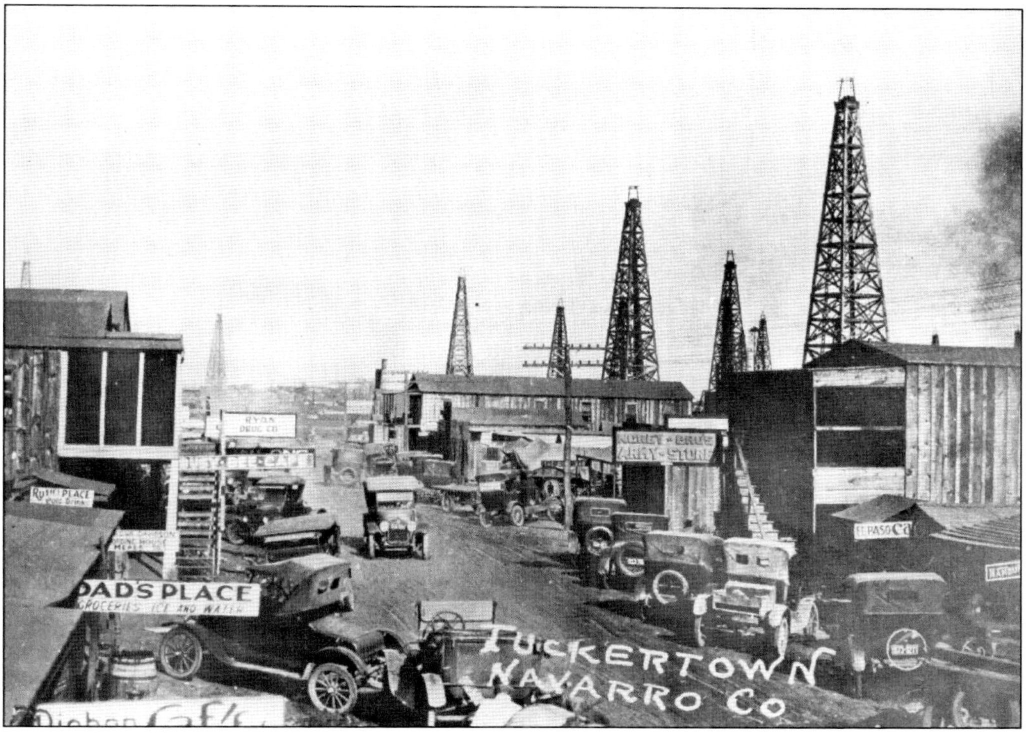

During the oil boom, which began in 1923, boomtowns sprang up all over Navarro County. The most notable was Tuckertown, southeast of Corsicana. With a population of 6,000 within three months of its beginnings, Tuckertown was the epitome of lawlessness. The town was destroyed by fire in 1927.

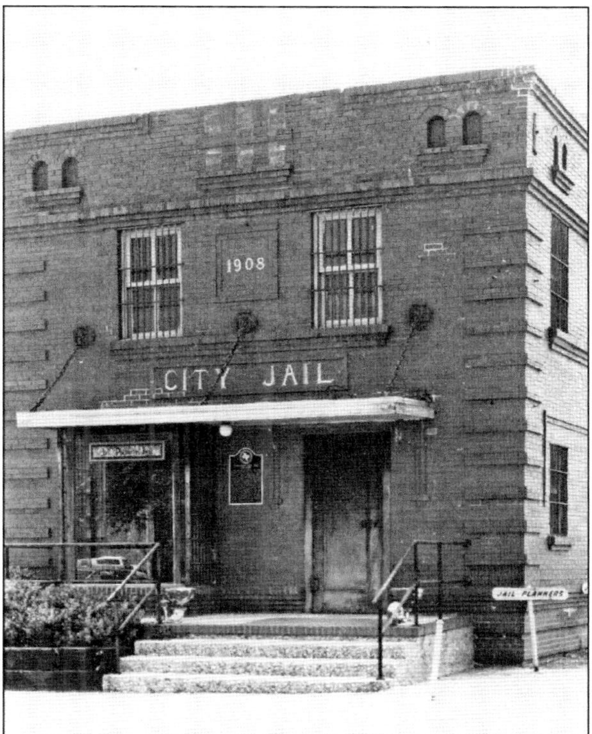

Built in 1908, the city jail, located at 207 West Fifth Avenue, could comfortably accommodate 12 prisoners. However, with the crime related to the oil boom, it frequently was well over capacity, holding as many as 80 inmates on occasions. The overflow was handcuffed together outside and confined to a tree in an arrangement referred to as a trotline.

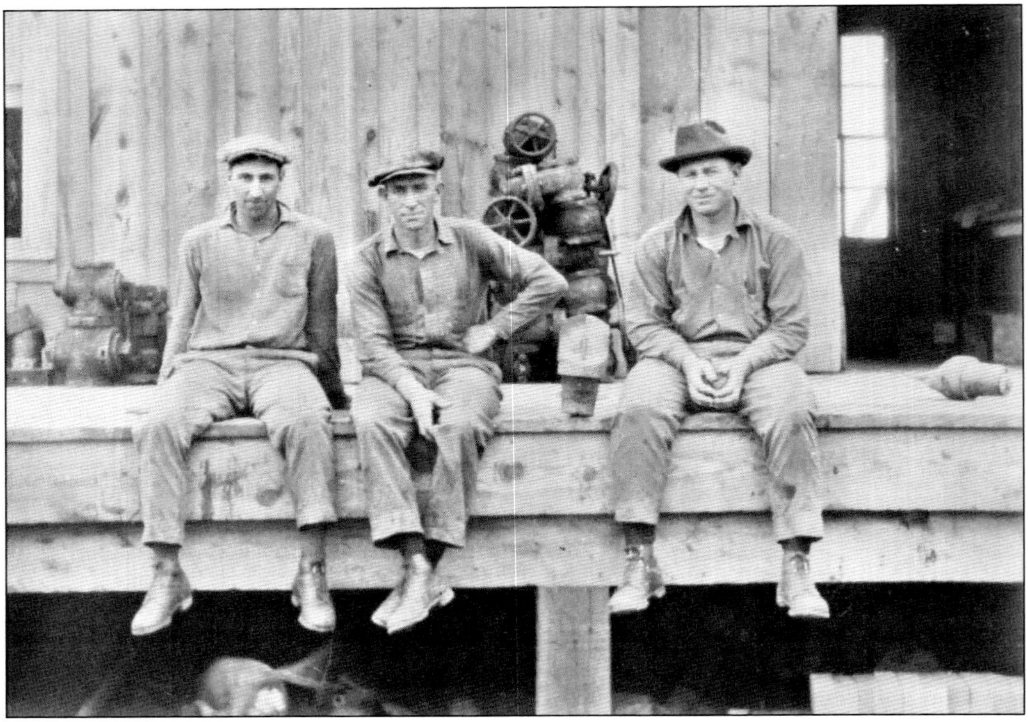

Pictured from left to right are Frank McNally and brothers W. C. "Cornie" and H. R. "Bill" Stroube. McNally was a half brother. In 1924, the Stroube brothers drilled a wildcat gusher well near Mildred that provided the foundation for their highly successful oil business. Among H. R. Stroube's many civic contributions was leading the drive to build the Navarro Regional Hospital in 1951. (Courtesy of Navarro County Oil Museum.)

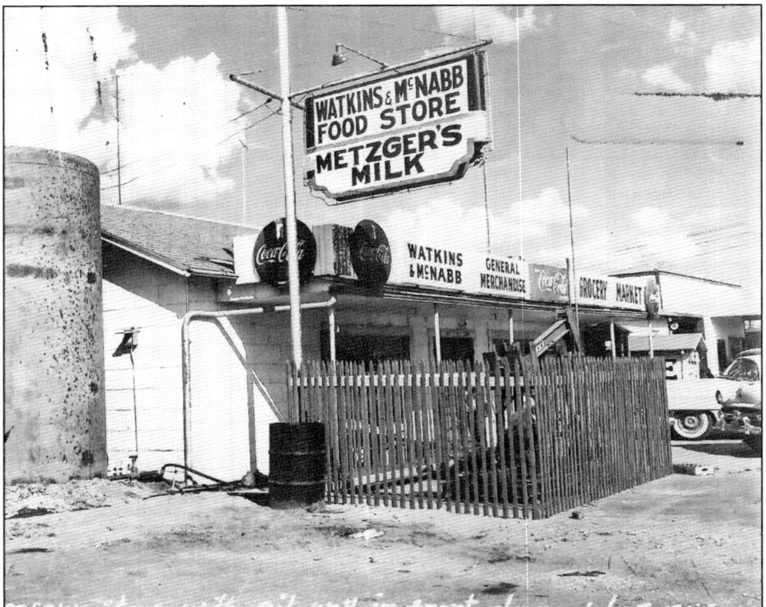

The Corsicana area experienced a minor resurgence in oil production during the 1950s. As in previous boom periods, wells were drilled in some rather unusual places, such as in front of the Watkins and McNabb Food Store owned by Otie Watkins and Lousie McNabb, located at 711 South Seventh Street. (Courtesy of City of Corsicana, Stroube Collection.)

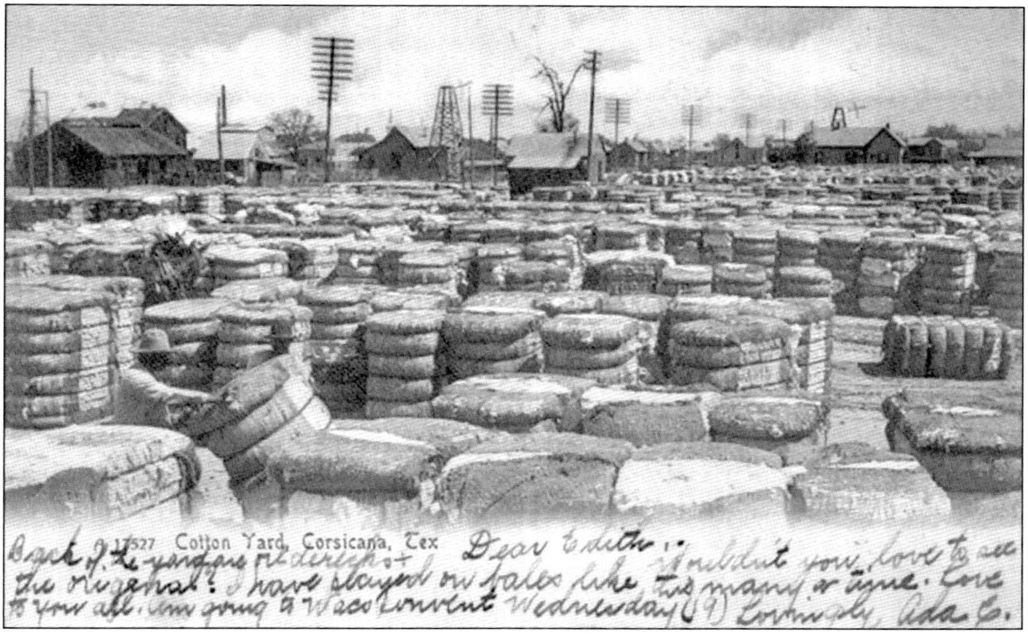

Cotton was king of Navarro County for many decades. During its peak production years, the county boasted 60 cotton gins. In the 1920s, there were 300,000 acres under cultivation, and 90,000 bales of cotton were ginned in a single year. Farmers hauled their cotton by wagon to the courthouse square where bidding and trading occurred in a type of cotton exchange. Open yards, such as the one pictured here, replaced the area around the courthouse. (Courtesy of Tresa Darby.)

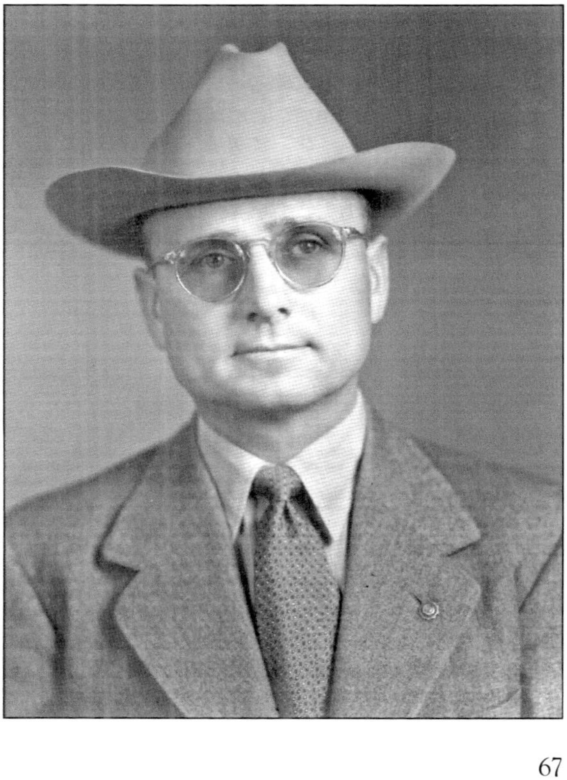

J. Afton Burke was born near Corsicana in 1897. After serving in World War I, Burke returned to Navarro County, where he engaged in two endeavors that are synonymous with Texas, namely oil and cattle. In the 1920s, Burke helped develop oilfields at Mexia, Wortham, and Powell. In addition to his oil interests, Burke introduced Brahman cattle into Navarro County. (Courtesy of Kathryn Zack.)

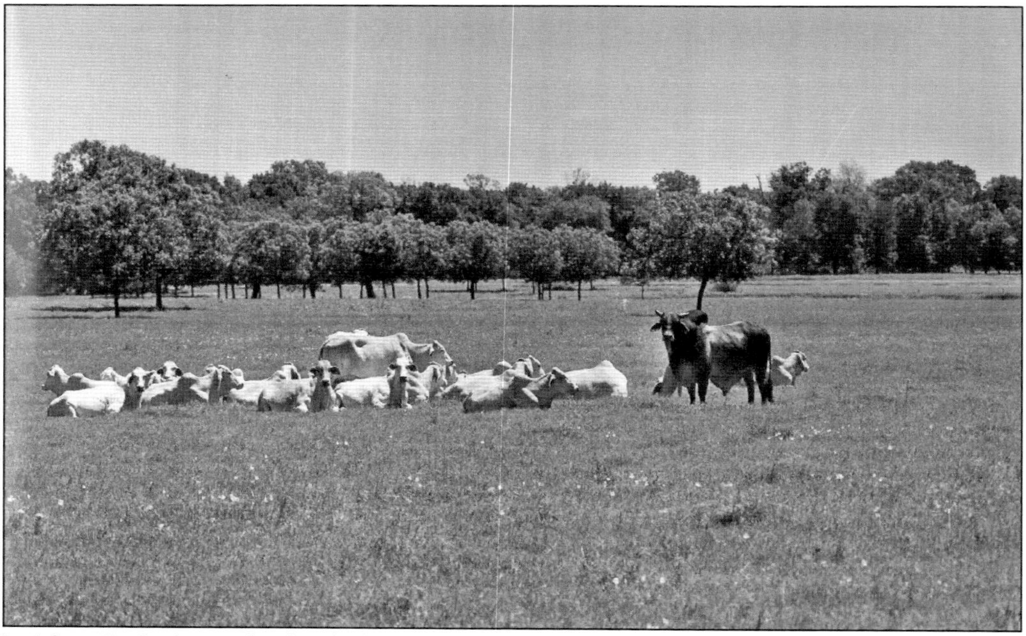

J. Afton Burke began his herd of registered Brahmans in 1932, an operation that eventually expanded to more than 1,000 cows and 175 bulls. From the ranch on Highway 31, east of downtown Corsicana, Burke shipped registered Brahmans to South America, Cuba, and Southeast Asia. (Courtesy of Kathryn Zack.)

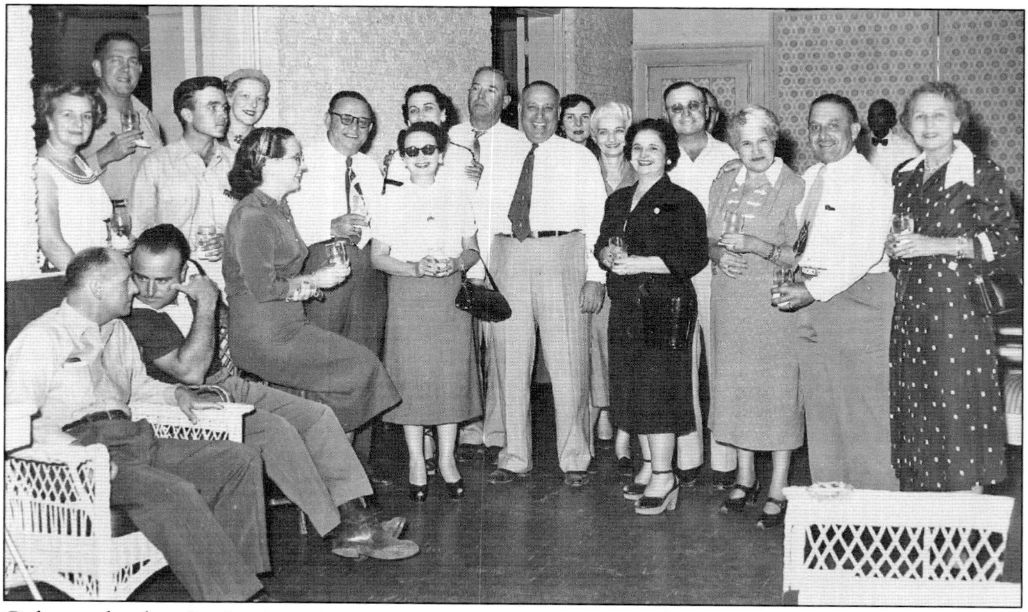

Cuba and other Latin American countries were major markets for Burke bulls, which were transported by airplanes to those destinations. Ranchers and government officials from those countries were frequent guests at the Burke Ranch on East Highway 31. Depicted here is a group of Cuban visitors being entertained by J. Afton Burke at the Corsicana Country Club in 1947. (Courtesy of Kathryn Zack.)

Three

Churches, Schools, and Clubs

Corsicana's Cultural Scene

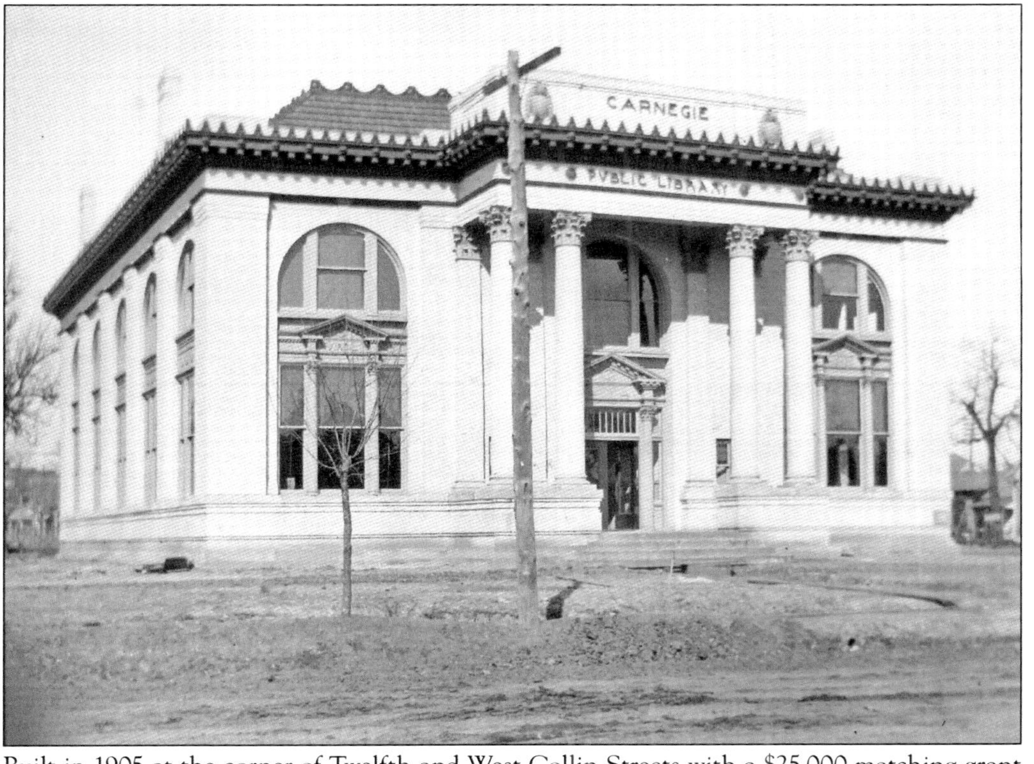

Built in 1905 at the corner of Twelfth and West Collin Streets with a $25,000 matching grant from steel magnate Andrew Carnegie, the library housed the book collection on the first floor, while the second floor was an auditorium that served as a community meeting room. The building was demolished in the 1960s and replaced by the current facility at the same location.

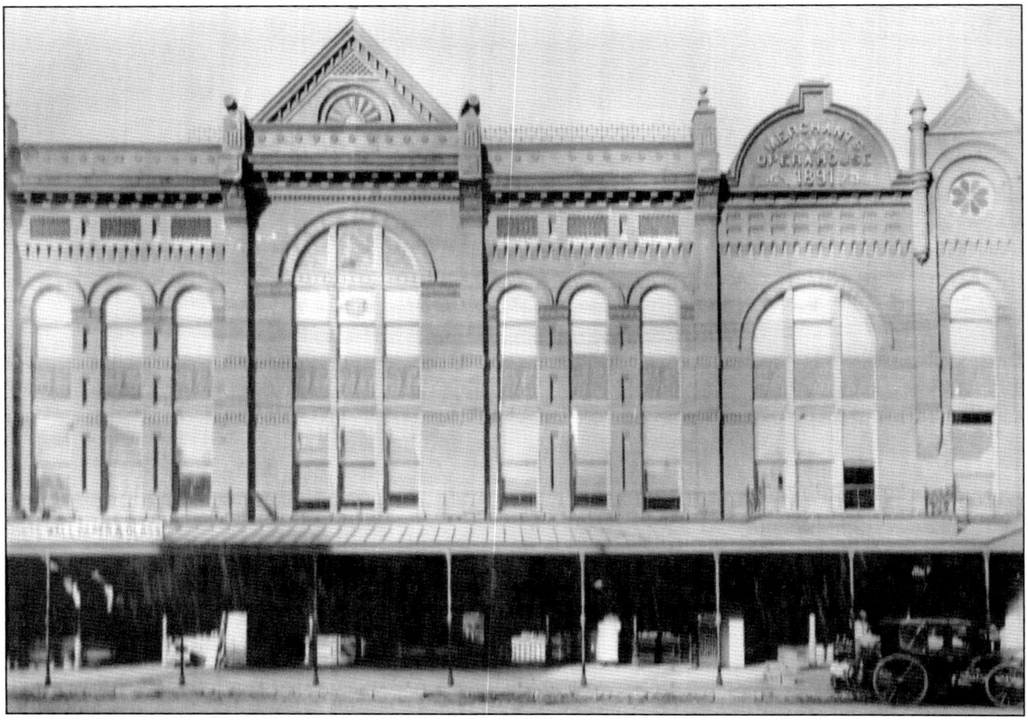

The Merchants Opera House, located at 117 South Beaton Street, was opened in 1891. A three-story structure, the opera house claimed to be the finest such facility between Dallas and Houston. The third-floor auditorium had a seating capacity of 1,000. Notable acts that performed at the opera house included Lillian Russell and George M. Cohan. When the building burned in April 1914 (below) it was not rebuilt, since the popularity of motion pictures was on the rise and interest in live theater was diminishing.

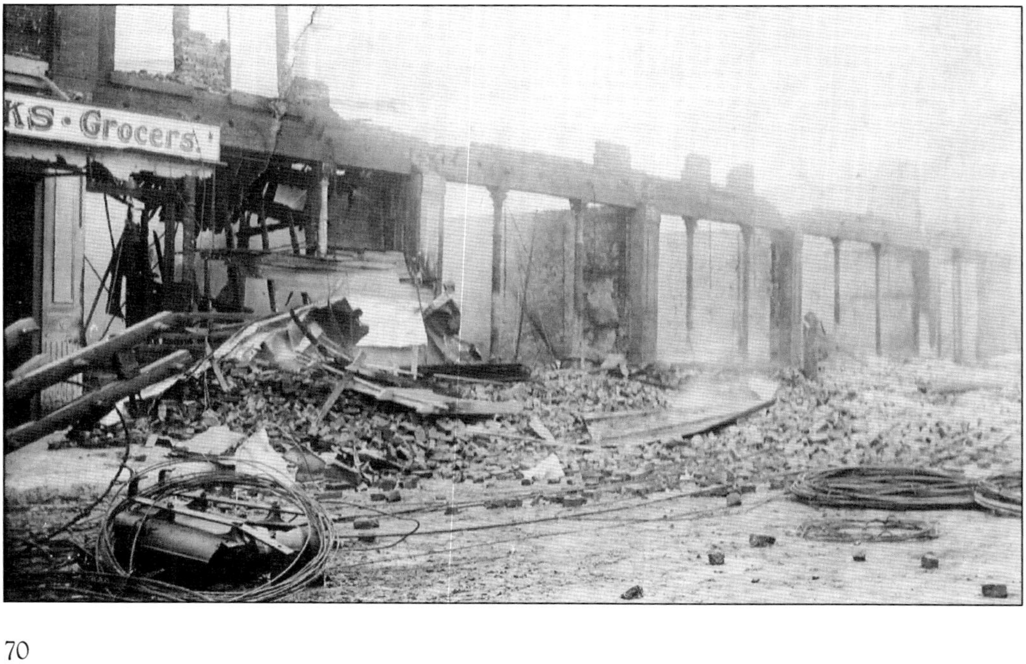

Because of its location between Dallas and Houston, Corsicana was able to attract some of the most prominent entertainers of the late 19th and early 20th centuries. As seen in this playbill, march king John Phillip Sousa and his band performed at the Corsicana High School auditorium in 1925. During his Corsicana visit, Sousa met with the band members of the Corsicana State Home and the IOOF Home.

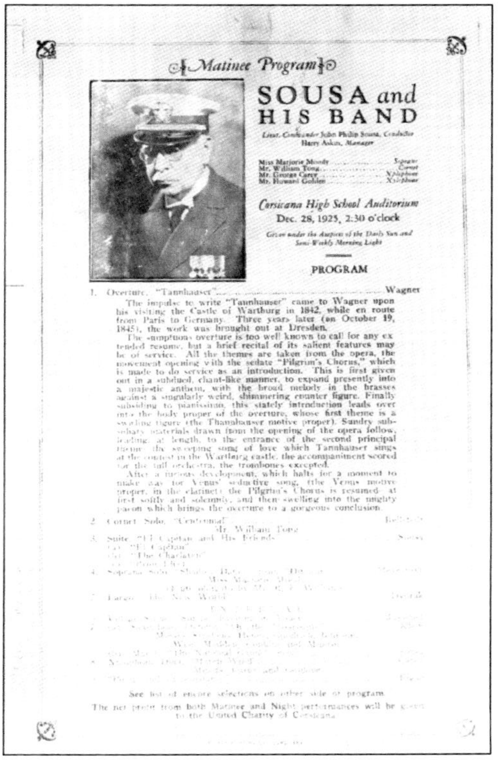

Matinee Program

SOUSA *and* HIS BAND

Lieut. Commander John Philip Sousa, Conductor
Harry Askin, *Manager*

Miss Marjorie Moody .... *Soprano*
Mr. William Tong .... *Cornet*
Mr. George Carey .... *Xylophone*
Mr. Howard Goulden .... *Xylophone*

Corsicana High School Auditorium
Dec. 28, 1925, 2:30 o'clock

Given under the Auspices of the Daily Sun and Semi-Weekly Morning Light

PROGRAM

1. Overture, "Tannhauser" .... Wagner

The impulse to write "Tannhauser" came to Wagner upon his visiting the Castle of Wartburg in 1842, while en route from Paris to Germany. Three years later (on October 19, 1845), the work was brought out at Dresden.

The sumptuous overture is too well known to call for any extended resume, but a brief recital of its salient features may be of service. All the themes are taken from the opera, the movement opening with the sedate "Pilgrim's Chorus," which is made to do service as an introduction. This is first given out in a subdued, chant-like manner, to expand presently into a majestic anthem, with the broad melody in the brasses against a singularly weird, shimmering counter figure. Finally subsiding to pianissimo, this stately introduction leads over into the body proper of the overture, whose first theme is a swaling figure (the Thannhauser motive proper). Sandry subsidiary materials drawn from the opening of the opera follow, leading, at length, to the entrance of the second principal theme: the sweeping song of love which Tannhauser sings at the contest in the Wartburg castle, the accompaniment scored for the full orchestra, the trombones excepted.

After a furious development, which halts for a moment to make way for Venus' seductive song, (the Venus motive proper, in the clarinet) the Pilgrim's Chorus is resumed: at first softly and solemnly, and then swelling into the mighty paeon which brings the overture to a gorgeous conclusion.

2. Cornet Solo, "Centennial" [illegible]
Mr. William Tong

3. Suite, "El Capitan and His Friends" .... Sousa
(a) "El Capitan"
(b) "The Charlatan"

[illegible]

See list of encore selections on other side of program.

The net profit from both Matinee and Night performances will be given to the United Charity of Corsicana.

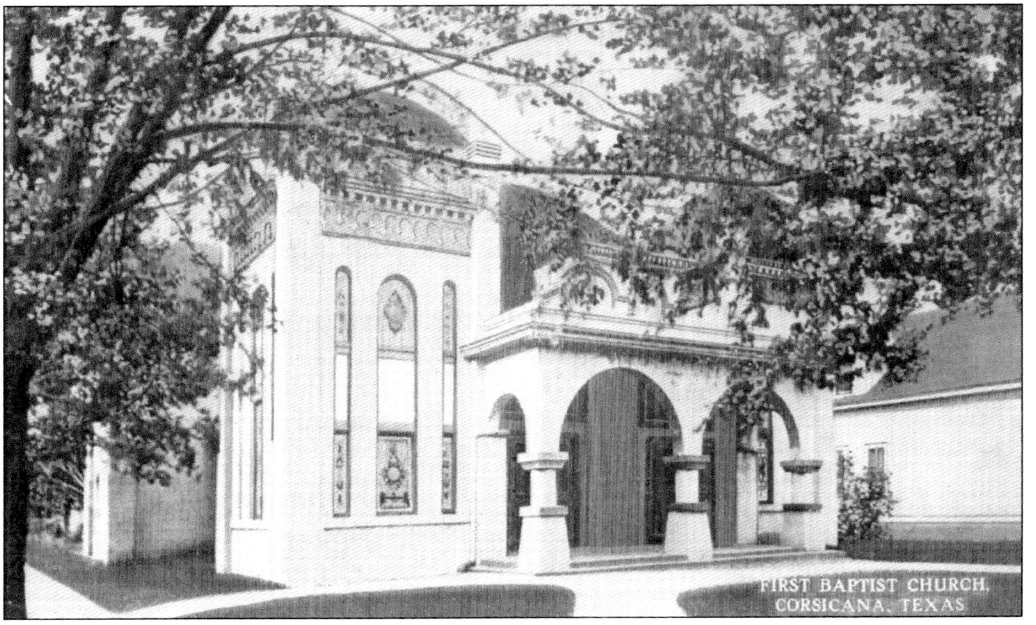

The Baptists had a presence in Corsicana from the beginning of the town's existence in 1848. After meeting in various locations, they erected this building at the corner of Fourteenth and West Collin Streets in 1901. It served the congregation until 1921, when the current sanctuary was constructed at Fifteenth and West Collin Streets.

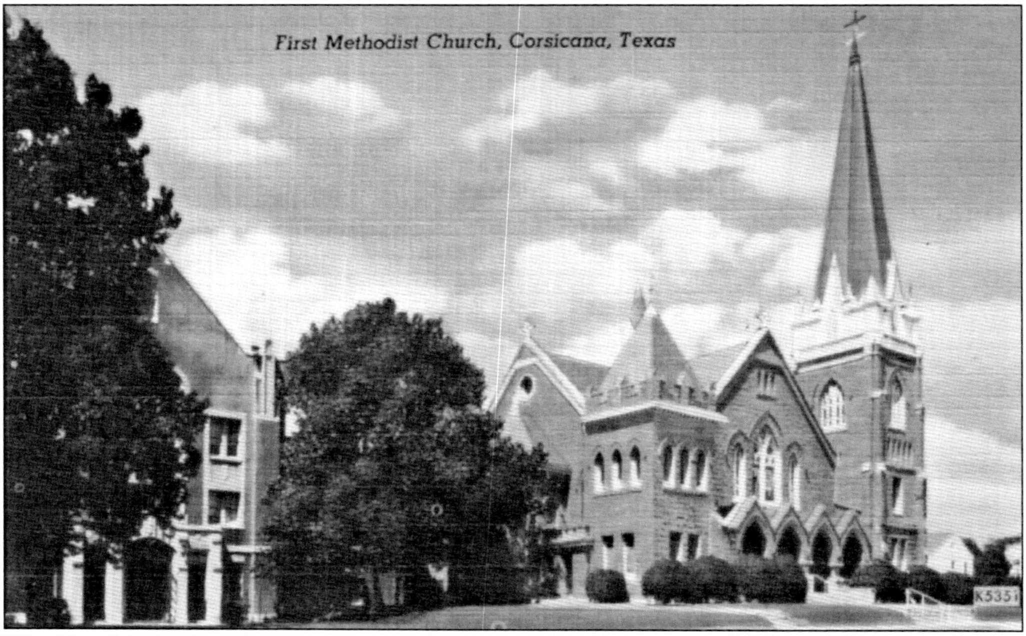

The First Methodist Church acquired the property at the corner of Fifteenth Street and West Third Avenue in 1851, but the first building was not erected until 20 years later. Construction began in 1896 on the current building, depicted in this photograph. Four thousand dollars short of the $40,000 needed to complete the project, minster Abe Mulkey called the congregation together, locked the church doors, and placed a washtub at the altar for a collection plate. As a result of this unusual "altar call," the needed funds were raised in 20 minutes.

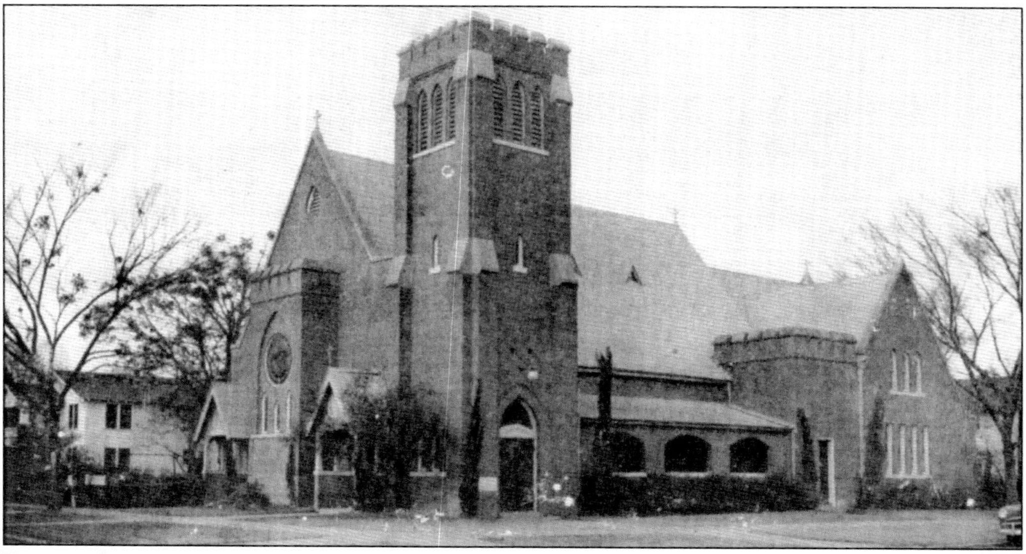

Episcopal services were first conducted in Corsicana in 1855, only seven years after the town's founding. They met in the log courthouse and later in the Masonic lodge before acquiring a permanent location. St. John Episcopal Church has occupied the corner of West Collin and North Fourteenth Streets since 1874. Construction began on the facility pictured here in 1905, and it was dedicated on November 15, 1908

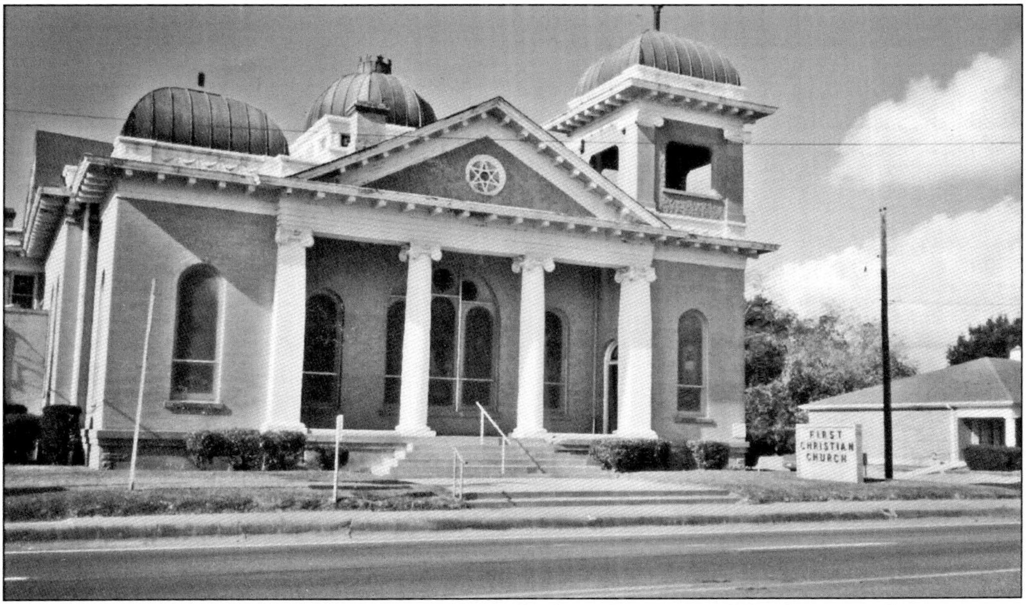

The First Christian Church occupied the corner of Fifteenth Street and Sixth Avenue beginning in 1888. This building was constructed in 1905 at a cost of $20,000. A devastating fire in April 1999 destroyed everything except the exterior walls and the columned porch. The congregation constructed a new meeting place on West Highway 22. The old building was refurbished into condominiums.

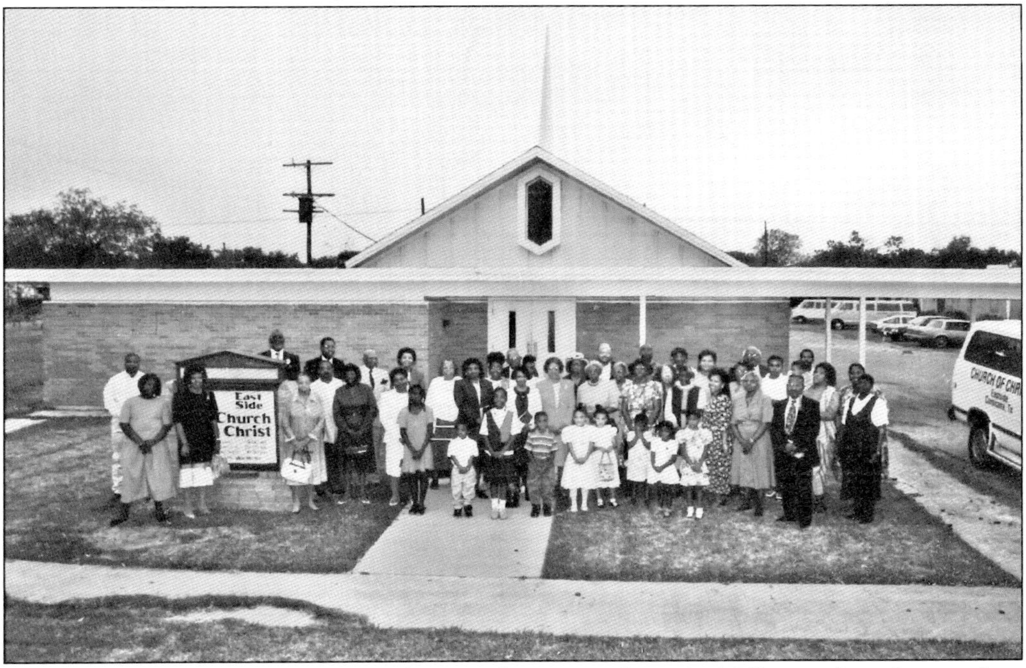

Eastside Church of Christ began in July 1933 when evangelist Luke Miller conducted an outdoor revival meeting at the 1100 block of East Sixth Avenue, resulting in 218 baptisms. In 1948, the congregation moved to 1501 East Seventh Avenue, and in 1972, they dedicated a new facility at 906 East Thirteenth Avenue. Willie Wilmore has served as minister since 1961.

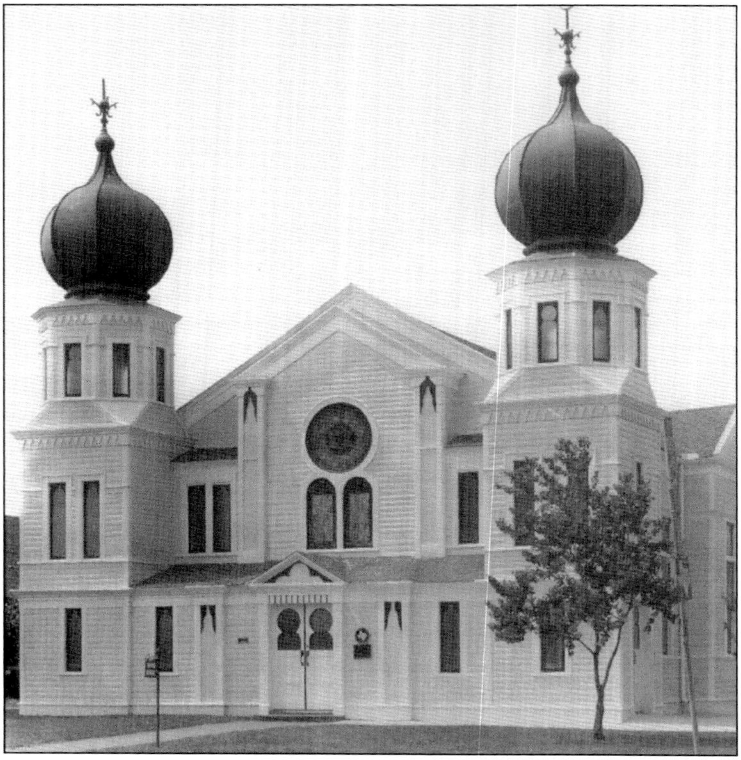

Temple Beth El was constructed on Fifteenth Street between Sixth Avenue and Collin Street in 1898 by the Jewish Reform congregation. When the congregation disbanded in the mid-1980s, plans were to demolish the structure, but a "Save-the Temple" committee comprised of local citizens and the Navarro County Historical Society raised funds to purchase and restore the building. Listed on the National Registry of Historic Places, the temple is now owned by the City of Corsicana and is used as a community center.

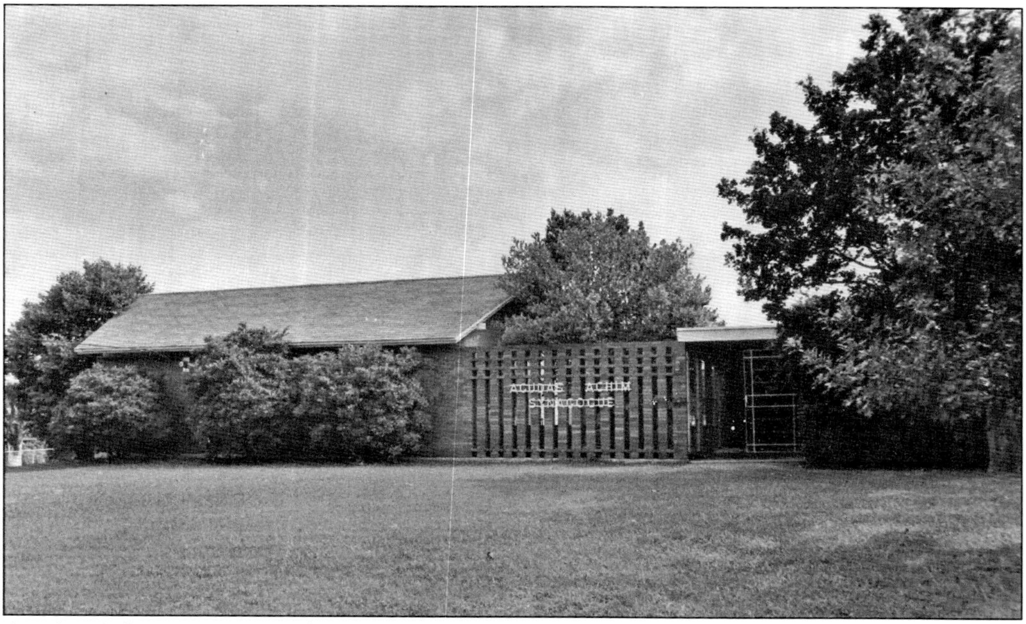

Agudas Achim Synagogue, located at 919 West Park Avenue, was the place of worship of the Orthodox Jewish congregation. They originally met on North Twelfth Street but constructed this facility in 1957. When the congregation dissolved in the 1990s, the building was acquired by the City of Corsicana and is now used as a senior citizens center.

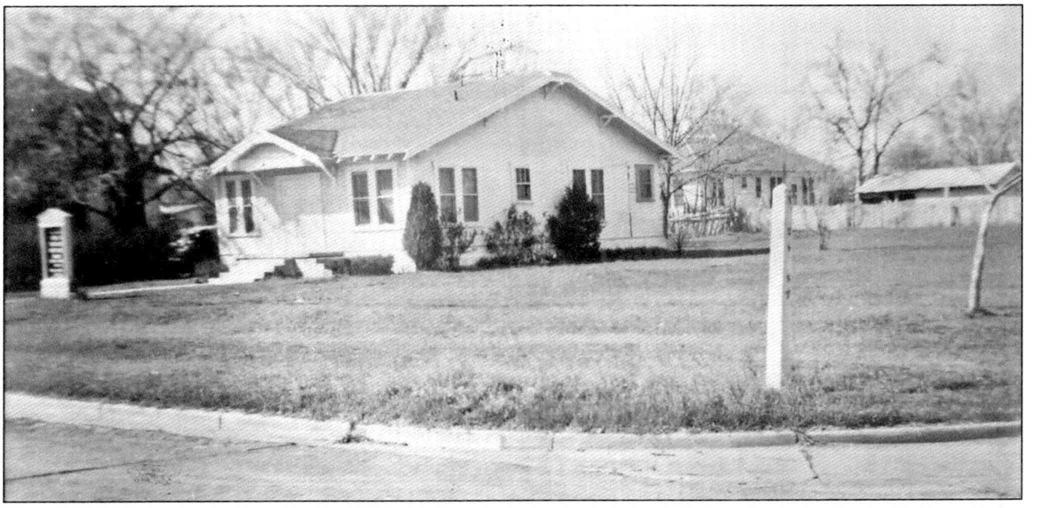

The Lutherans began meeting in Corsicana in 1886 in a saloon. The pastor had to "clean up" the facility on Sunday mornings and set up for worship services. At various times over the years, they met in a trailer and the YMCA, until the first permanent building, shown in this photograph, was constructed in the late 1940s at 1902 West Fifth Avenue. The church moved to its current location on West Highway 22 in 1980. (Courtesy of Bruce Hale.)

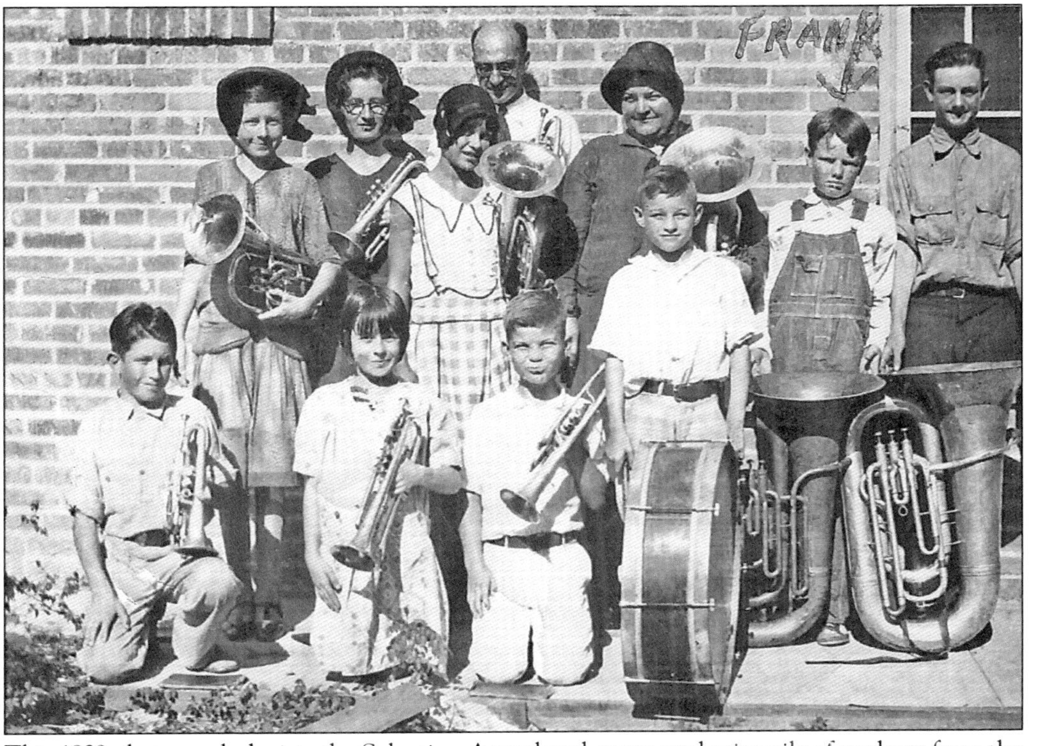

This 1929 photograph depicts the Salvation Army band, composed primarily of students from the area around William B. Travis Elementary School. At the time, the Salvation Army met at 211 West Collin Street, holding services on Sundays and Wednesdays. On Saturday nights on Beaton Street, there was music from the band and preaching on the street corner. (Courtesy of Lona Hines.)

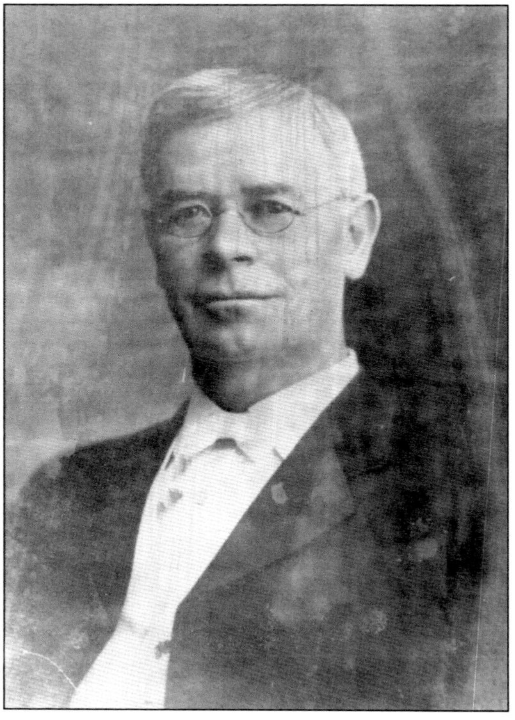

Abe Mulkey was in the grocery business in Corsicana before entering the Methodist ministry in 1885. A dynamic speaker, Mulkey conducted more than 500 revival meetings in 20 states, preached more than 16,000 sermons, and had more than 54,000 conversions. In addition, Mulkey raised thousands of dollars to help build churches and retire debts of local congregations. He was a strong supporter of the Methodist Boys Home of Waco. He died in 1919.

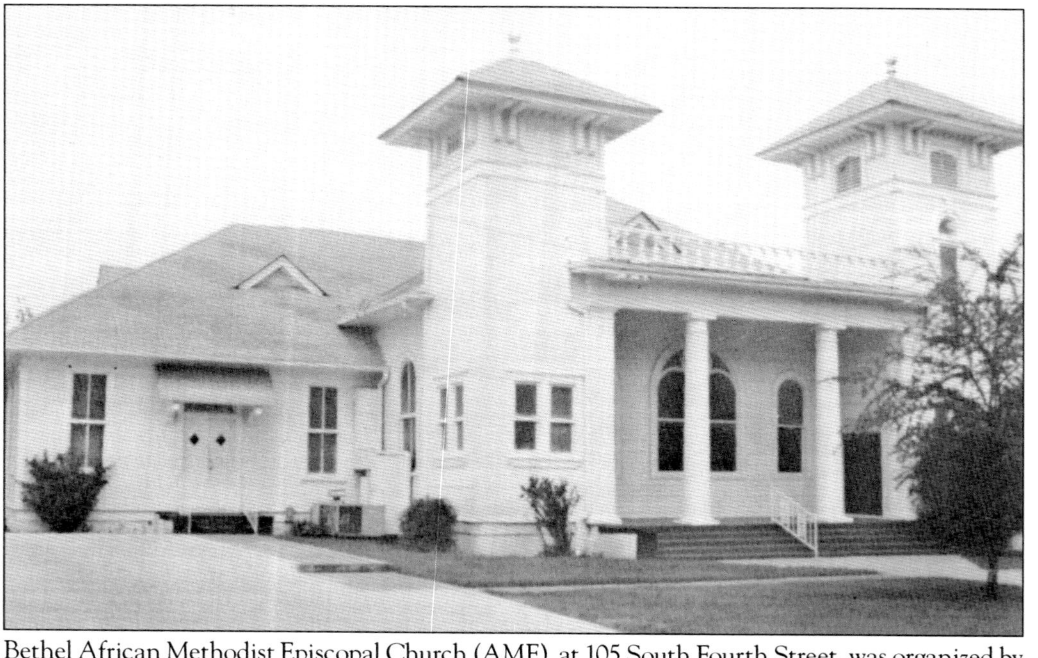

Bethel African Methodist Episcopal Church (AME), at 105 South Fourth Street, was organized by former slaves during the Reconstruction period following the Civil War. The congregation initially met in a tent near the present location of the courthouse until they constructed a permanent building at the present site of the church at the corner of East Collin and North Fourth Streets. (Courtesy of Mabel Scott.)

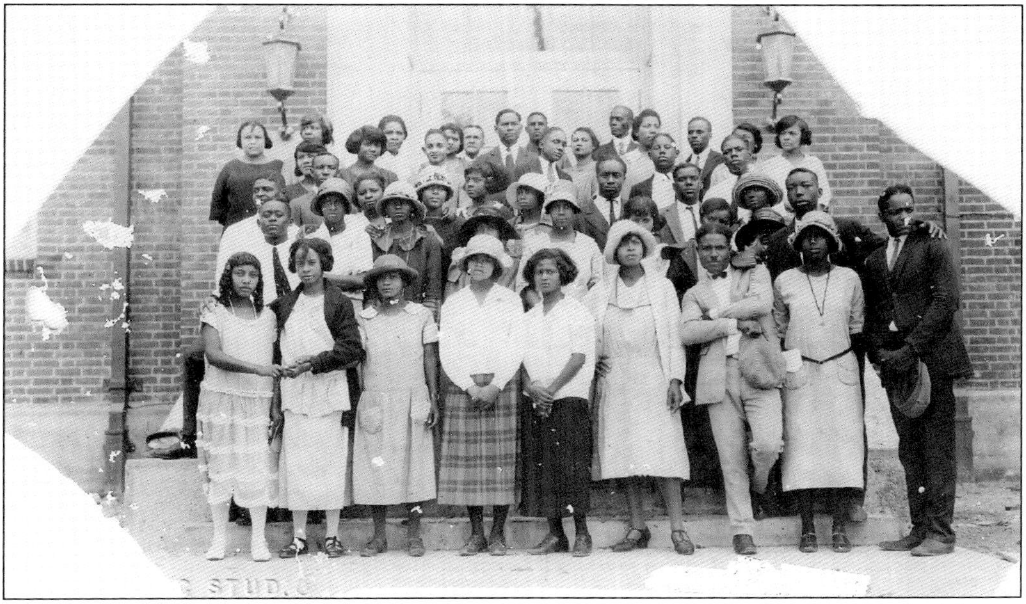

This 1930s-era photograph depicts the members of the Sixth Avenue Baptist Church, which began in 1904 with 25 members. Rev. R. T. Pardee was the first pastor of the congregation. The original building faced Sixth Avenue, but when a new facility was constructed, it faced Fifth Street. L. F. Hardee served effectively as the minister in the 1940s, and James Chaney pastored the church for 28 years. Today the membership consists of 100 families. (Courtesy of Mabel Scott.)

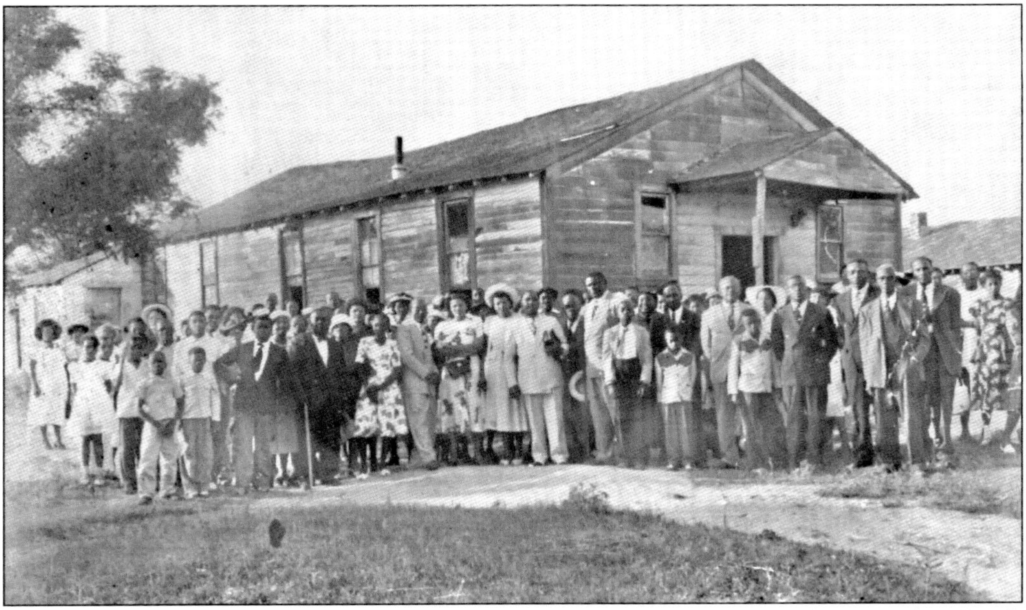

Bethlehem Missionary Baptist Church began in June 1921 when a group gathered under a brush arbor in Bob Bell's yard. After formally organizing, the congregation met for a time in the Masonic lodge hall before constructing this building at 409 North Third Street. It was replaced by a new structure on the same site in 1940, and the current meeting place was built in 1972. (Courtesy of Dairy Johnson Jr.)

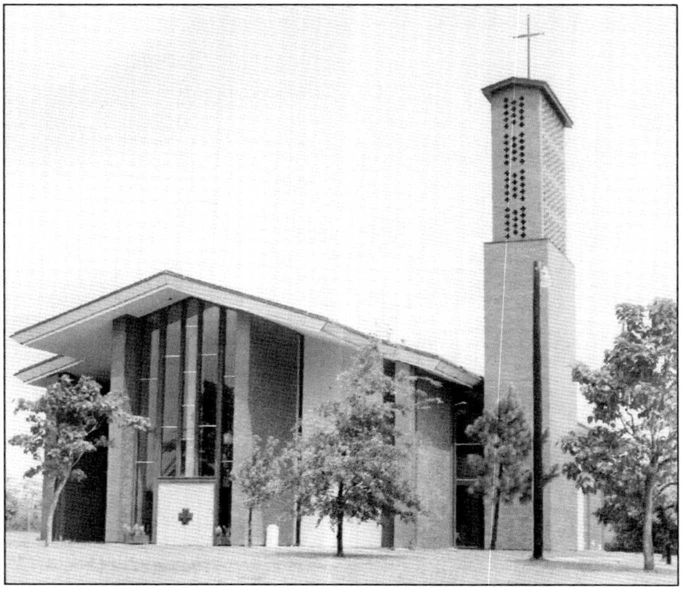

The Catholic Church was organized in Corsicana in 1871, and shortly thereafter, the congregation constructed a house of worship at Fifteenth and Collin Streets. The church also operated a parochial school nearby. The building pictured here was constructed in 1955 on a 22-acre site on West Highway 22. A generous bequest in the will of oilman and philanthropist James L. Collins provided much of the funding for the facility, along with the James L. Collins Catholic School adjacent to the church.

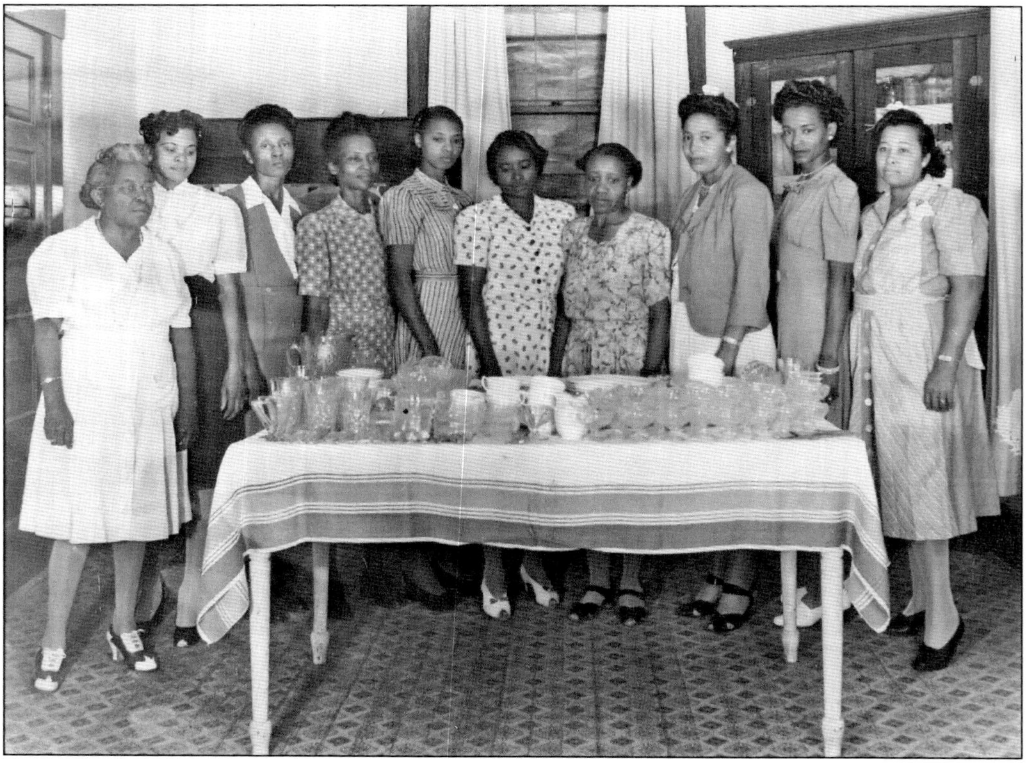

The First Independent Baptist Church was organized in 1868 by former slaves. The congregation incorporated the term" independent" into their name to distinguish themselves from the Baptist movement being led by whites at that time. The current building, located at 701 East Fifth Street, was erected in 1918. Depicted in this photograph is the Young Women's Christian Missionary Society. (Courtesy of Mabel Scott.)

Born in Brooklyn, New York, in 1854, Katie Kinsloe lived in Corsicana for 47 years with her husband, Harris, who managed the Corsicana Bottling Works. She was a longtime member of St. John's Episcopal Church. She died in 1937 at the age of 82. As was customary in those days, her funeral was conducted at the family home at 618 West Third Avenue.

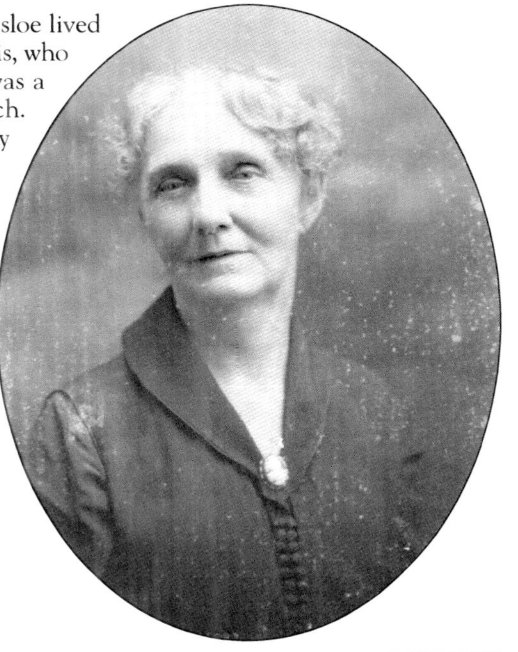

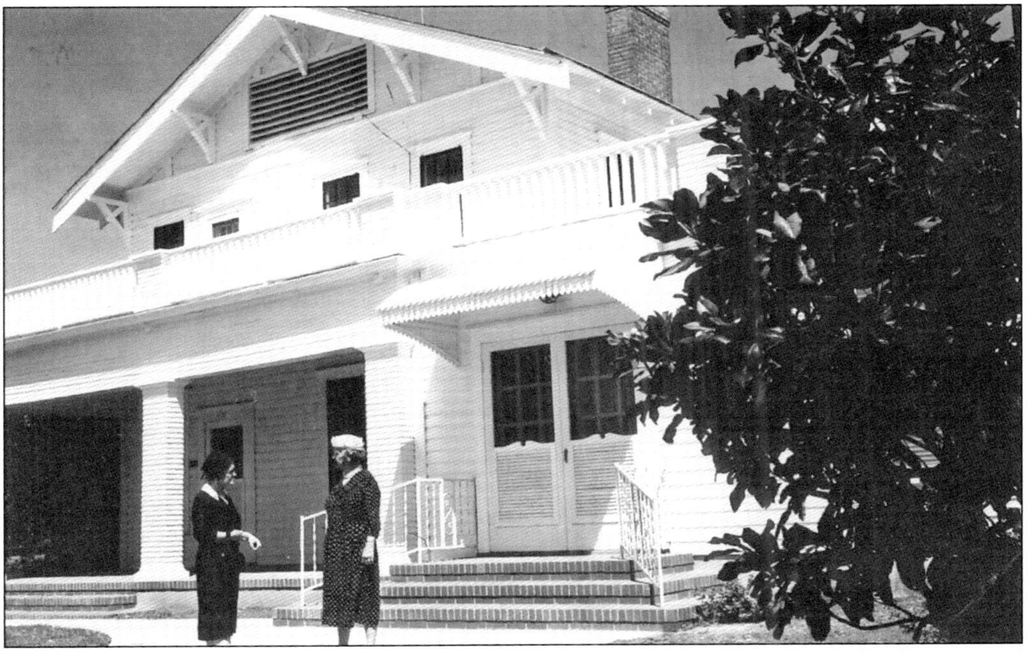

In 1937, the United Daughters of the Confederacy planned to meet in Corsicana for their annual state convention but lacked an adequate facility to host the event. Consequently, Kathleen Steele and other members of the group began exploring prospective locations for a home for the Corsicana Women's Clubs. Autry Kelley of Houston donated the home of her late grandmother H. E "Katie" Kinsloe at 618 West Third Avenue for that purpose. Ethel Wortham (left) and Winnie Lee Rankin are shown in front of the Kinsloe House in this 1950s-era photograph. The original building was destroyed by fire in 1988 and was replaced with a new structure on the same site.

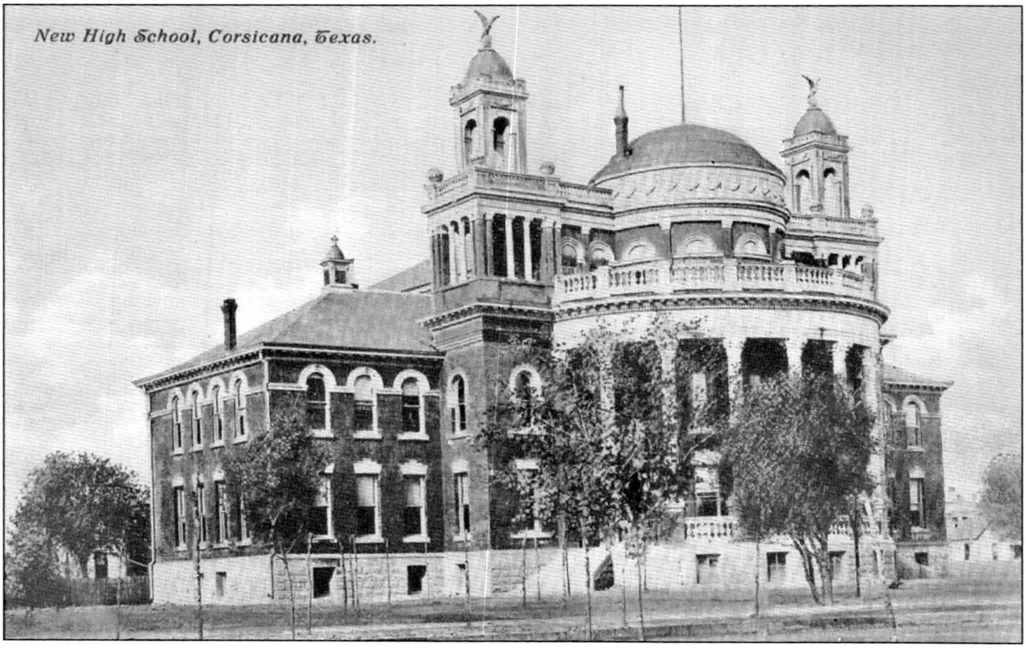

The Corsicana Independent School District was established in 1881 with J. T. Hand as the first superintendent and two schools for white students and one for African Americans. This building, which housed Corsicana High School, was built in 1902 at a cost of $30,000 and occupied the site where Drane Middle School is currently located.

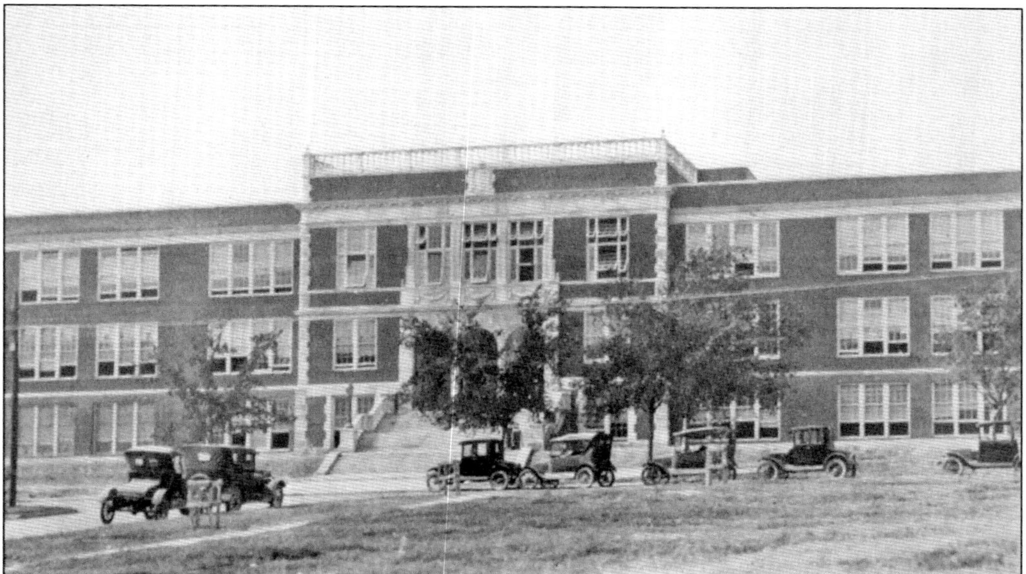

This photograph was taken in 1923 while a new high school was under construction. The economic prosperity generated by the oil boom provided significant revenue increases for this and other building projects. Classes met for the first time in this facility in 1924. When a new high school was constructed on West Highway 22, this building was converted into Drane Junior High School. (Courtesy of Tresa Darby.)

Prior to rulings by the federal courts in the 1950s and 1960s, Corsicana schools were segregated by race. G. W. Jackson High School, the African American high school, was in operation from 1881 to 1970. It was located at 1012 East Fifth Avenue. It was closed when the new Corsicana High School opened on West Highway 22 in 1970, and the black and white schools were merged. Depicted here is a granite marker noting the site of Jackson High, expressing the loyalty of the students to their school.

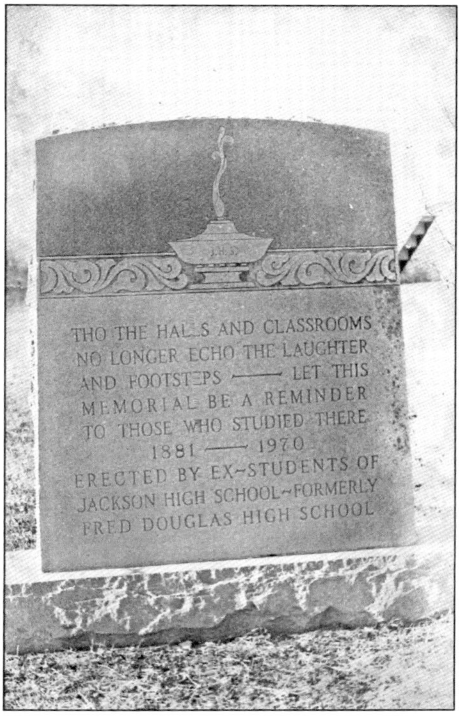

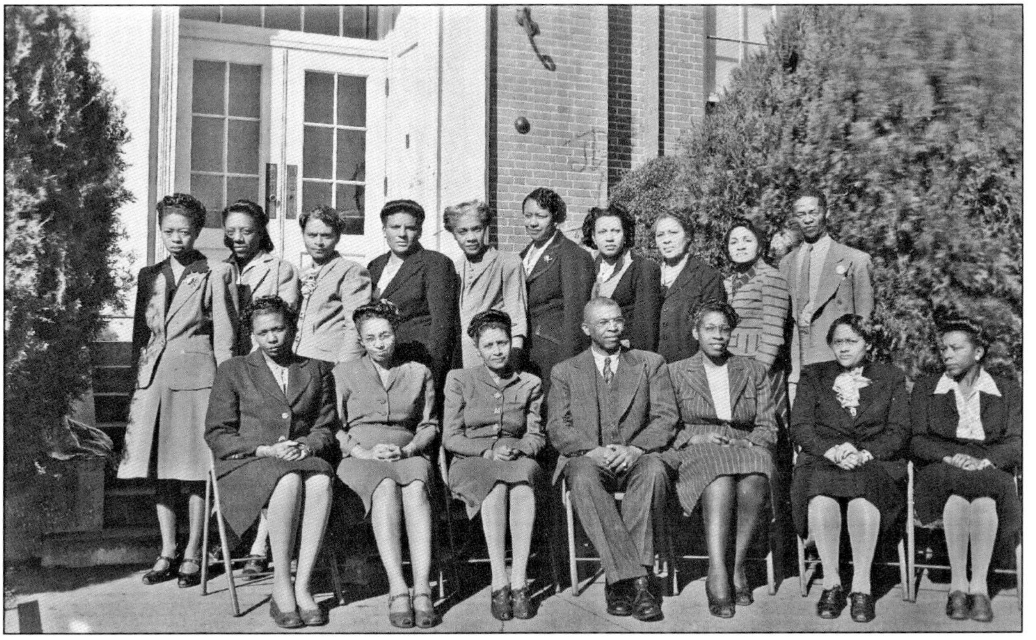

Pictured in front of G. W. Jackson High School are members of the 1947–1948 faculty. From left to right are (first row) Margarita Springfield, Alva Jean Smith, Jimmie Dee Powell, principal Walter Cotton, Zenobia Dobbs, Martha Moody, and Izez Rhodes; (second row) Catherine Britton, Willie Mae Sparks, Marie Hudson, Roxie Cooksey, Johnnie Mae Moore, Zadie (Z. B.) Moore, Johnnie Hardee, Ollie Jones, Christine Orr, and Samuel Smith. (Courtesy of Mabel Scott.)

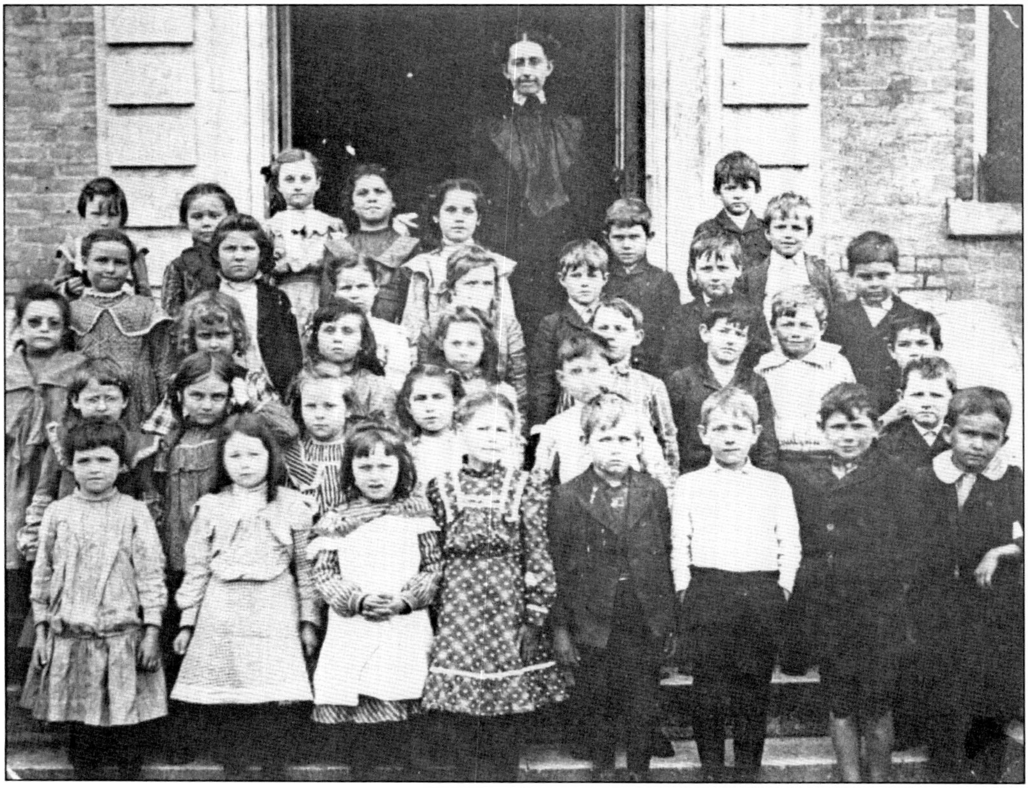

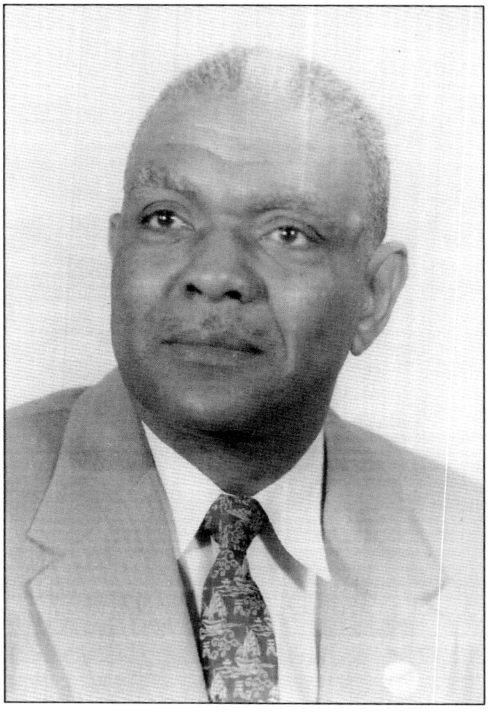

Shown in this photograph are students at the Sacred Heart Parochial School, which was established in 1874 by Fr. Peter Chandy. The school, which was located at 630 West Collin Street, initially enrolled five girls and six boys. Eventually it became a boarding and day school for girls with male students occupying another building down the street. The school closed in 1905.

Harlon Powell was born in Corsicana in 1910. He earned degrees from Paul Quinn College and Texas Southern University. Powell was the first and only principal of the Jackson Elementary School. He was also president of the Colored Teachers Association. A World War II veteran and an ordained minister, Powell was active in the Bethel AME Church, serving on its board of trustees. (Courtesy of Mabel Scott.)

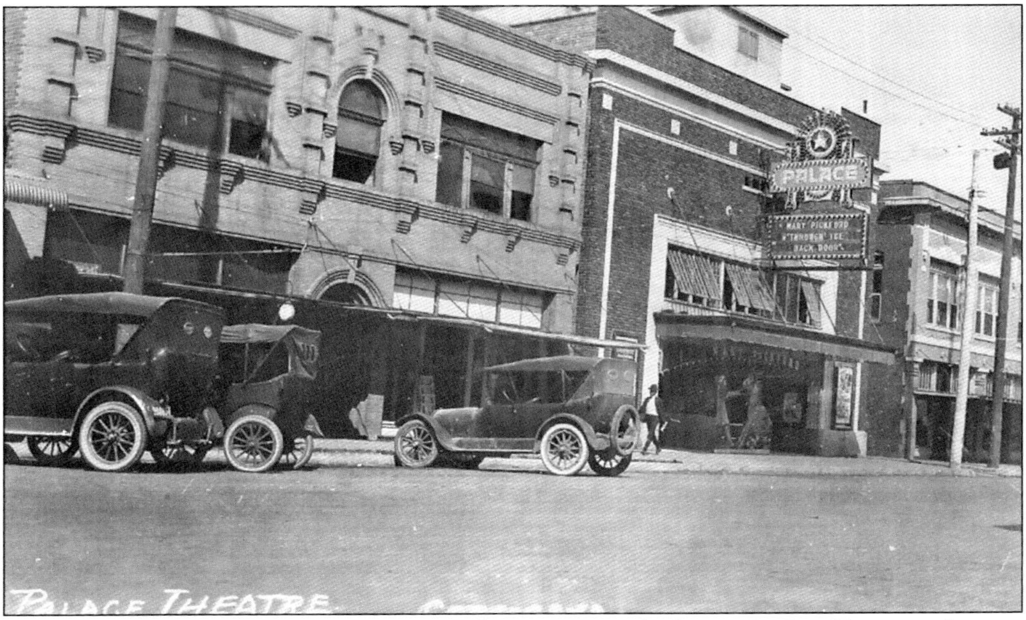

The Palace Theater, located at 112 West Sixth Avenue, was built in 1921 In addition to showing silent films, the theater also hosted live vaudevillian acts. The "talkies" came in the 1930s, and for the next two decades, the Palace Theater enjoyed its golden years. It closed in the early 1970s and remained vacant for two decades until a group of interested citizens began a restoration project in 1999. It reopened in 2002, and today hosts headline entertainers. (Courtesy of Kathryn Zack.)

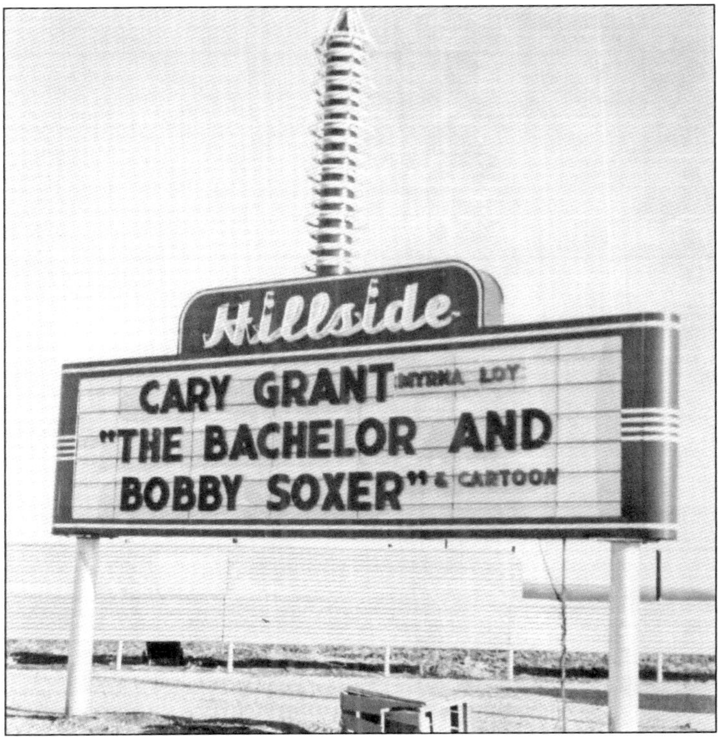

The Hillside Drive-In Theater was a popular form of entertainment for Corsicana residents during the post–World War II years. Owned by Sidney Miller, the Hillside was located on South Fifteenth Street near the current location of the Carmack Watkins Construction Company. With the emergence of television and air-conditioning, drive-in movies became less appealing, resulting in the theater being closed in the 1970s. (Courtesy of Sidney and Jane Miller.)

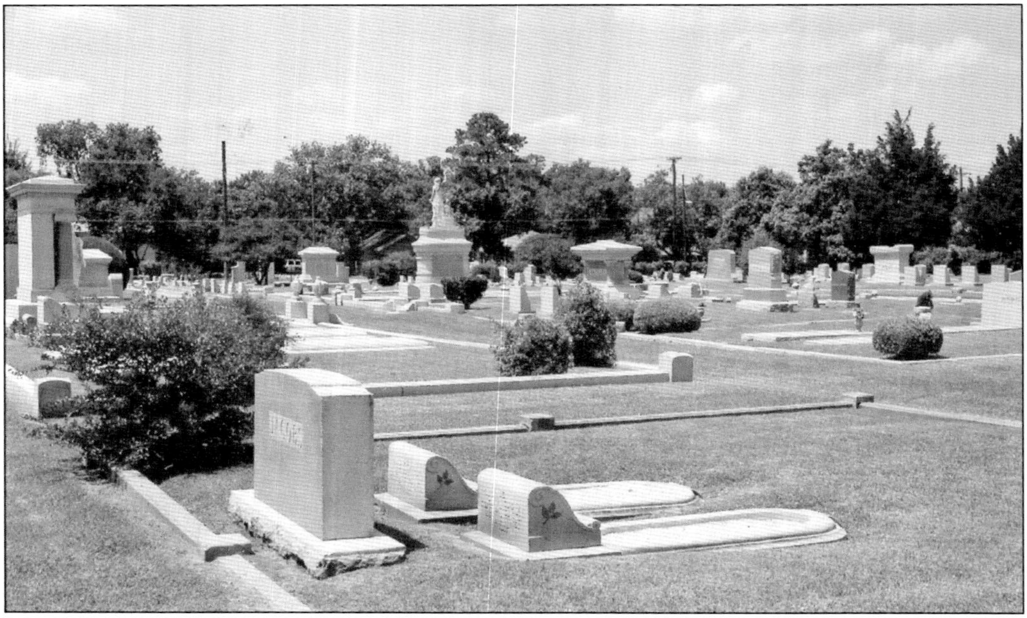

The first burial in the Corsicana Hebrew Cemetery occurred in 1877, with six more during the following three years. The property, which is located on Second Avenue 2 miles west of downtown, was formally purchased in 1881, and the cemetery association was organized the following year to maintain the facility. Of the 402 graves in the cemetery, the most unique is that of the Rope Walker (shown below). A traveling salesman with a peg leg hoping to promote his wares fell while walking a tightrope stretched across Beaton Street in 1884, resulting in his death. Shortly before his demise, he announced he was Jewish but gave no other information about himself, including his name. Because efforts to determine his identity proved fruitless, he was laid to rest in the Hebrew cemetery with the inscription "Rope Walker" on his tombstone. (Both, courtesy of Babette Samuels.)

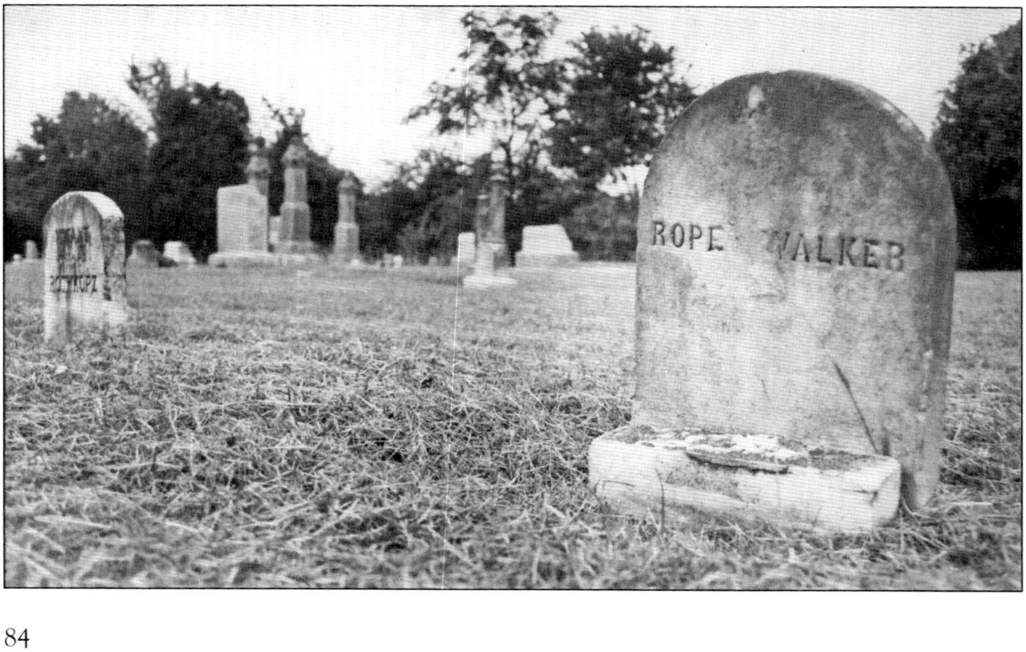

Named for Presbyterian minister N. P. Modrall, this cemetery is located at Twenty-second and Hackberry Streets. Shortly after Modrall's daughter Ellen married, her new husband, J. R. Love, was killed in a Civil War battle. Before word of his death reached Texas, Ellen Love died herself. To comfort the grieving minister, Roger Mills, who was one of Modrall's parishioners, donated the land to bury her. The cemetery is still active today.

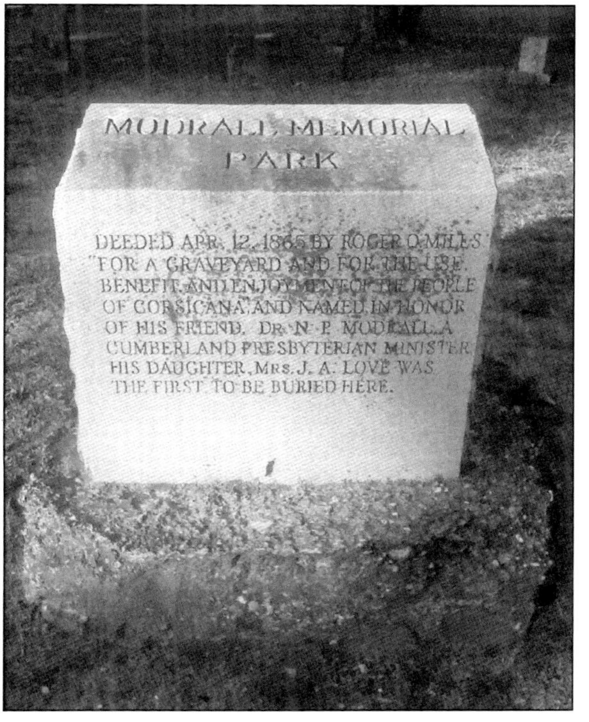

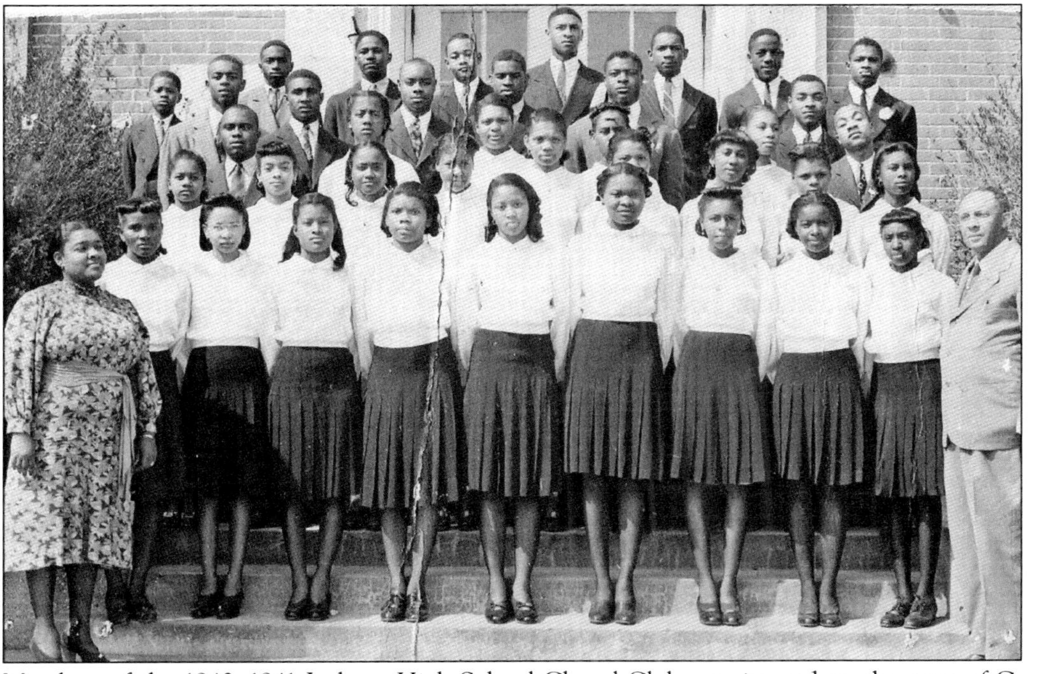

Members of the 1940–1941 Jackson High School Choral Club are pictured on the steps of G. W. Jackson High School. The group's director, Selma Butler, is shown on the far left of the first row. Walter Day, who coached the Jackson High Bears to three state football championships, is shown second from the left on the fifth row. (Courtesy of Mabel Scott.)

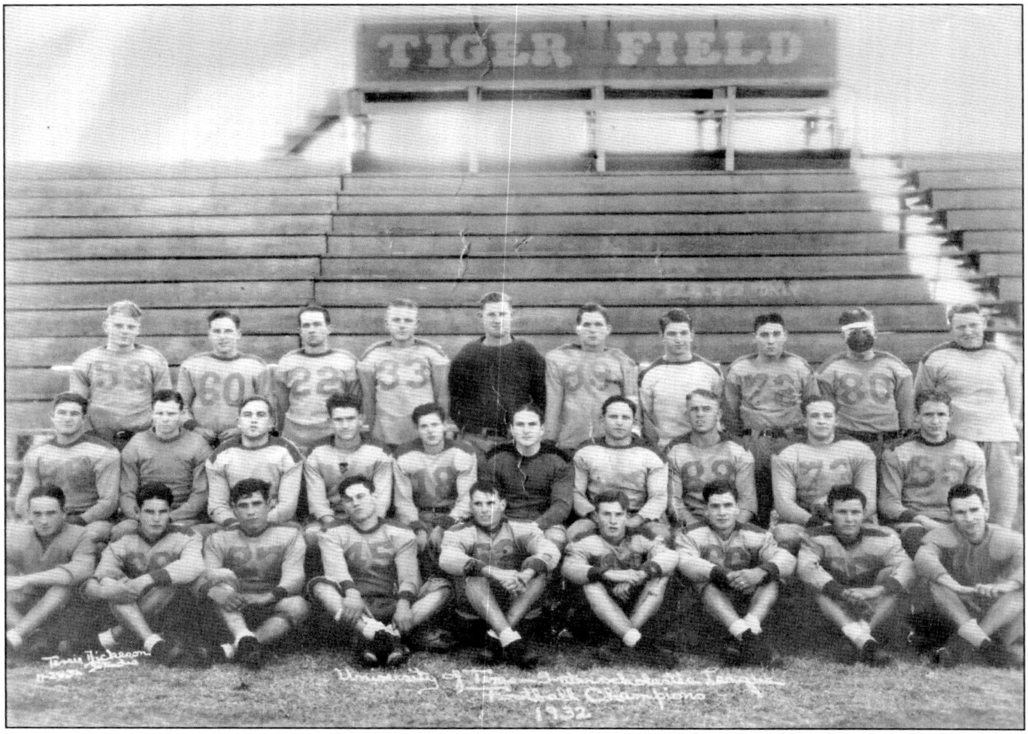

In 1932, the Corsicana Tigers played the famed Fort Worth Masonic Home Mighty Mites for the state championship. The two teams battled to a 0-0 tie, with the Tigers claiming the title on penetrations. According to the 1933 Corsicana High School yearbook, the Tigers were on the opponents's 6-inch line when the game ended. The game, which was played in Corsicana, was interrupted when a section of the bleachers collapsed because of the overflow crowd. (Courtesy of Babette Samuels.)

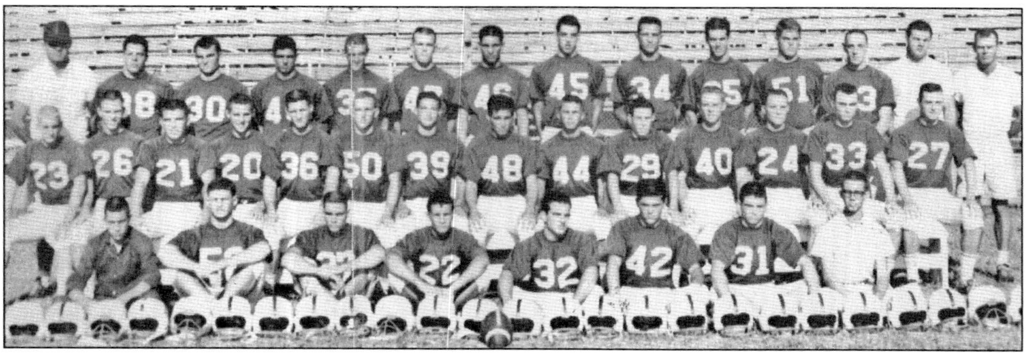

The Corsicana Tigers claimed the AAA state championship in 1963, defeating Pharr San Juan Alamo 7-0 in the title game. Led by head coach Jim Acree, the Tigers compiled a record of 14-0 and were the only undefeated and untied high school team at any classification in Texas high school football for the 1963 season. (Courtesy of Jim Wood.)

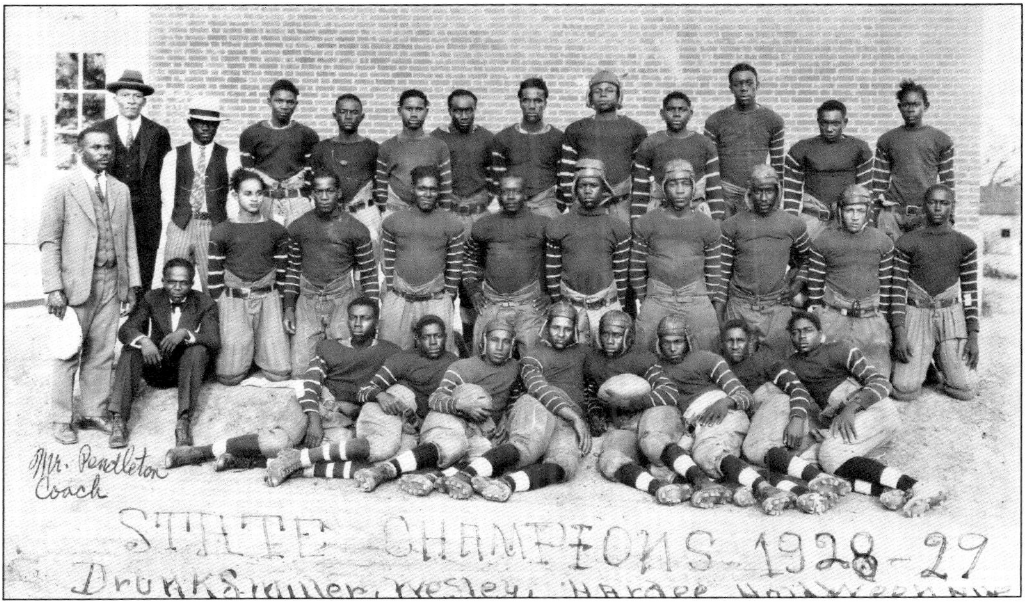

The Jackson High School Bears established a long winning tradition on the gridiron. The 1928 team, coached by N. H. Pendleton (second row, far left), claimed the state championship, defeating Houston Wheatley. During their undefeated season, the Bears outscored their opponents 351 to 44. The 1927 team, also state champions, outscored their opponents 341 to 6. (Courtesy of Mabel Scott.)

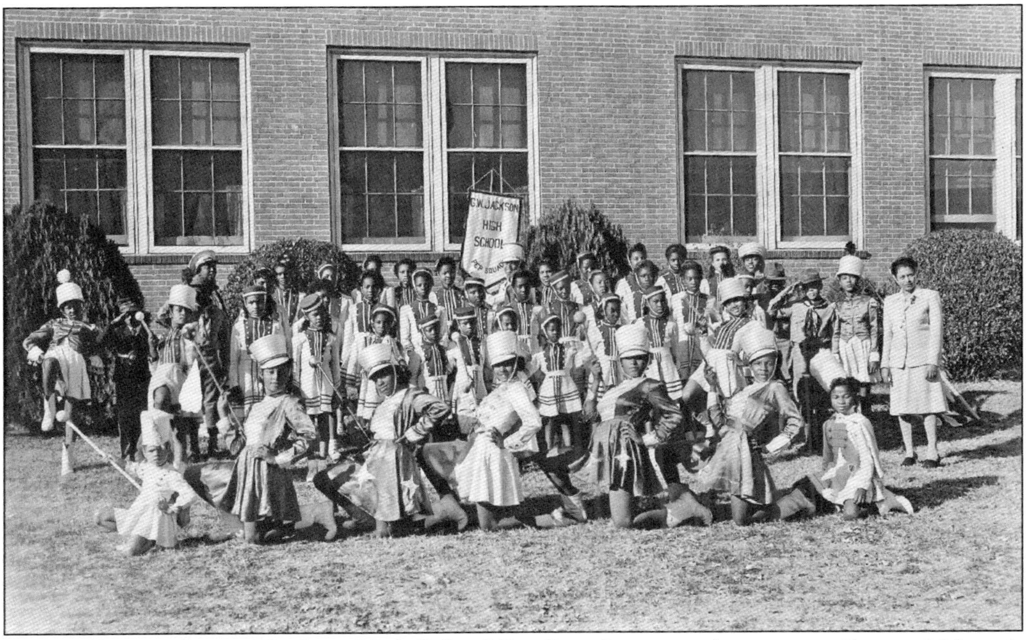

Pictured here is the 1947 Jackson High School Pep Squad wearing their new uniforms. Although the football team dominated the African American high school ranks, they rarely got new uniforms. The school colors were purple and white, but the Bears often dressed in blue and gold since their uniforms were hand-me-downs from the Corsicana High School Tigers, whose colors were blue and gold. (Courtesy of Mabel Scott.)

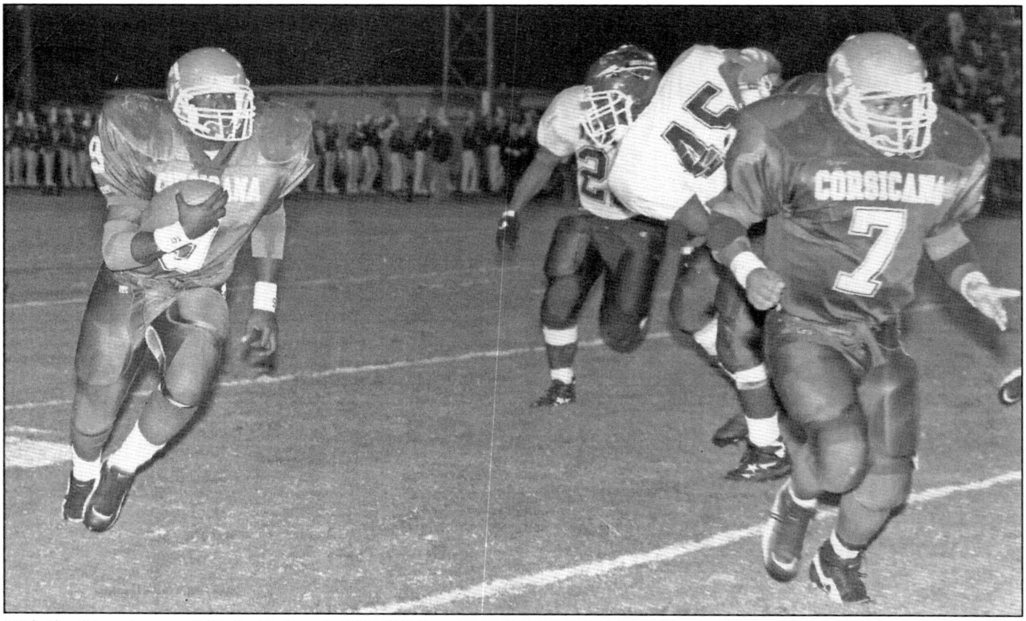

While Corsicana High School (CHS) has produced many outstanding athletes, the name that appears most in the record books is Ketrick Sanford. During his three varsity seasons with the Tigers, he rushed 1,058 times for 6,762 yards and 69 touchdowns. His 376 yards in 30 carries in a 1995 game is the highest single game–rushing total in CHS football history. Sanford also set several rushing records at the University of Houston.

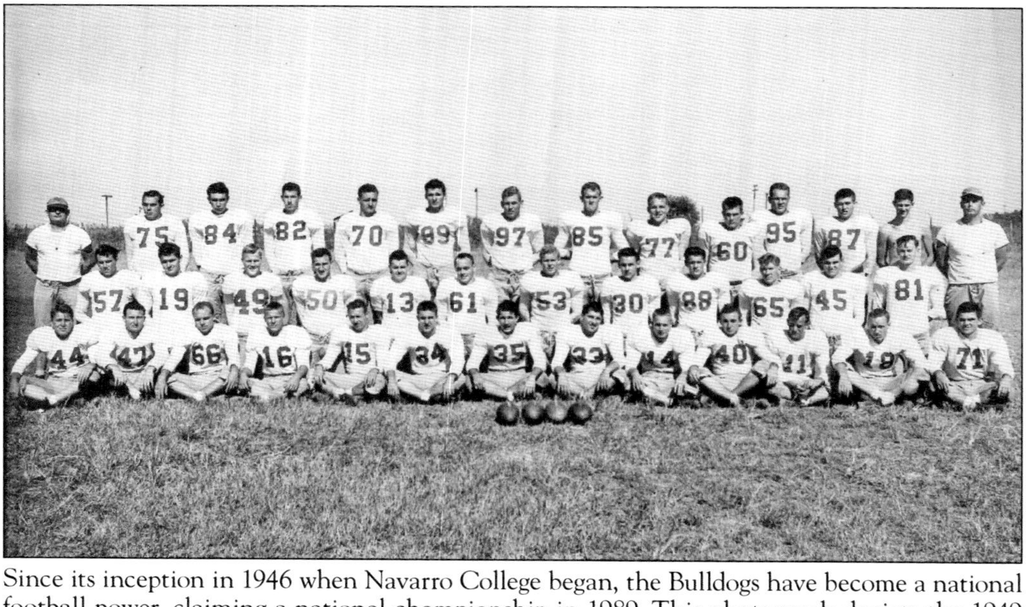

Since its inception in 1946 when Navarro College began, the Bulldogs have become a national football power, claiming a national championship in 1989. This photograph depicts the 1949 team. Head coach Ken Clark (third row, far left) was the entire coaching staff during the team's inaugural season. Over the years, many former Bulldogs continued on to successful careers at major universities, and some enjoyed careers in the National Football League. (Courtesy of Navarro College Archives.)

During the 1950s, Navarro College baseball teams dominated Texas junior college circles. The 1958 team, depicted in this photograph, were coached by Bill Carnes and advanced to the national junior college tournament, finishing third in the nation. The 1959 team repeated the state champion streak but declined the invitation to the national tournament since the dates conflicted with final exams. (Courtesy of Needom Muns.)

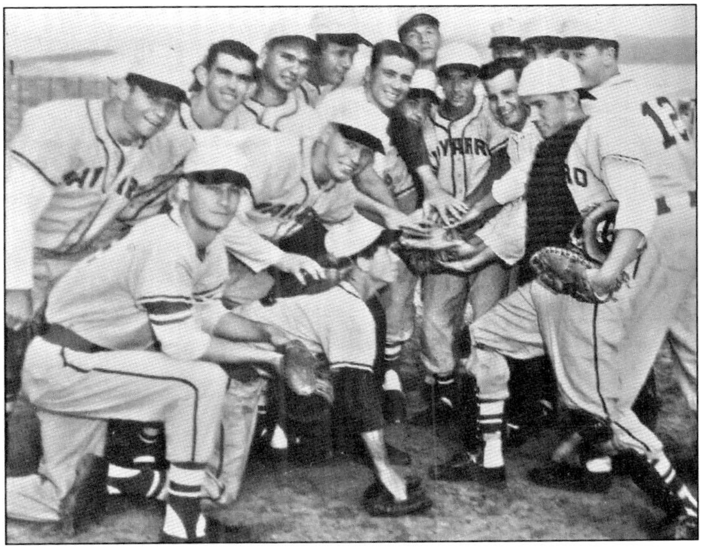

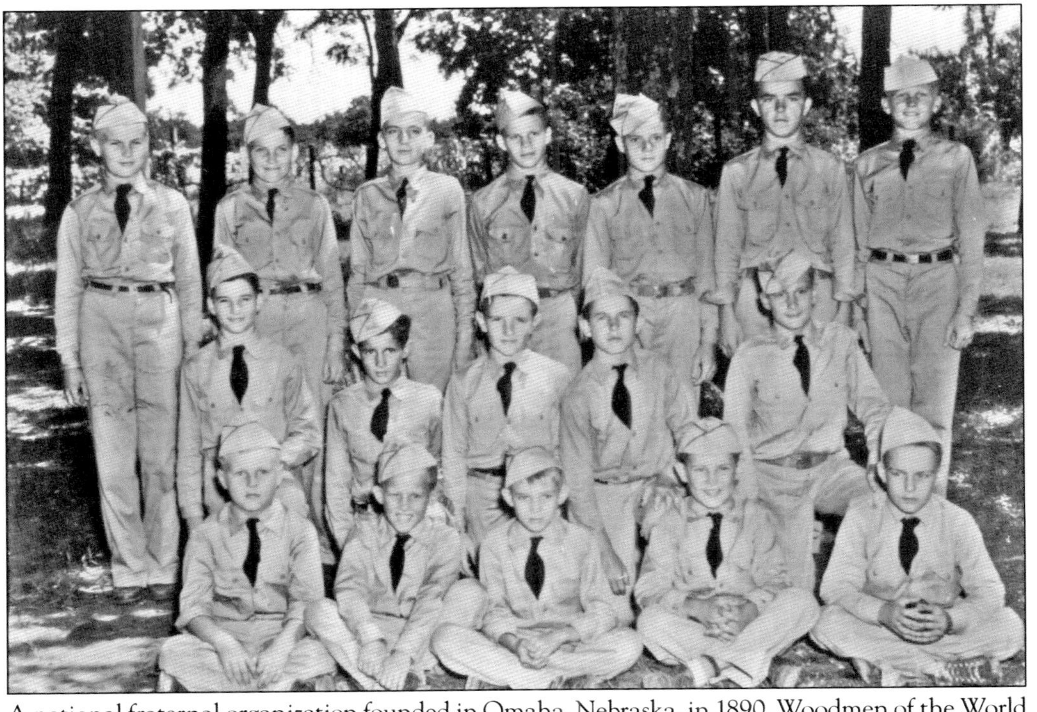

A national fraternal organization founded in Omaha, Nebraska, in 1890, Woodmen of the World is best known for its insurance program for its members. In 1946, the organization provided funds for recreation and youth programs. A group of Corsicana boys, shown here, benefitted from that program through an organization patterned after the Boy Scouts, which provided camping and other outdoor activities. (Courtesy of John Barron.)

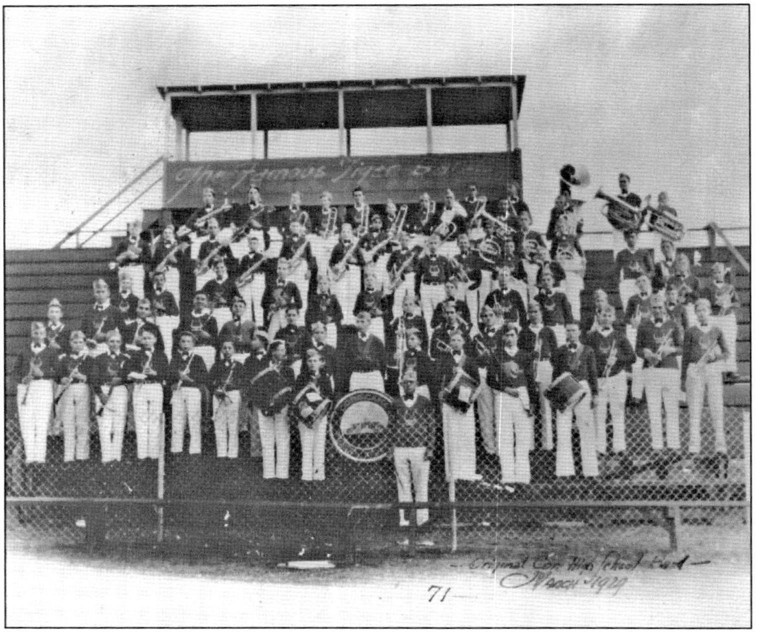

Although Corsicana High School offered some music programs such as a glee club and orchestra, the Tiger marching band was not organized until 1928, with Joel Trimble as the director. This photograph, taken in March 1929, depicts the 71 members of the original band. Although they had been in existence only six months at the time of the picture, they claimed to be the "famous Tiger band."

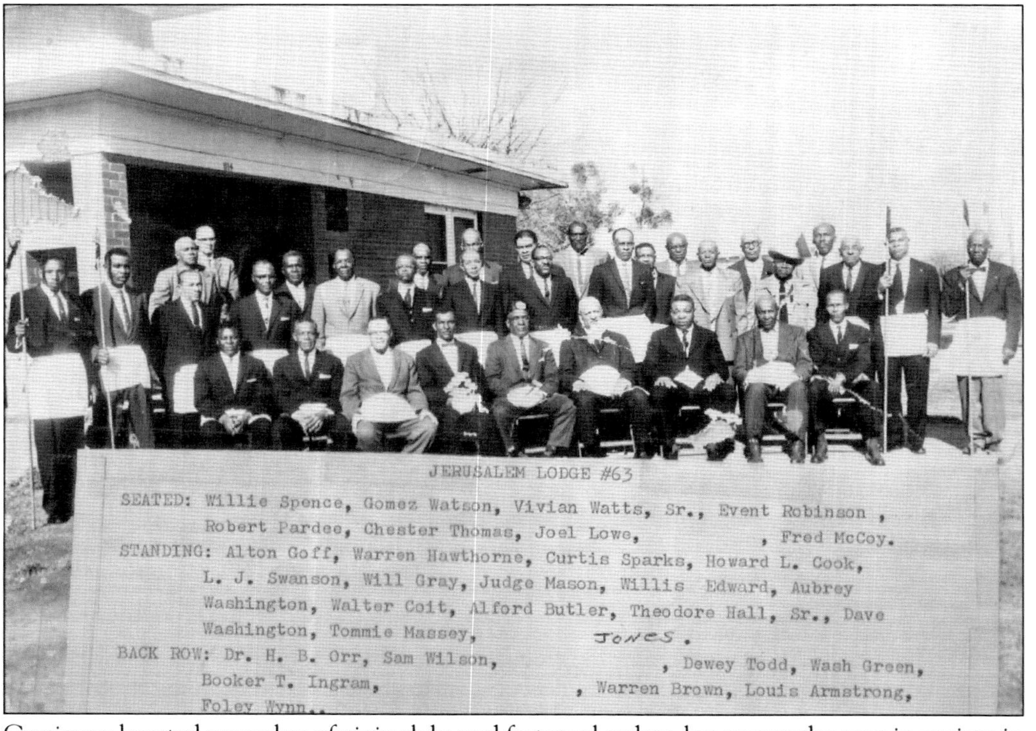

Corsicana boasted a number of civic clubs and fraternal orders, but as was the case in society in general, those organizations were segregated by race. Depicted here in this 1930s-era photograph is Jerusalem Lodge No. 63, a Masonic order for African Americans. The group met in the lodge hall at the corner of Fourth Avenue and Fifth Street. The organization disbanded in the 1960s. (Courtesy of Mabel Scott.)

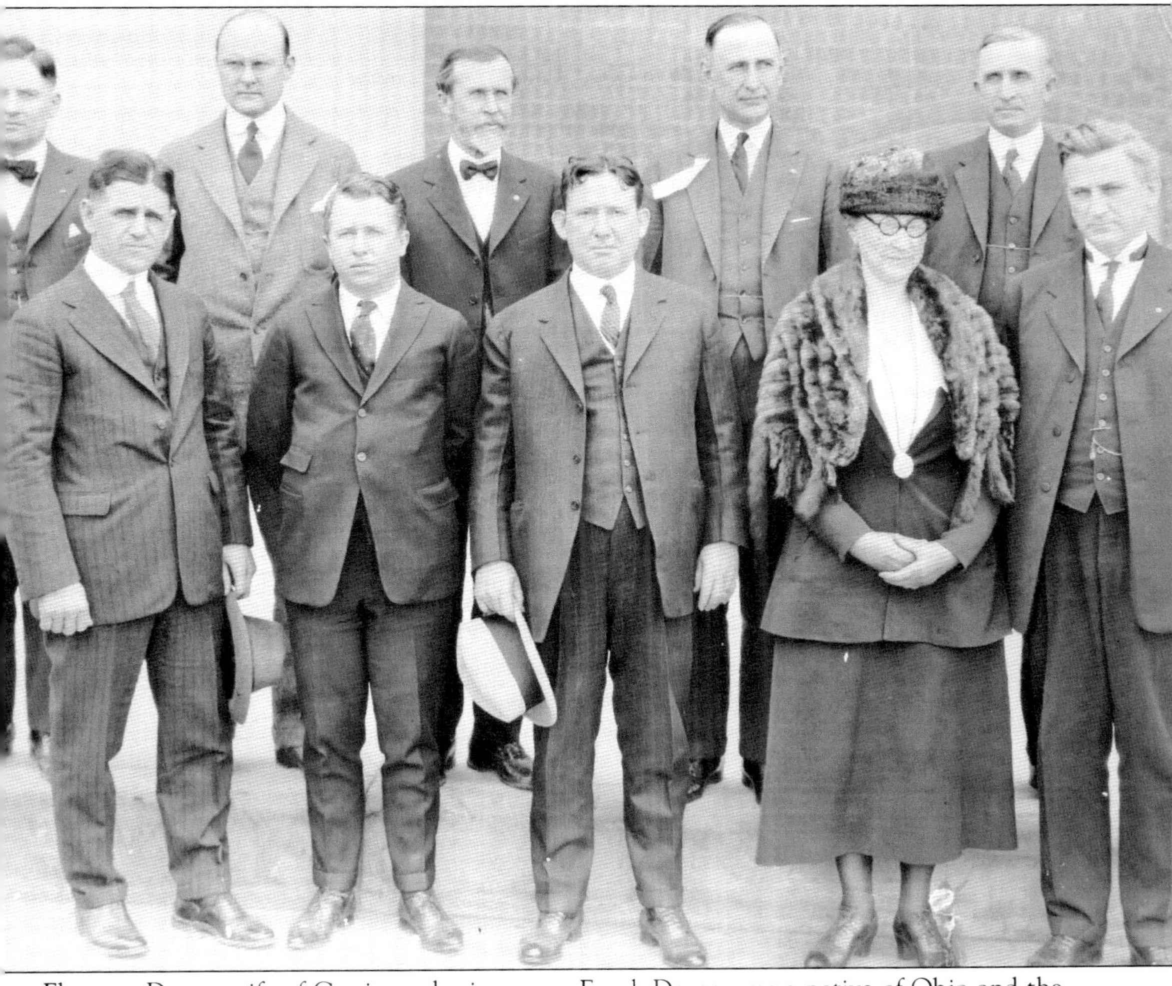

Florence Drane, wife of Corsicana businessman Frank Drane, was a native of Ohio and the daughter of a minister. Active in various community organizations, Florence served on the local school board as well as the board of Trinity University when it was located in Waxahachie. She was an active member of the Third Avenue Presbyterian Church and chaired the Navarro County Fair Association. In 1923, she was named to the board of directors of the newly created Texas Technological College in Lubbock. Pictured from left to right are (first row) C. W. Meadows, Stillman Evans, W. P. Hobby, Florence Drane, and Gov. Pat Neff; (second row) R. A. Underwood, Clifford Jones, J. E. Nunn, Amon Carter, and John Carpenter. Carpenter was a Navarro County native, but at the time of his service on the Texas Tech Board, he was president of Texas Power and Light Company in Dallas. (Courtesy of Jon Ketcham.)

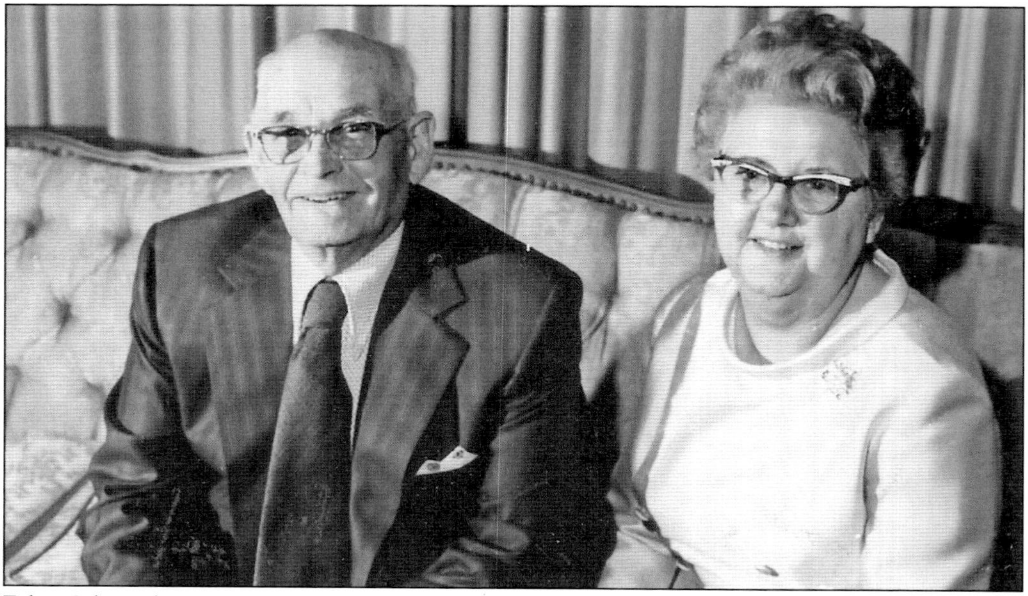

Felix Gibson began working in Texas oil fields at age 14. He met and married Jewel Henson when he came to Bald Prairie, Texas, to drill an oil well. During the 43 years he worked in the oil fields, she taught at various public schools as well as at the University of Houston and at Sam Houston State University. She also published several plays and best-selling novels. The Gibsons spent their retirement years in Corsicana near their son, Dr. Louis Gibson, one of the founders of the Medical Arts Clinic.

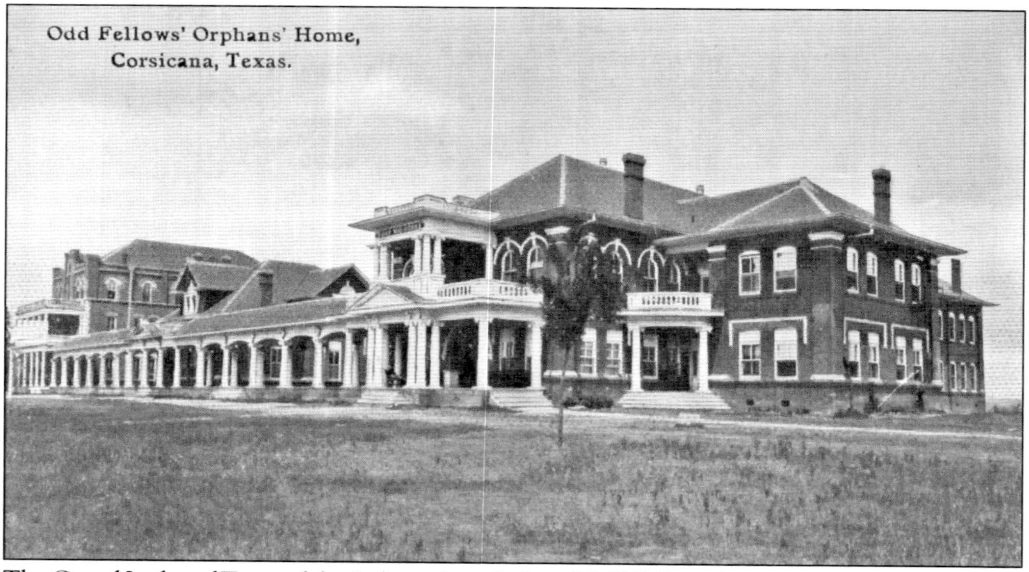

The Grand Lodge of Texas of the Independent Order of Odd Fellows (IOOF) designated Corsicana as the location for a widows and orphans home. The Corsicana lodge and private citizens donated 200 acres of land 3 miles east of downtown for a permanent campus. The facility opened in 1885, and by the 1920s, more than 400 resided at the home. A self-contained community, the IOOF home had its own school system, farm and dairy operation, power plant, and water system. It closed in the 1990s, having cared for thousands of needy children during its 110-year history.

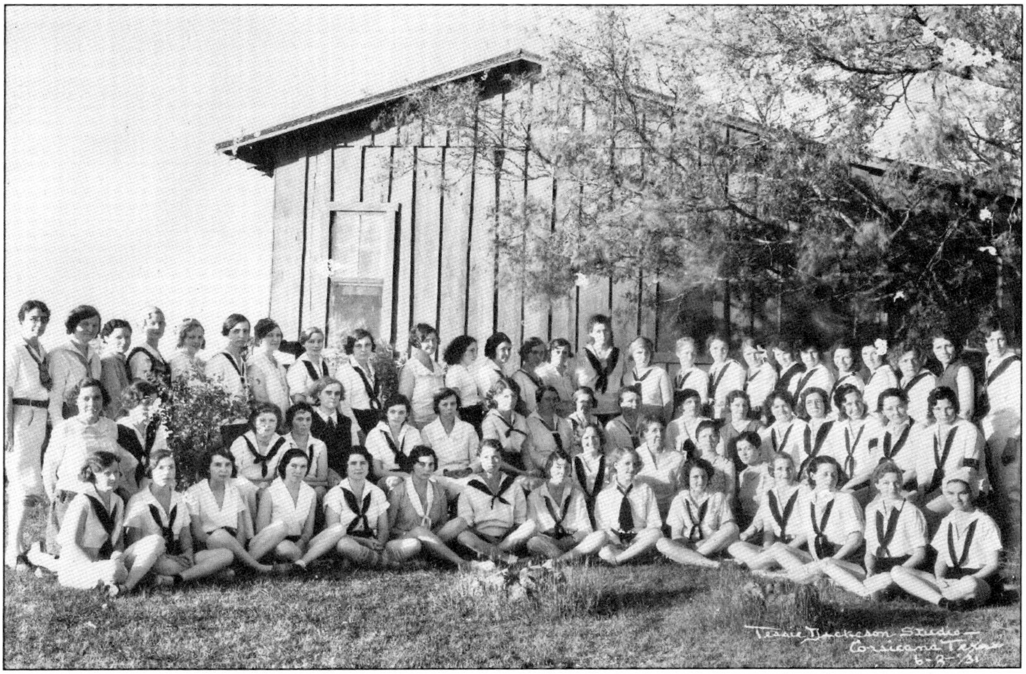

The Corsicana Camp Fire began in 1925. Four years later, the W. J. McKie family donated 10 acres south of town to the local group to hold summer retreats. The focal point of the grounds, which were named Camp Wanica, was the McElwee Lodge, named for Tom McElwee, co-owner of the Collin Street Bakery. Other businesses and service clubs sponsored cabins on the campgrounds. The above photograph from 1931 shows a Camp Fire group gathered at Camp Wanica for a summer outing. Candy sales provided revenue for Camp Fire activities, as depicted in this 1955 photograph below that shows Ralph Stell at his office of the Stroud and Stell Wholesale Grocery Company buying Camp Fire candy from Ann Ruth (left), Elizabeth Settle (center), and Amy Lou Settle (seated on Stell's lap). (Both, courtesy of Lynda Green.)

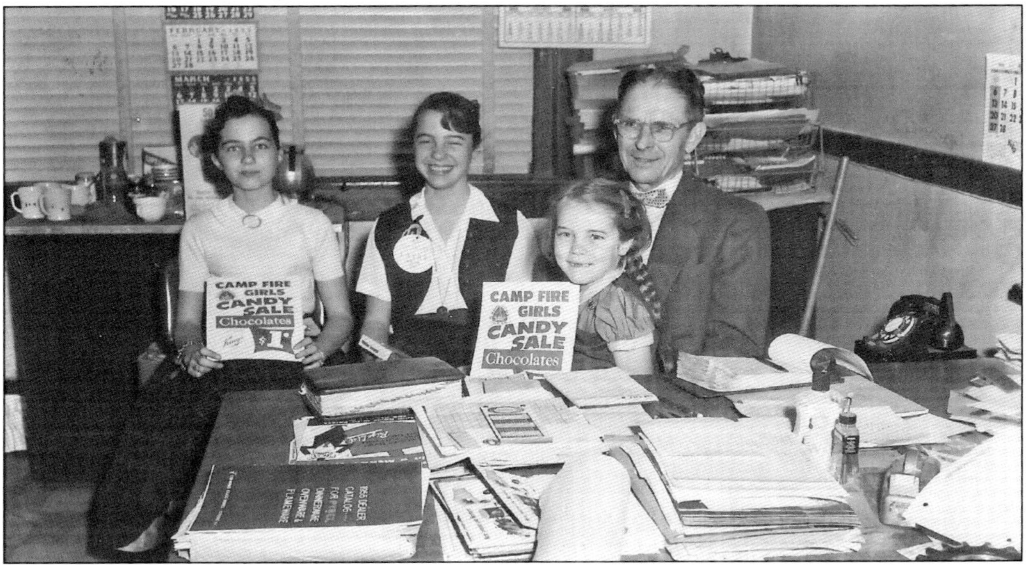

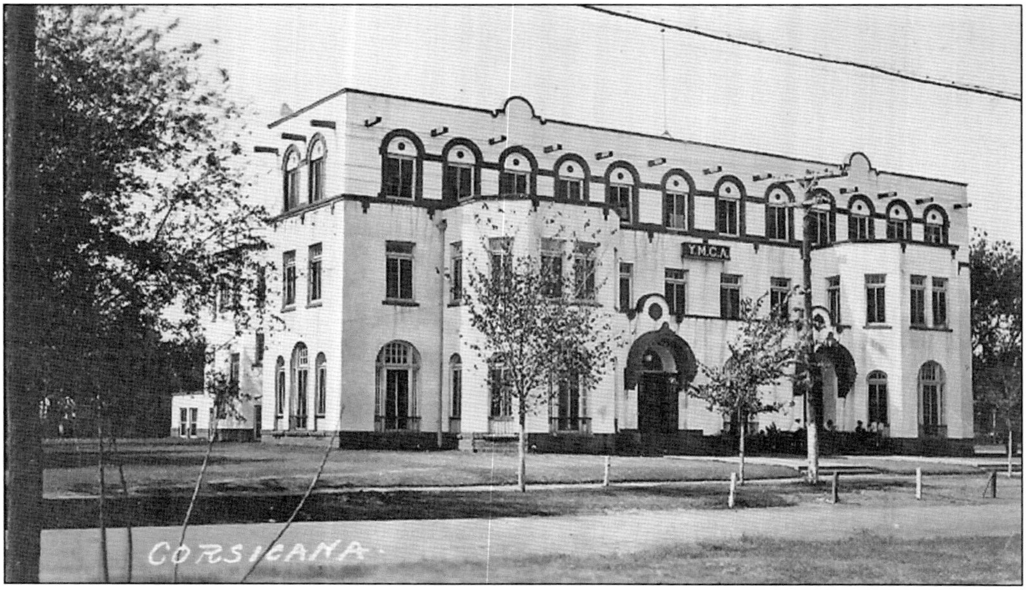

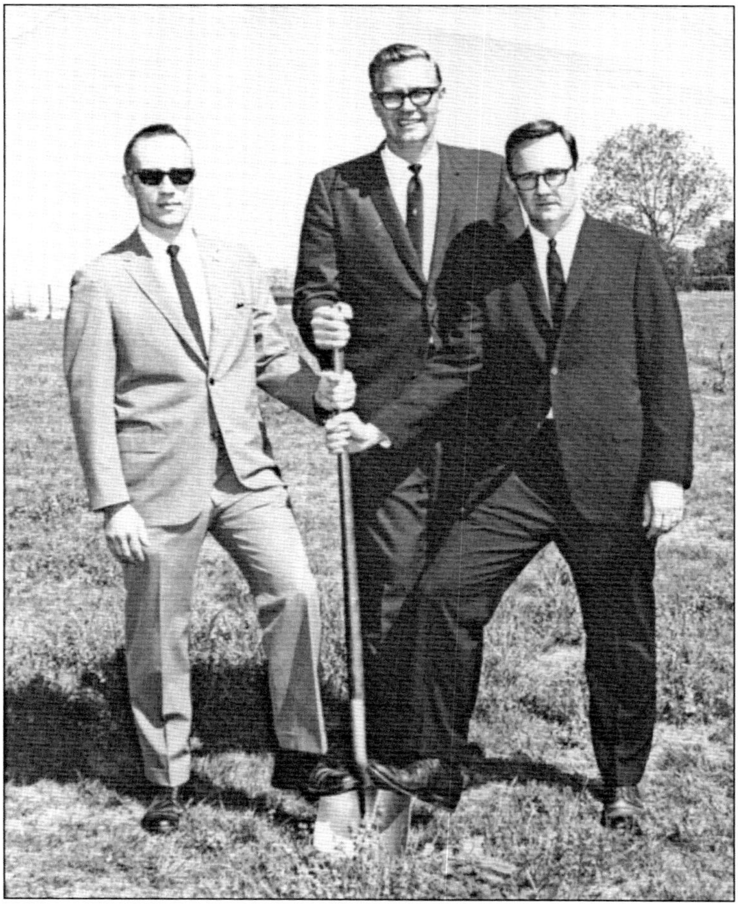

Wiley Johnson and Frank Neal Drane were the driving forces behind the establishment of the Corsicana YMCA in 1884. This building was constructed at the corner of Fifth Avenue and Twelfth Street, and opened in April 1915. In addition to 22 sleeping rooms, the facility housed a swimming pool, a gymnasium, a jogging track, and a meeting room. The building was razed in the 1960s and replaced with a modern structure located at 400 Oaklawn Drive. At left, Jim Stephenson (left), Gene Bullard (center), and David Brown are depicted at the ground-breaking for the new YMCA, which opened in 1968.

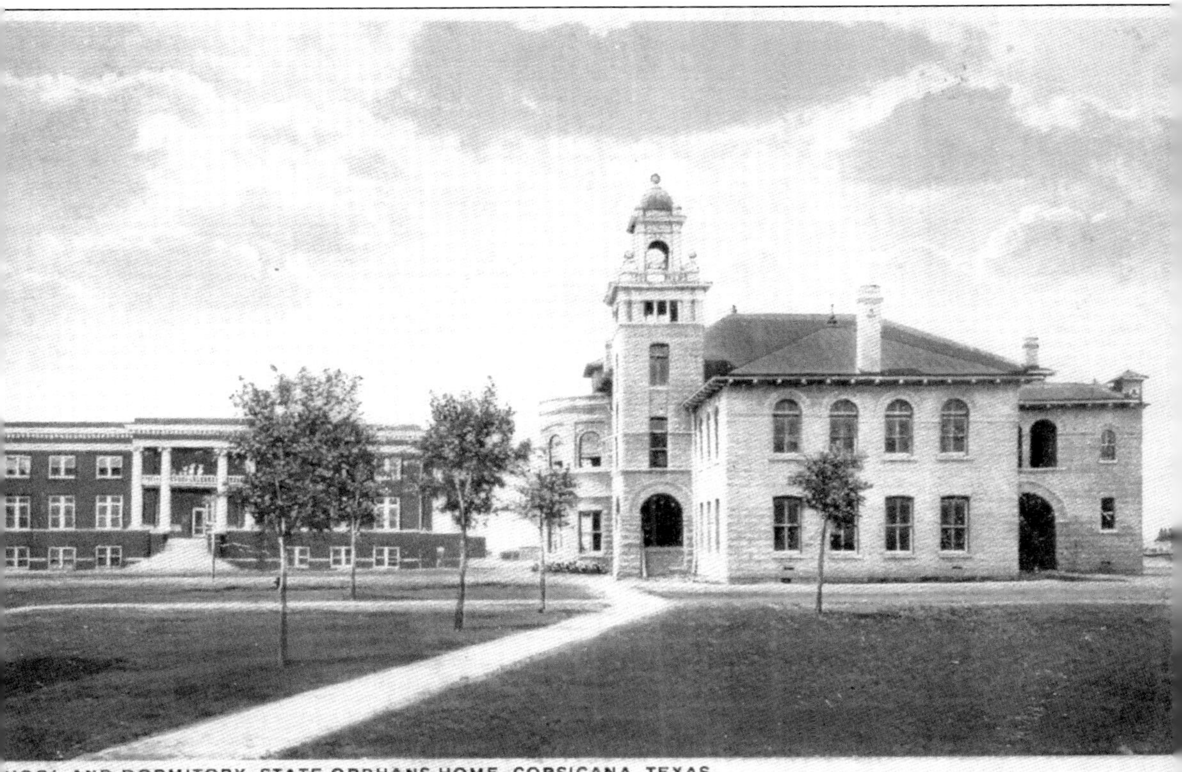

HOOL AND DORMITORY, STATE ORPHANS HOME, CORSICANA, TEXAS.

In 1887, Sen. Charles Bell introduced a bill in the 12th Texas Legislature to create the Texas Orphans Home and Asylum. The first 54 students arrived two years later to occupy the 200-acre campus located 3 miles west of downtown between state highways 22 and 31. By 1900, the facility housed 400 students. A self-contained community, the state home had its own school system, which included both academic courses as well as courses in various vocational fields. There were also farming and dairy operations. In 1932, during the depths of the Great Depression, the state home cared for 890 students. By 1948, the campus had expanded to 417 acres. As numbers declined, the school system was discontinued, and the children attended classes in the Corsicana Independent School District. In 1957, the name was changed to the Corsicana State Home and was placed under jurisdiction of the Texas Youth Commission. Today it is a correctional facility for troubled youths.

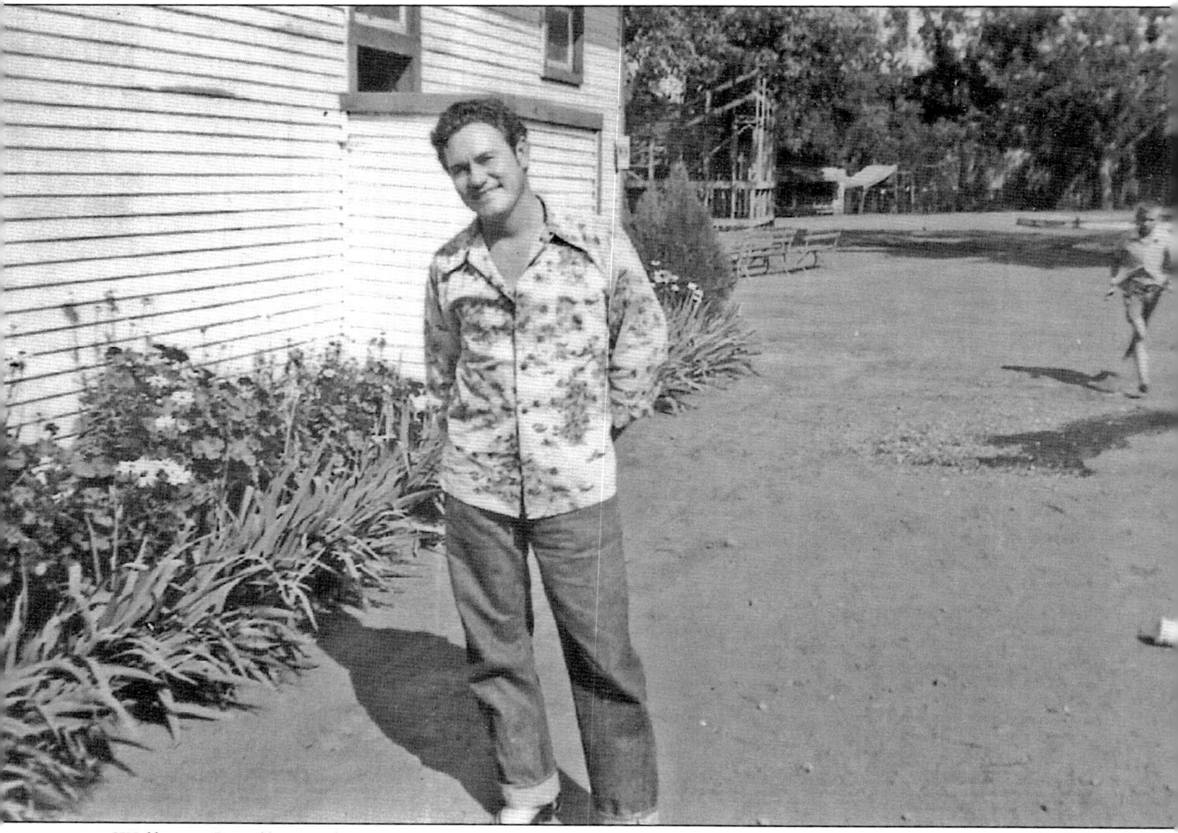

William Orville "Lefty" Frizzell (shown here during a visit to California in the 1950s) was born in Tuckertown—an oil boomtown east of Corsicana—in 1928 while his father was working as a roustabout in the oil fields in the area. The family moved to other parts of Texas, Oklahoma, and Arkansas, following the oil fields. Frizzell launched his successful recording career in 1952. During his career, Frizzell had 13 songs that made the Top 10 list, three of which were No. 1 on the charts. Among his most popular songs were, "If You've Got the Money, Honey, I've Got the Time." His unique style influenced such performers as George Jones and Willie Nelson. He was inducted in the Songwriters Hall of Fame in 1972 and the Country Music Hall of Fame in 1982. He is also a member of the Texas Country Music Hall of Fame. Frizzell died in 1975. His life and accomplishments are memorialized in a museum at Pioneer Village in Corsicana.

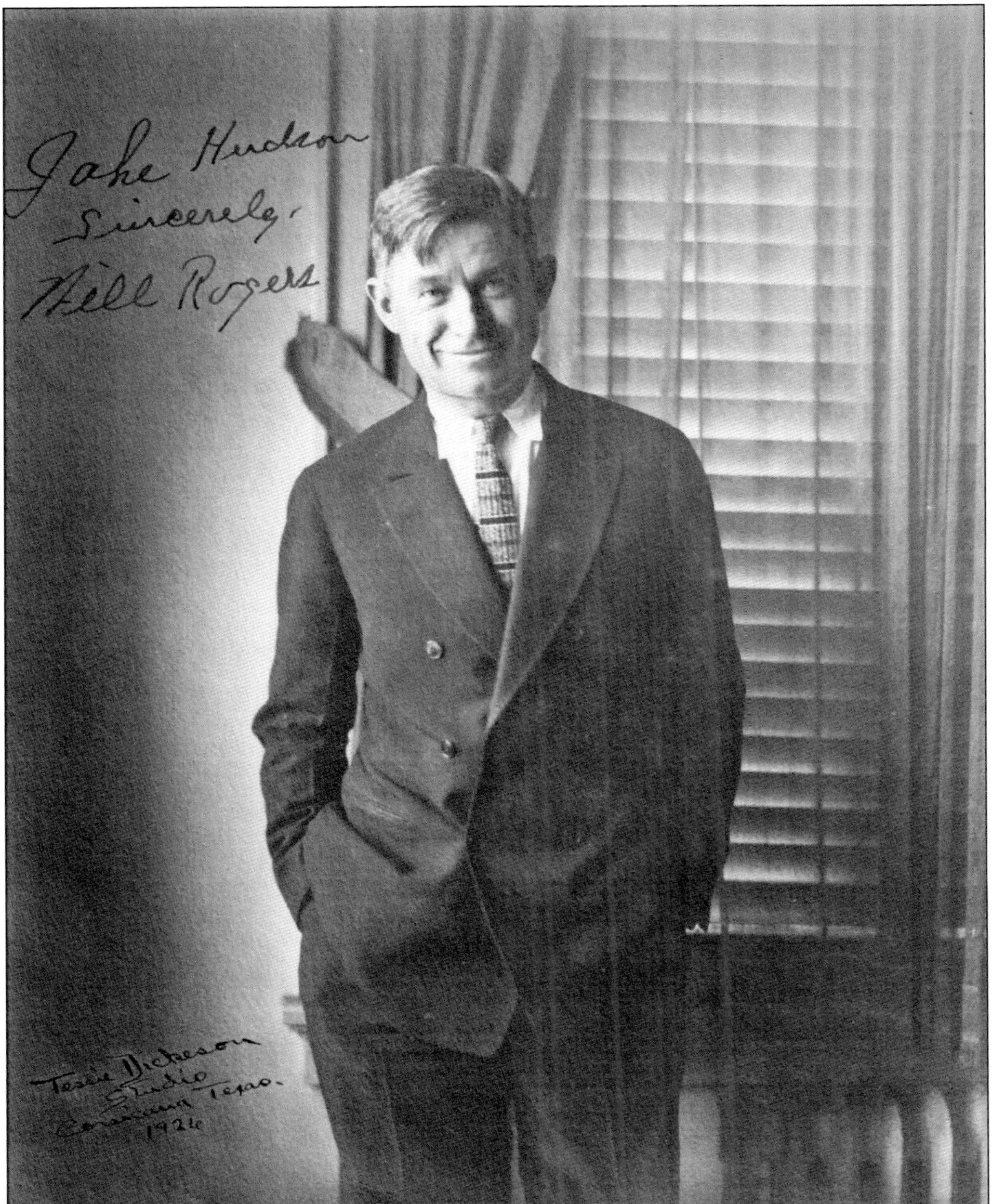

Noted humorist, newspaper columnist, and movie star Will Rogers was a die-hard "chili head." During his extensive travels, he would order Wolf Brand from the company, and during his visits to Texas, he would arrange his itinerary to come through Corsicana to personally pick up ample supplies of chili. Rogers was also a guest at Tom McElwee's private hotel above the Collin Street Bakery. His untimely death in a 1931 airplane crash in Alaska saddened the community along with the entire country. This 1925 photograph was taken by Corsicana photographer Tressie Dickerson, whose studio was located at 202 North Beaton Street. Her photographs recorded much of Corsicana's history. (Courtesy of City of Corsicana, Stroube Collection.)

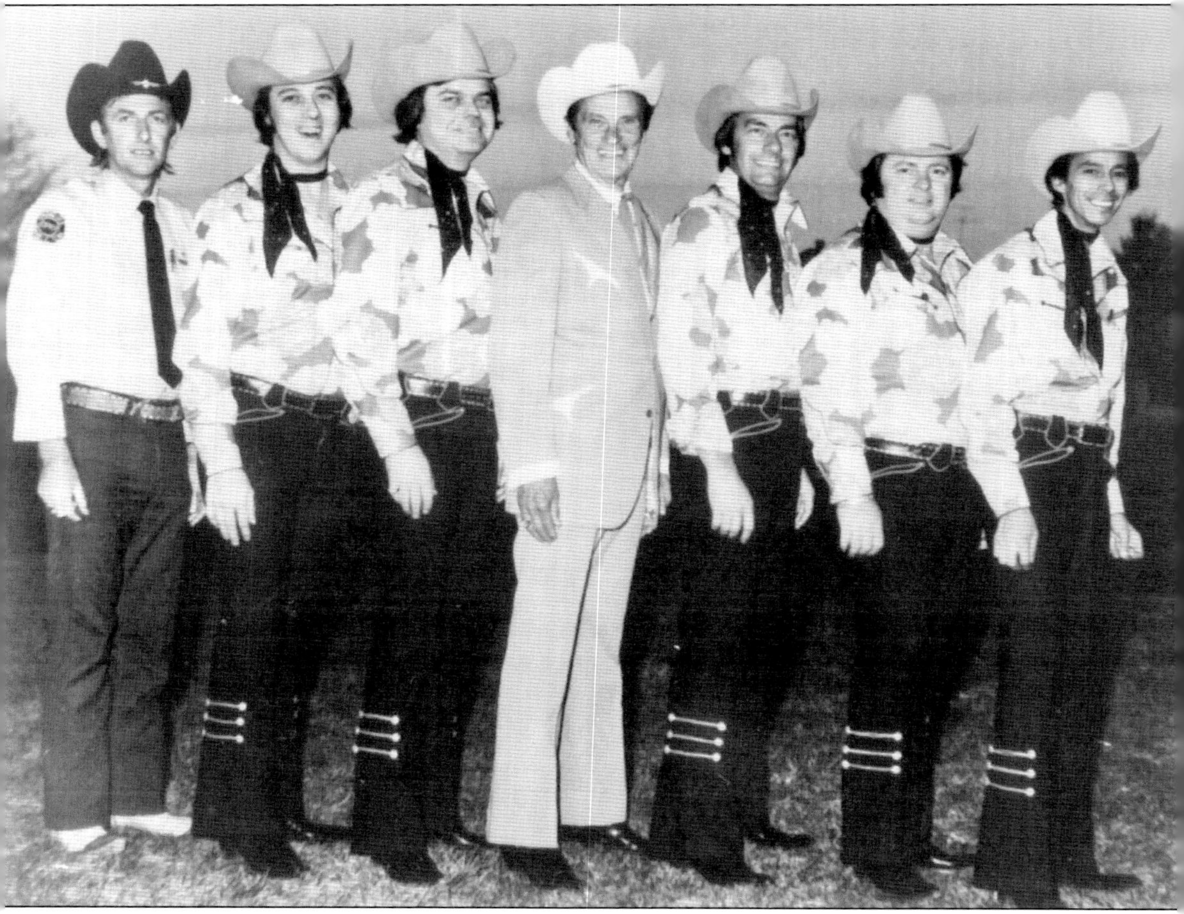

County music legend Ernest Tubb (center, wearing suit) was born in neighboring Ellis County in 1914. As his career was being launched, Tubb stopped by the Wolf Brand Chili plant in 1941. Having just signed a recording contract, he was hitting the road for his first tour. Since he would be in various states where the chili might not be available, he wanted to pick up several cases to carry him over. A lifelong Wolf Brand fan, Tubb commented that his favorite meal was a bowl of Wolf Brand and a bologna sandwich. During his illustrious career, Tubb sold more than 30 million records. He and his band, the Texas Troubadours, maintained a rigorous tour schedule across the United States. A 40-year performer at the Grand Ole Opry, Tubb was inducted into the Country Music Hall of Fame in 1965 and the Songwriters Hall of Fame in 1970. He died in 1984. (Courtesy of Al Hopkins.)

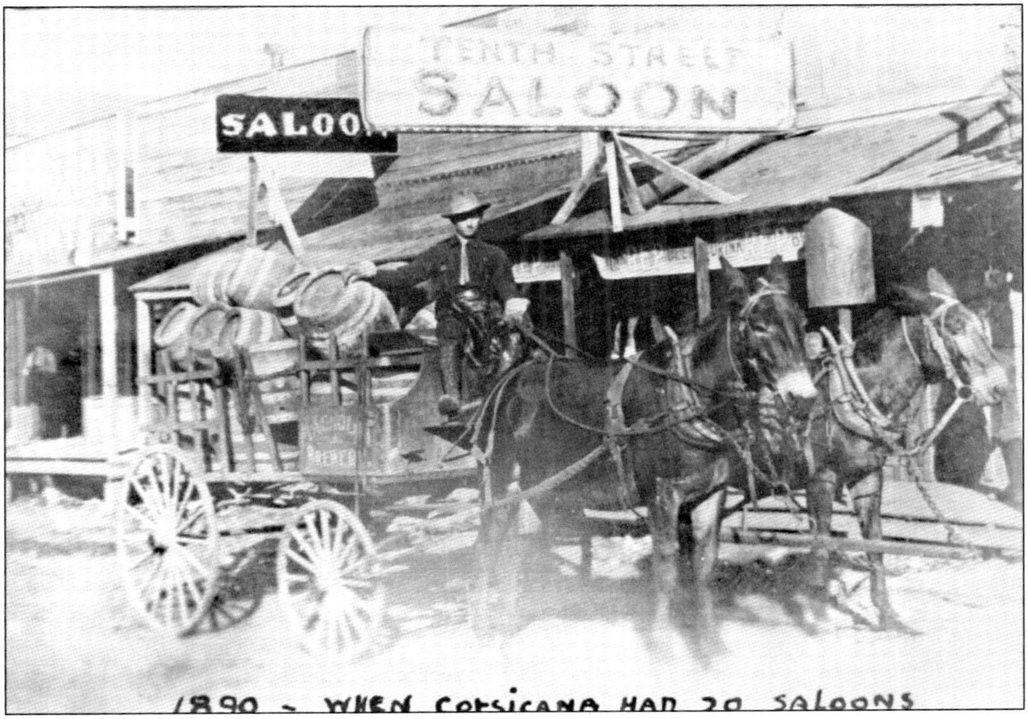

As noted on the inscription of the above photograph of the Tenth Street Saloon, the 1894 city directory listed 21 liquor dealers and saloons in Corsicana. By 1901, that number had grown to 36. In 1904, citizens voted to outlaw the sale of alcohol, and Corsicana remained legally dry until 2004 when voters reversed the "dry" status that had been in place for 100 years. However, bootlegging remained an ongoing practice, as shown below, with local law enforcement officials on the jailhouse yard displaying a recently confiscated illegal whiskey still.

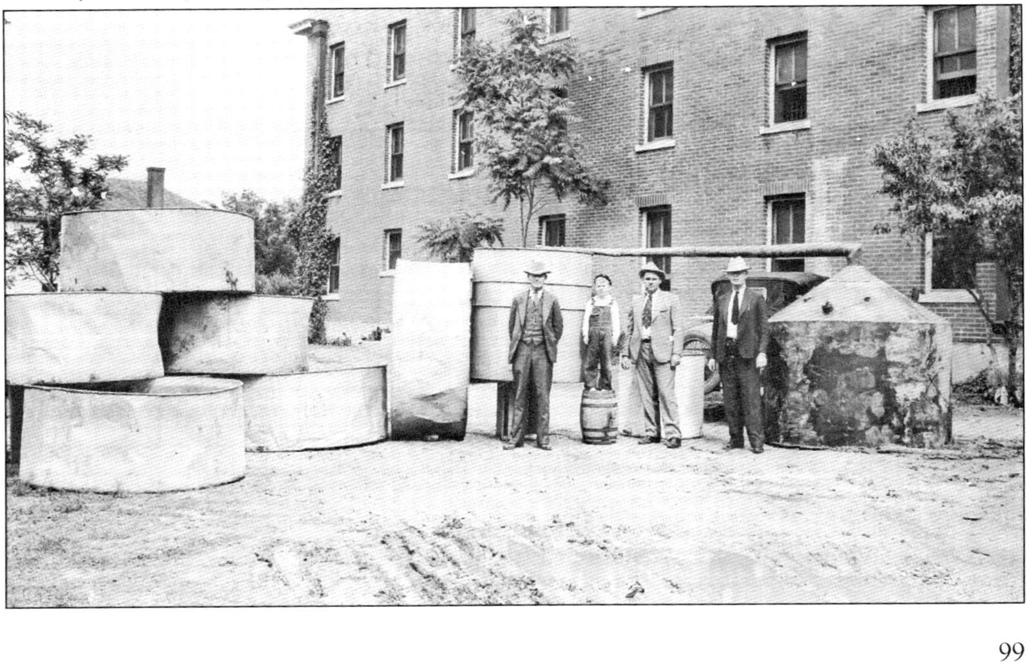

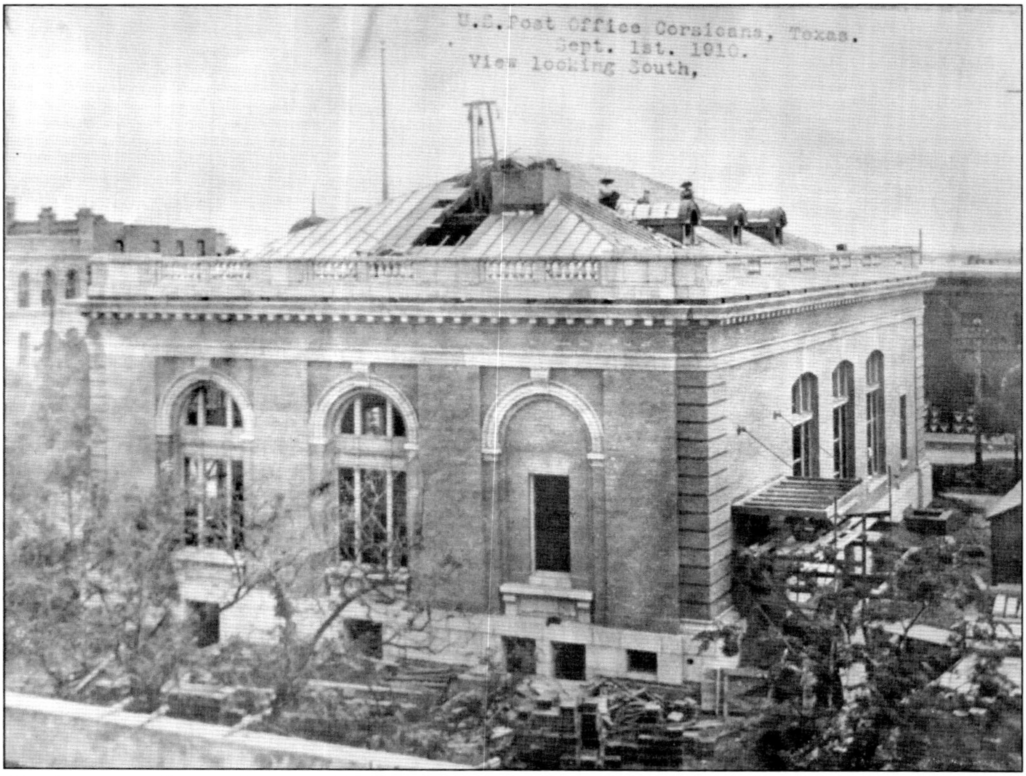

The first post office in Navarro County was established in 1846 in the home of Ethan Melton near Dresden. According to Navarro County historian Annie Carpenter Love, in the early days letters were not placed in envelopes but were tied with string or sealed with wax and accompanied with money for postage. The current Corsicana post office (pictured above), located at 116 South Main Street, was constructed in 1909. Mail carrier Walter Roberts makes his rounds in the photograph below. Delivering mail in the rural areas around Corsicana could be especially challenging due to less-than-desirable roads and the long distances between residences.

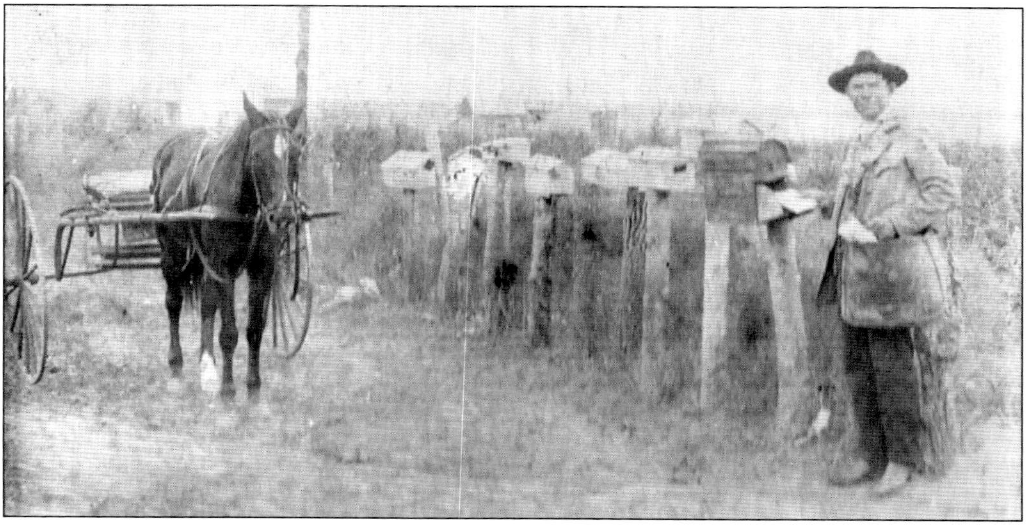

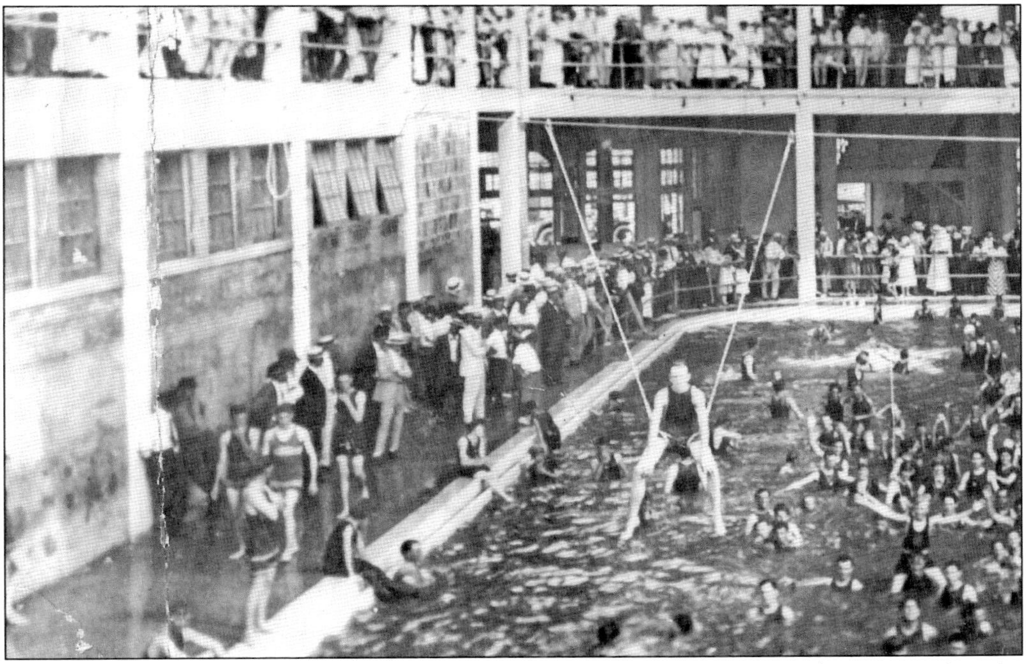

Opened in the summer of 1911, the Natatorium was operated by C. D. Speed Sr. Located in the 200 block of North Main Street near the current site of Corsicana Cleaners, it was billed as a hot mineral spa offering steam treatments with experienced masseurs. Lifeguards were on duty at all times, and bathing suits were available for rent. Devastated by the drowning deaths of two boys, Speed closed the facility in 1913. A second natatorium operated in the mid-1920s at 425 South Twelfth Street.

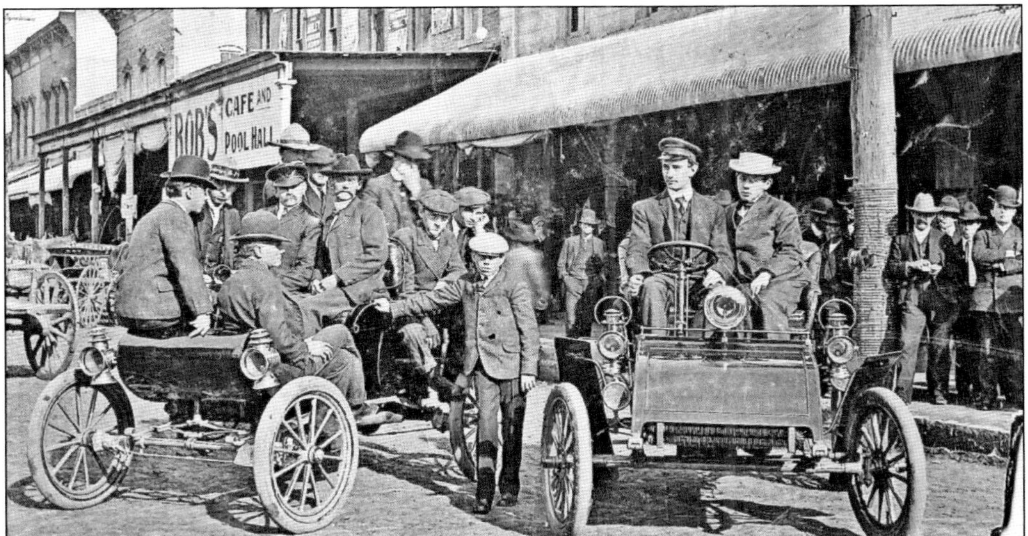

The arrival of the automobile brought drastic economic and social changes to Corsicana. The first horseless carriage in town was owned by Robert Peck, as shown in this 1897 photograph in downtown Corsicana. Allegedly, the contraption could reach a top speed of 20 miles per hour. Peck had a business at 119 West Sixth Avenue in the Hardy-Peck Building.

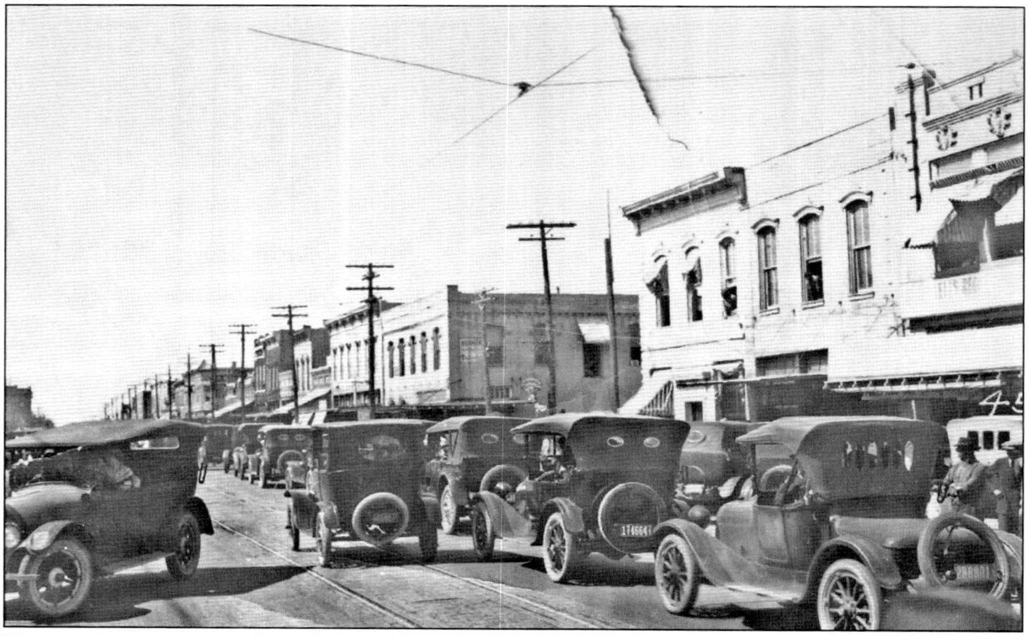

During the prosperous days of the oil boom, the streets of Corsicana were filled with people and automobiles, as seen in this photograph of Beaton Street in the 1920s. It is estimated that the population may have reached 40,000 during the peak of the boom, many of whom were transients who left with the decline of the oil production. (Courtesy of Babette Samuels.)

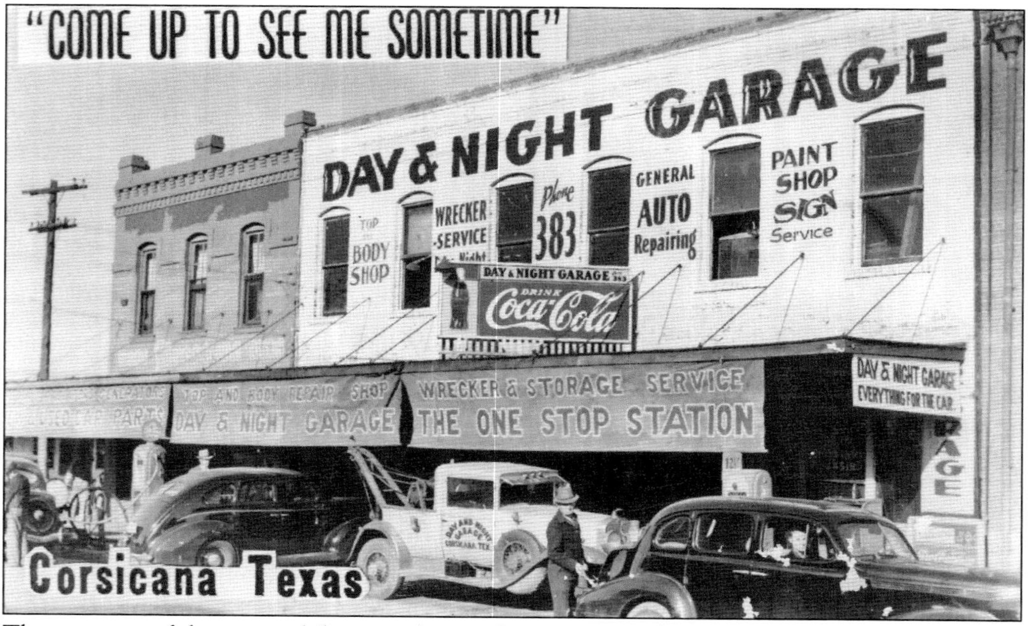

The presence of the automobile created a new business, namely automobile repairs. Claiming to be available every moment of the year, this 1940 photograph depicts the Day and Night Garage, located at 123 North Commerce Street, offering everything for the car, including wrecker service, body repair, and parts. (Courtesy of John Barron.)

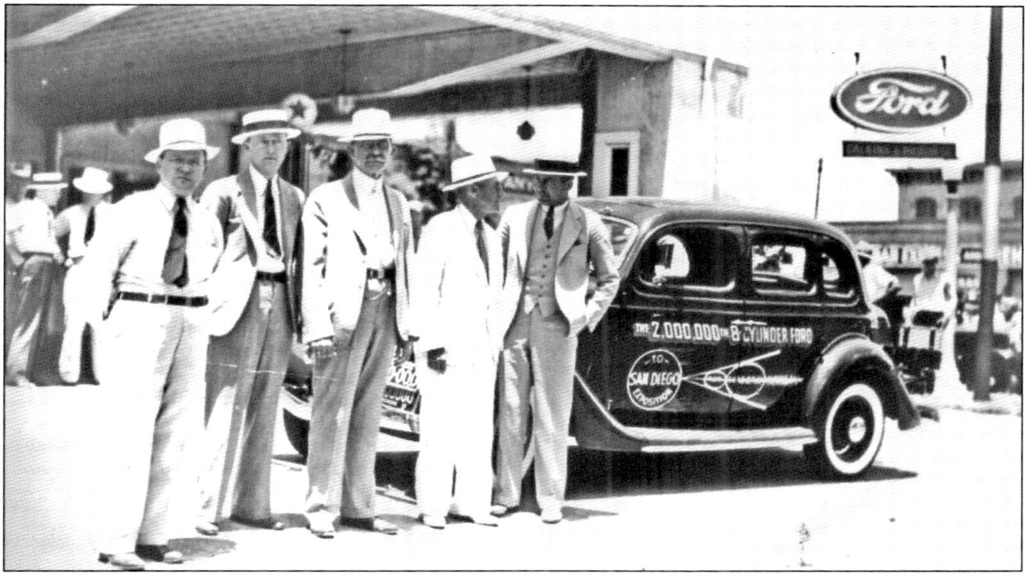

Corsicana residents could purchase automobiles from the Calkins-Dublin Ford dealership located at 112 West Fourth Avenue. The facility also had a service station on the premises. Shown in this 1935 photograph, from left to right, are Richard L. Calkins, S. L. Dublin, Corsicana chief of police Will Knight, Mayor John Murchison, and an unidentified official from the Ford Motor Company. (Courtesy of City of Corsicana, Stroube Collection.)

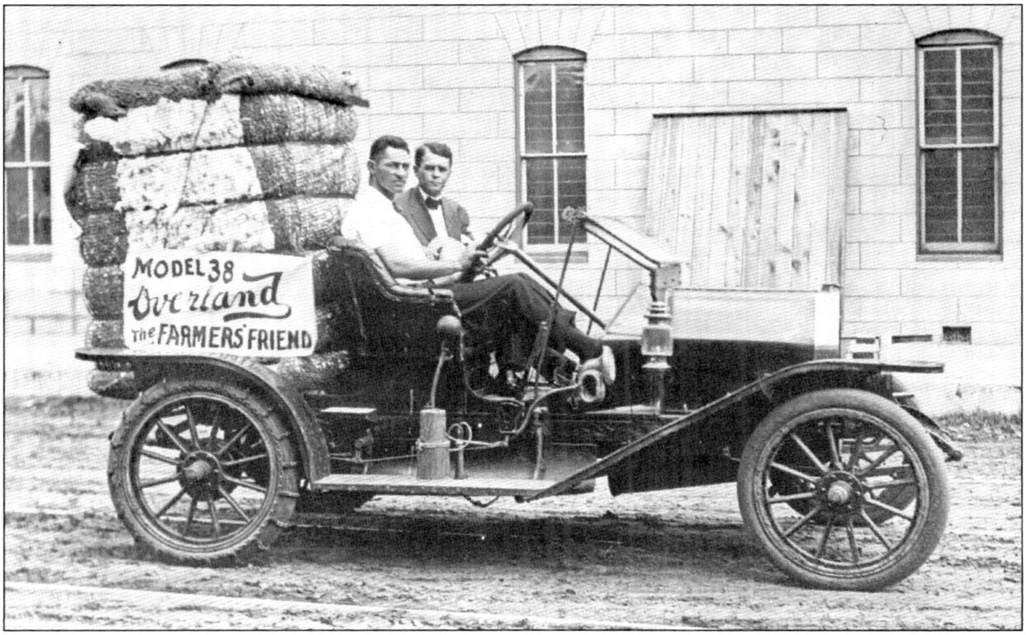

Hugh Drane Sr. (left) and Harry Williams are depicted in this photograph in a Model 38 Overlander. Drane was involved in numerous local businesses, including Drane and McKee automobile accessories, while Williams was a cashier at Corsicana National Bank. Manufactured by the Willys-Overland Company in Toledo, Ohio, in 1910, the vehicle sold for $1,000. (Courtesy of Jon Ketcham.)

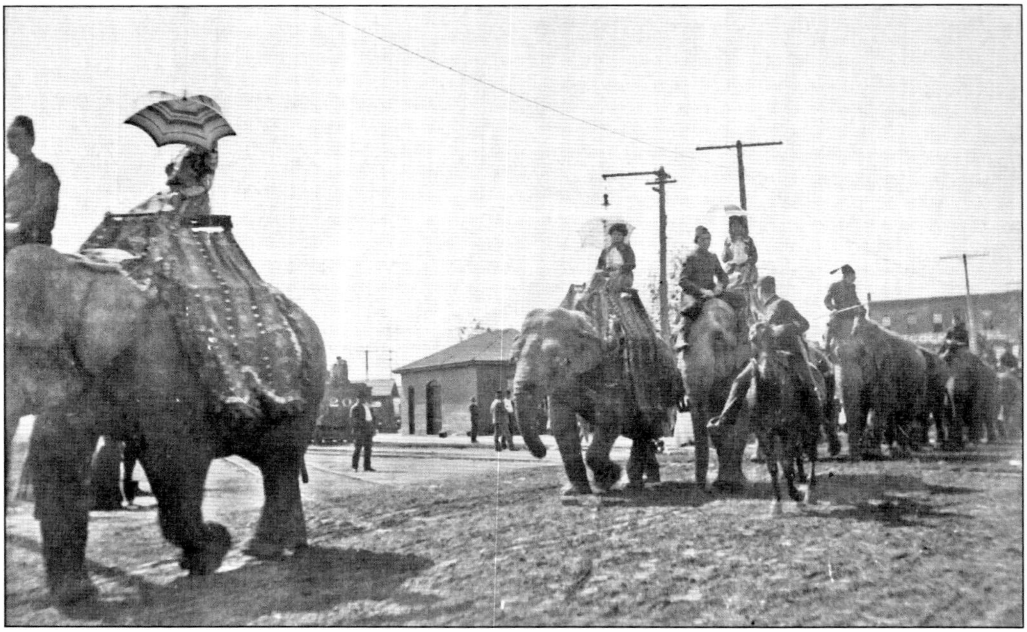

The circus provided entertainment for Corsicana residents from the town's earliest existence. The first circus came to town in 1857. As depicted in this photograph, locals came to watch the parade of animals as they were unloaded from the circus train and marched to the fairgrounds for their performance.

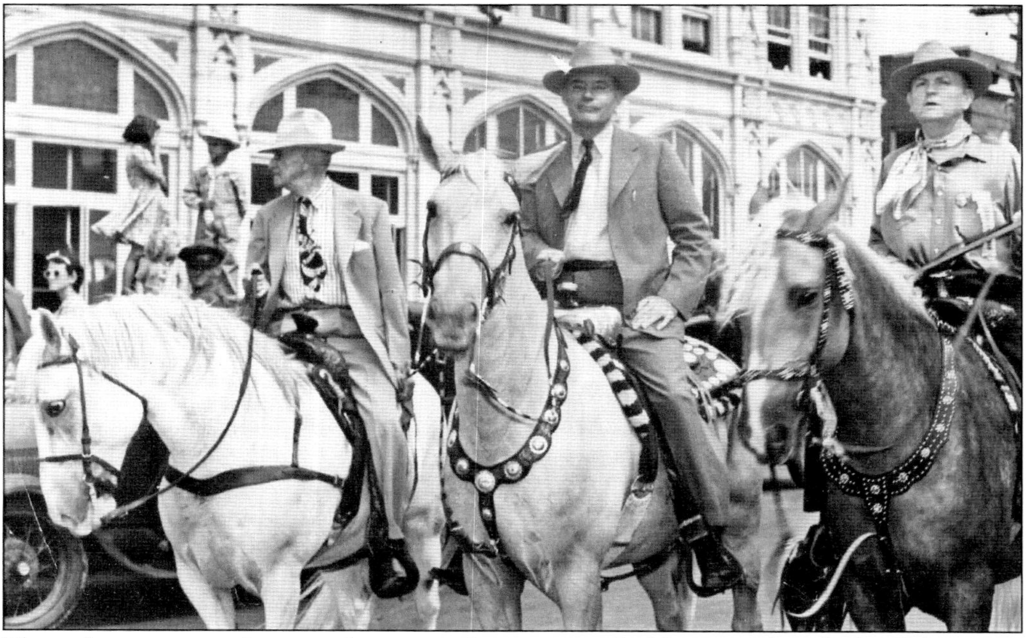

The rodeo was a popular annual event in Corsicana marked by a parade to kick off the event. Depicted in this 1940s-era photograph are, from left to right, J. N. "Pole" Edens, president of the First National Bank; Texas governor Coke Stevenson; and Fred Prince, local oilman and member of the Corsicana City Council.

On June 19, 1865, slavery officially ended in Texas with the arrival of Federal troops in Galveston. Consequently, African Americans celebrate the day, commonly called Juneteenth, with various festivities. This photograph from the 1940s depicts a Juneteenth parade in downtown Corsicana.

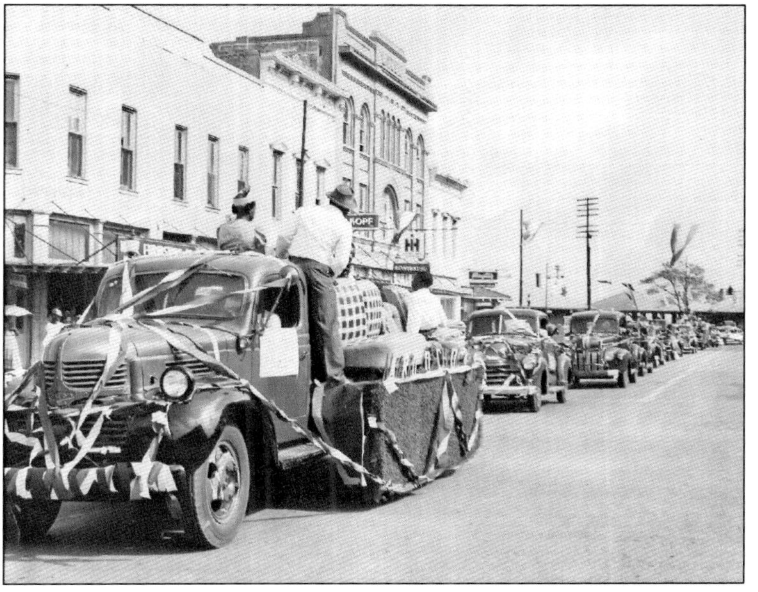

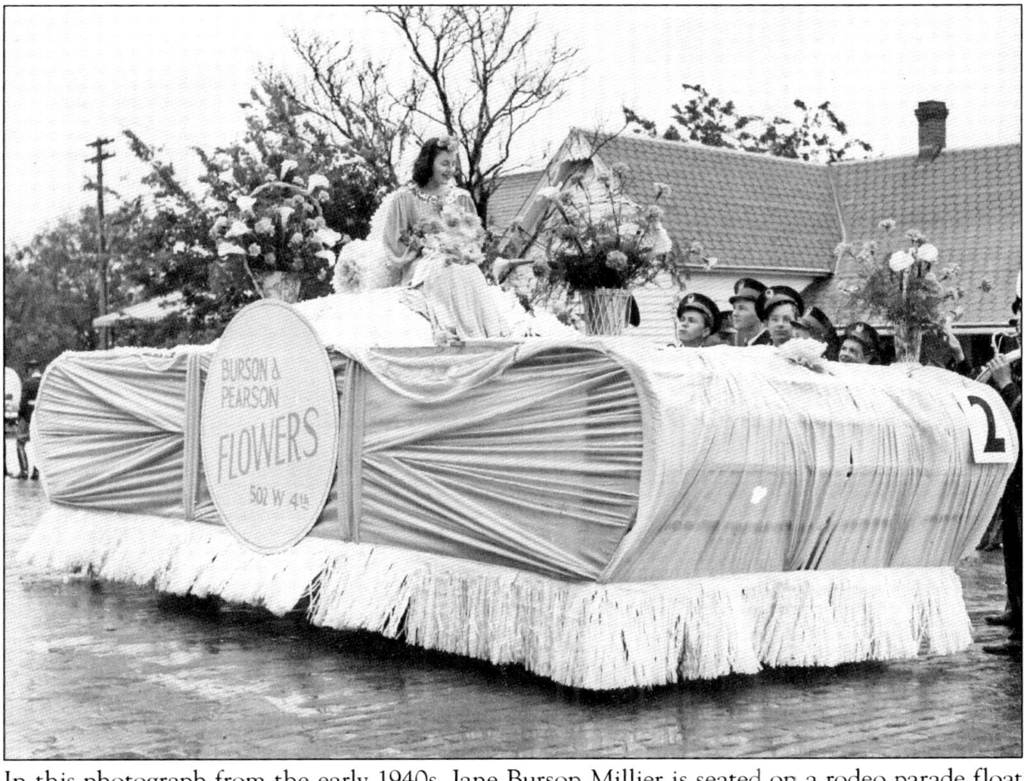

In this photograph from the early 1940s, Jane Burson Millier is seated on a rodeo parade float sponsored by Burson and Pearson Florist. Established in 1937 at 502 West Fourth Avenue, the business was owned and operated by Calesta Burson Pearson and her mother, Pearl Burson. The uniformed men near the float are cadets from the Air Activities of Texas. (Courtesy of Jane Burson Miller.)

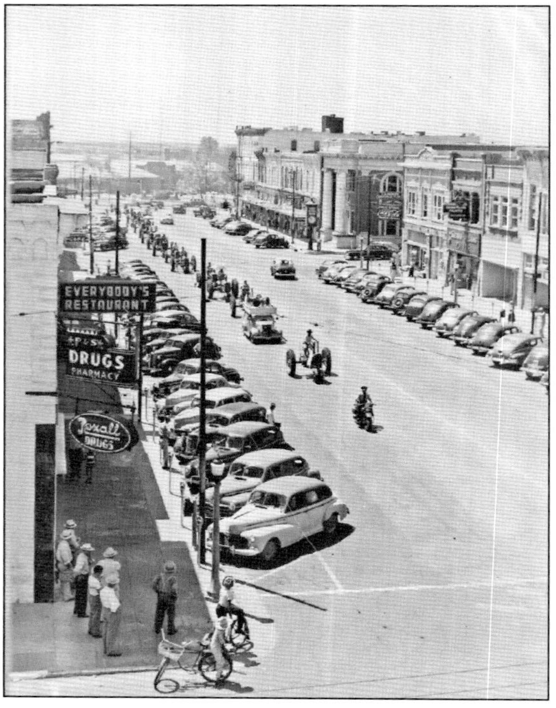

When the John Deere dealership, under the name Stroube Implements, opened in July 1948, the owners invited area famers to bring in their tractors for a free tune-up. They also drove tractors from the business's location at 1506 South Seventh Street for a parade down Beaton Street, as depicted in this photograph. (Courtesy of Steve Stroube.)

Corsicana celebrated the 100th anniversary of the town's founding in 1948. Mayor Hubert Braselton coordinated the event that included a downtown parade with Texas governor and Corsicana native son Beauford Jester as grand marshal. Corsicana native Anita Gordon, a singer on the Edgar Bergen radio program, was also featured. This photograph depicts a crew preparing barbecue for the event.

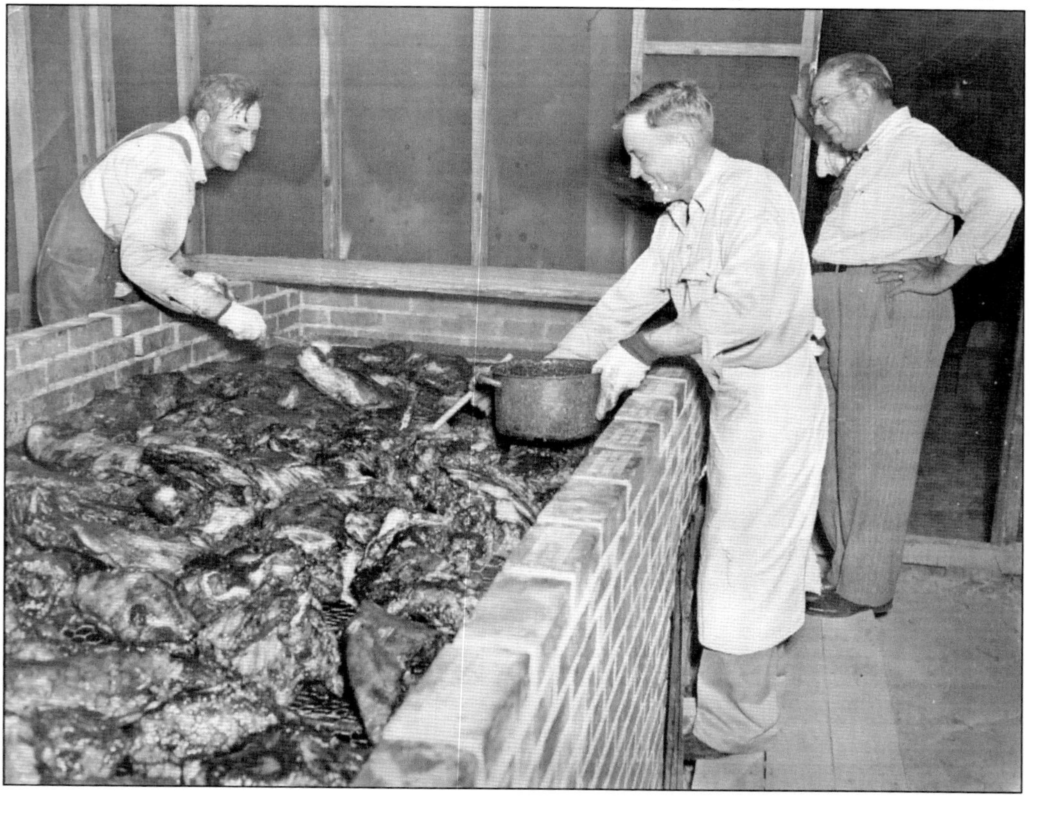

As was the case in many aspects of the community, the Corsicana Police Department employed white officers only. Theodore "Honey Bee" Hall was one of the first African American members of the Corsicana Police Department. One of the more familiar personalities in downtown Corsicana, Hall had shined shoes at George Baum's Big Four Shoe Store, as well as at Brooks Barber Shop. (Courtesy of Mabel Scott.)

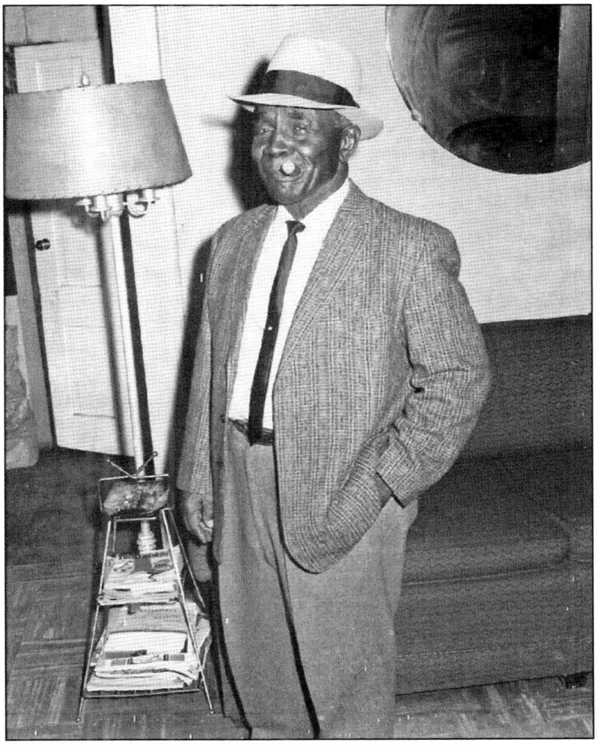

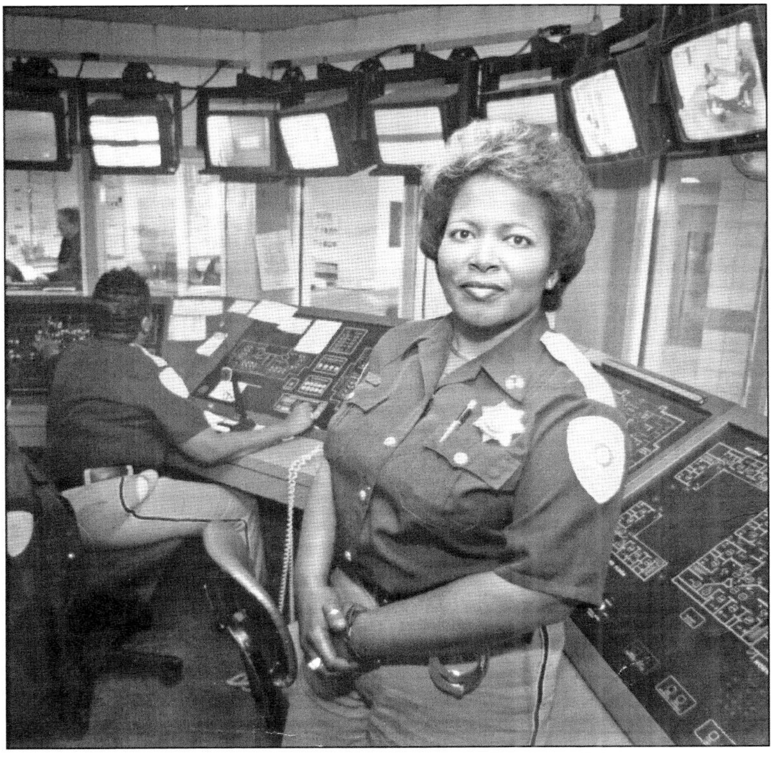

Faith Holt joined the Navarro County Sheriff's Department in 1984 as a dispatcher. Over time, she received promotions, eventually attaining the rank of captain. In 2004, she was appointed to the Navarro County Commissioners Court to replace Olin Nickleberry, who had been killed in an automobile accident. Faith was elected to a full term two years later. (Courtesy of Mabel Scott.)

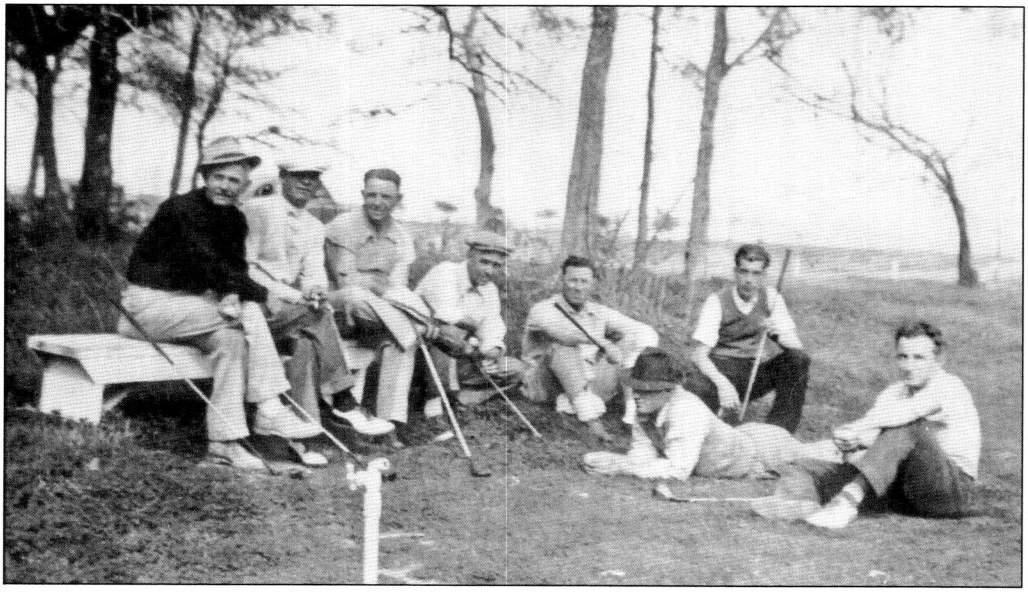

The Corsicana Country Club was established with 125 members in 1916 on a 148-acre tract of land north of town originally occupied by the Corsicana Fishing and Hunting Club. Charles Allyn served as the first president of the club. Shown in this photograph from the 1930s after a round of golf are, from left to right, Dr. Fred Owen, Porter Holloway, Rip Lang, Nick Garrity, H. R. Stroube, Joe Ezar, Charlie Holloway, and Alex Hickey. (Courtesy of Steve Stroube.)

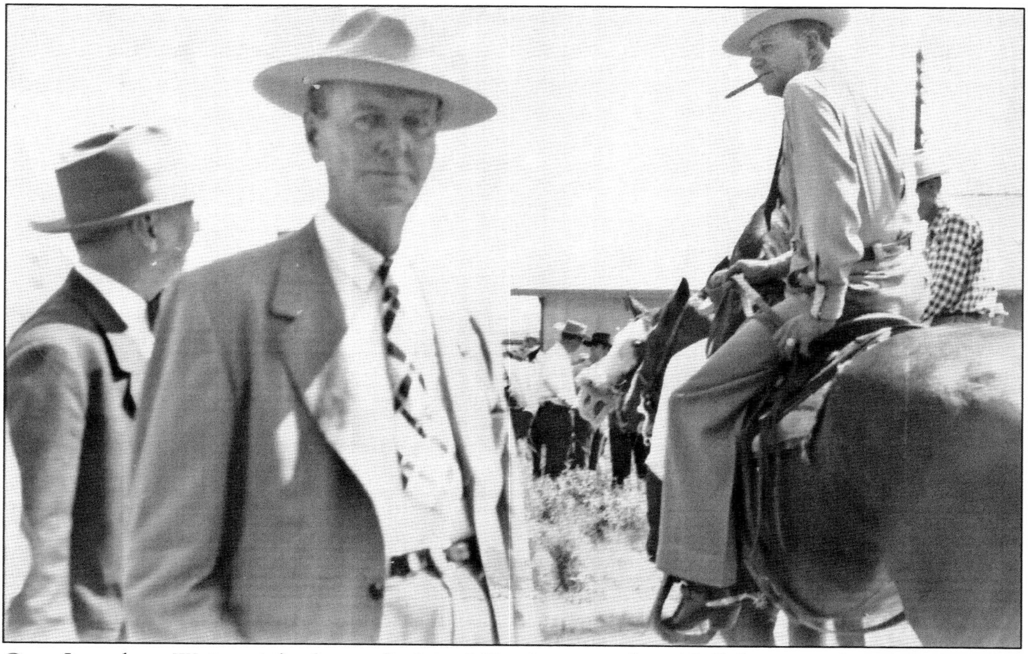

Gen. Jonathan Wainwright (center) visited Corsicana in late 1945 for a war bond drive, after having endured the infamous Bataan Death March. This photograph, which was taken behind the county jail near the courthouse, shows Ted Ferguson, an executive with Texas Power and Light, and Navarro County sheriff C. O. "Cap" Curington on horseback. (Courtesy of Paul Curington.)

Navarro Junior College was established in 1946 with a student body of 238 students, most of whom were veterans returning from service in World War II. The Air Activities of Texas, a World War II flight school, served as the first campus. Pictured here is Ray Waller, the first president of the college. During his 10-year administration, the college experienced growth and moved to a permanent campus 4 miles west of downtown on Highway 31. (Courtesy of Navarro College Archives.)

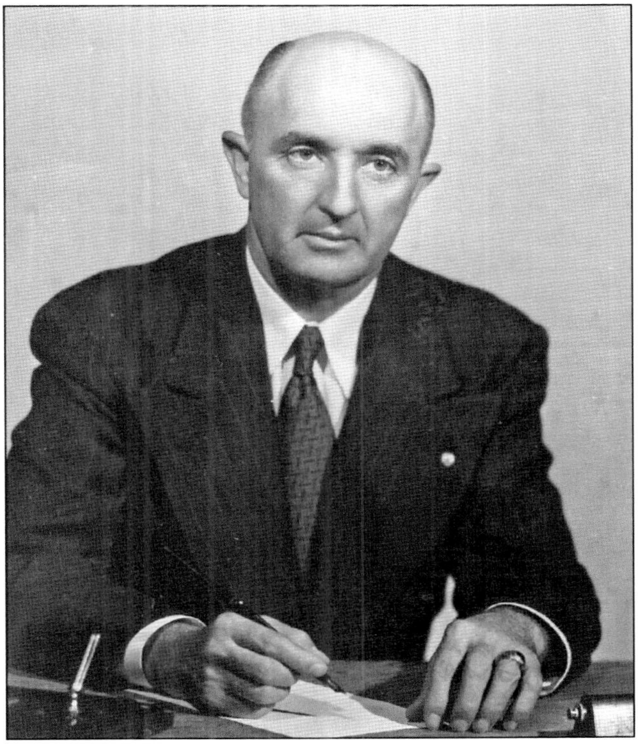

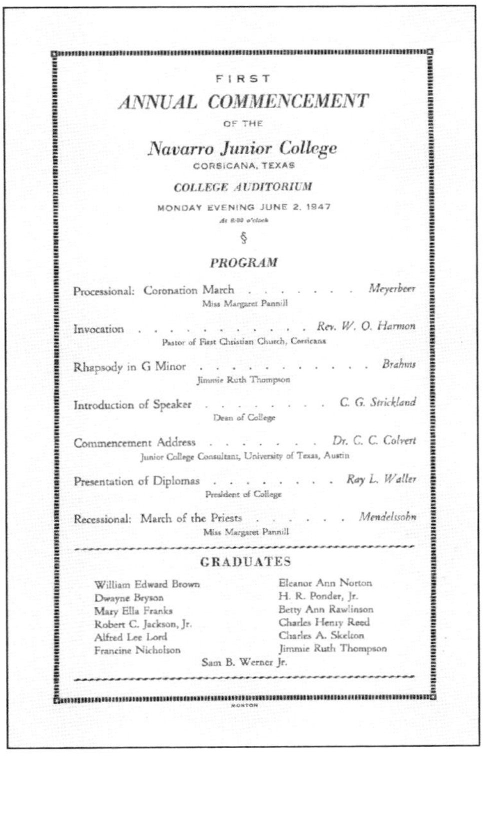

FIRST

ANNUAL COMMENCEMENT

OF THE

Navarro Junior College

CORSICANA, TEXAS

COLLEGE AUDITORIUM

MONDAY EVENING JUNE 2, 1947

At 8:00 o'clock

§

PROGRAM

Processional: Coronation March . . . . *Meyerbeer*
Miss Margaret Pannill

Invocation . . . . *Rev. W. O. Harmon*
Pastor of First Christian Church, Corsicana

Rhapsody in G Minor . . . . *Brahms*
Jimmie Ruth Thompson

Introduction of Speaker . . . . *C. G. Strickland*
Dean of College

Commencement Address . . . . *Dr. C. C. Colvert*
Junior College Consultant, University of Texas, Austin

Presentation of Diplomas . . . . *Ray L. Waller*
President of College

Recessional: March of the Priests . . . . . . *Mendelssohn*
Miss Margaret Pannill

GRADUATES

William Edward Brown
Dwayne Bryson
Mary Ella Franks
Robert C. Jackson, Jr.
Alfred Lee Lord
Francine Nicholson
Eleanor Ann Norton
H. R. Ponder, Jr.
Betty Ann Rawlinson
Charles Henry Reed
Charles A. Skelton
Jimmie Ruth Thompson
Sam B. Werner Jr.

NORTON

At the end of its first academic year, Navarro Junior College held a commencement ceremony to award associate degrees to 13 graduates. They had earned credits at other colleges or universities prior to enrolling at Navarro to meet the requirements for graduation. Noted junior college leader Dr. C. C. Calvert of the University of Texas was the speaker for the event, which was held on June 2, 1947. (Courtesy of Navarro College Archives.)

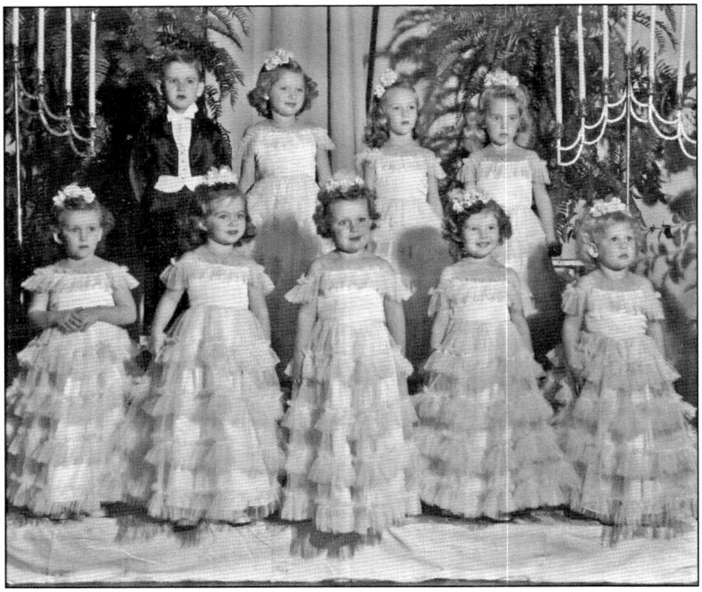

A highlight of each school year was the crowning of campus royalty. In addition to naming a king and queen of the high school, the ceremony also included elementary students as part of the court, as depicted in this 1947 photograph. From left to right are (first row) Cinda Cason, Ann Ruth, Mary Stroube, Mary Elizabeth Graham, and Molly Chilton; (second row) Pete Allen, Ann Sneed, Linda Landreth, and Elizabeth Settle. (Courtesy of Kathryn Zack.)

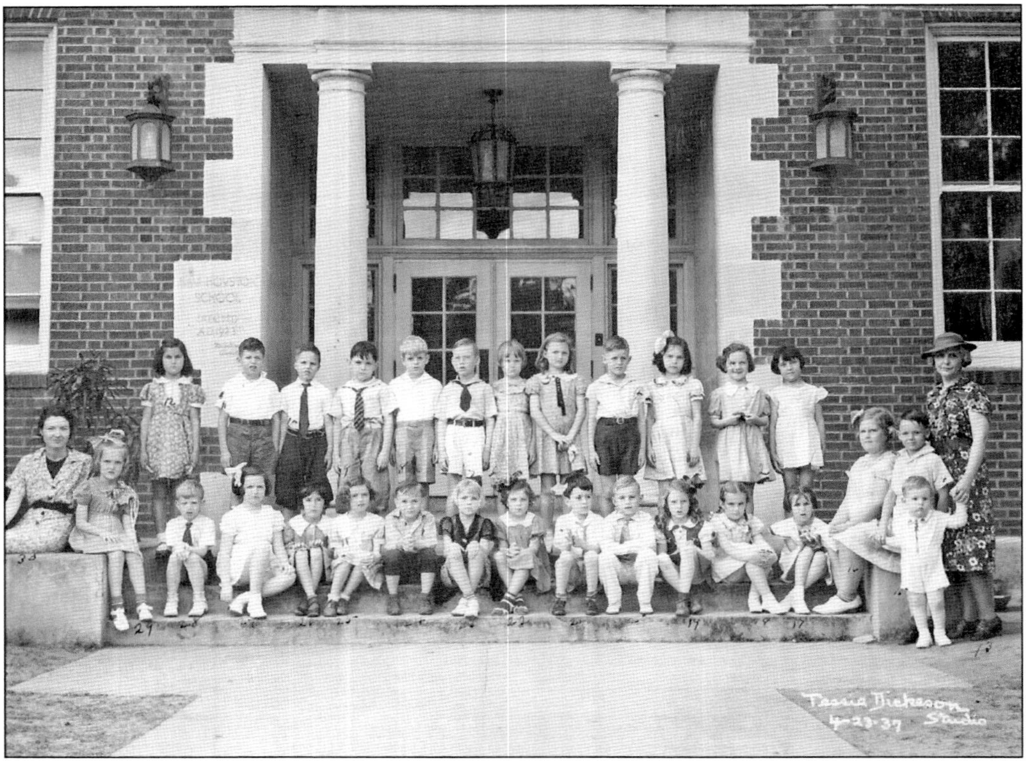

The Sam Houston School opened in 1905 in a building formerly housing the Academy of Our Lady of Sacred Heart. In 1923, that structure was demolished and replaced by a two-story brick building. Over the years, the building was expanded but was demolished in 1971, and Sam Houston moved to what had been Drane Junior High at 1213 West Fourth Avenue. Pictured here is Lillian Pearson's second grade class in 1937. (Courtesy of Katherine Zack.)

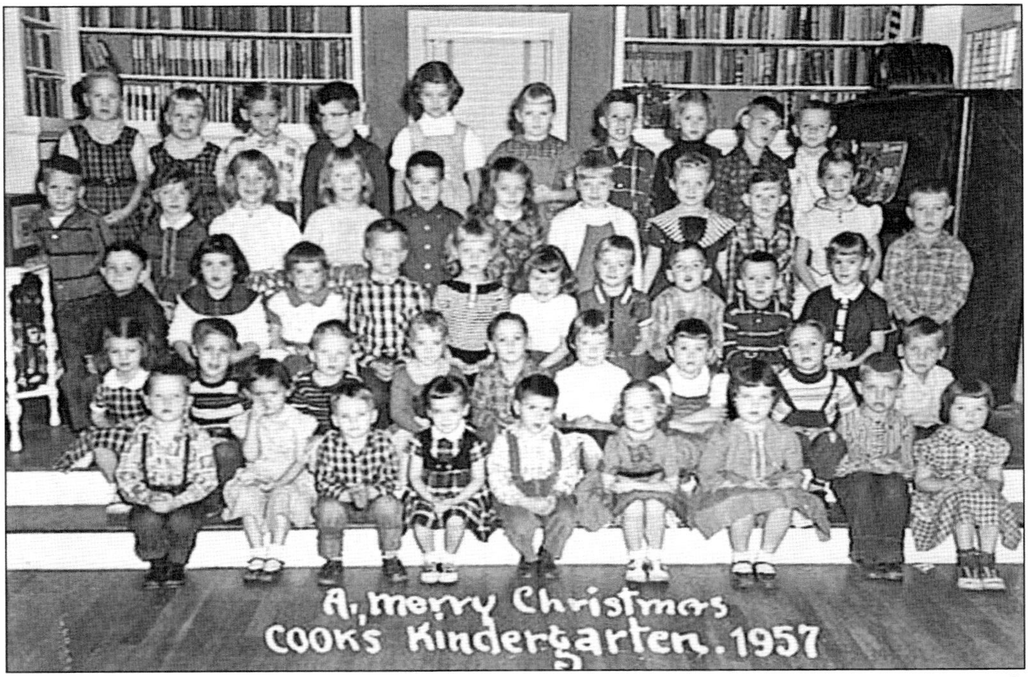

Cook's School of Speech and Dance, a private kindergarten located at 110 North Nineteenth Street, was owned by Sue Cook, affectionately known as "Cookie." In addition to her school, Cookie worked with her husband, Spruill Cook, who was a drama and English instructor at Navarro Junior College. Although never a paid employee, she was instrumental in many of the awards garnered by the college's theatrical productions. Shown above are students sending Christmas greetings in 1957. Below is a 1957 dance program with, from left to right, Stan Fletcher, Skipper Tullos, Larry Bowers, David Hansford, David Mesker, Bruce Mertz, Jim Breithaupt, Pat Gibson, Gary Summarall, and Matt Spikes. (Both, courtesy of Tresa Darby.)

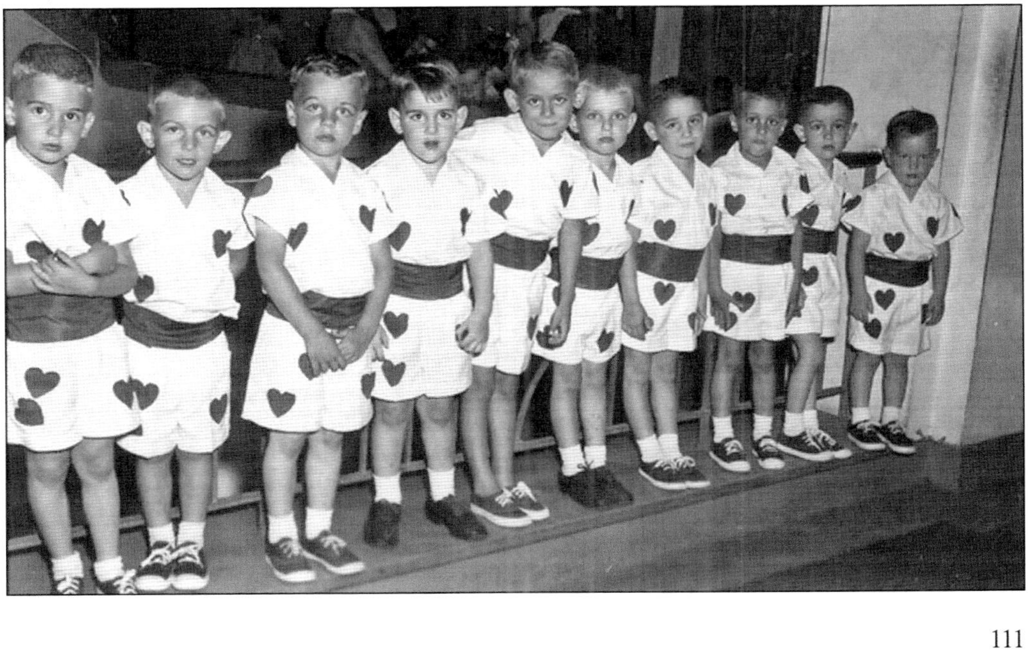

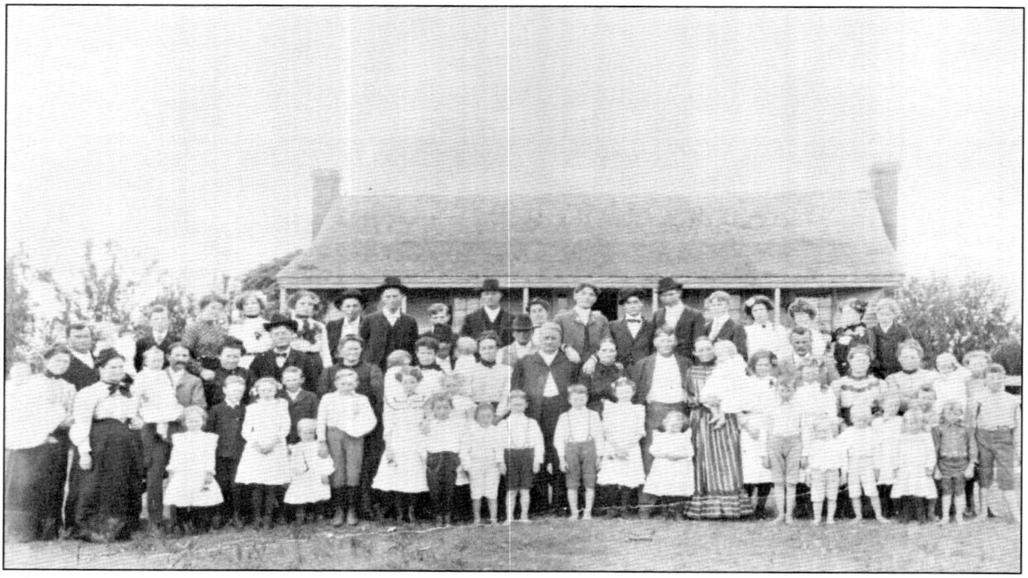

This photograph depicts the family of Matthew Ford Albritton. Born in Alabama in 1835, Albritton served in the Confederate army during the Civil War. Altogether Albritton fathered 17 children. He had 11 children by his first wife before her death. He then married Mary Paulina Gray Gaines, who had three children from a previous marriage. They had six more children together. (Courtesy of Jane Miller.)

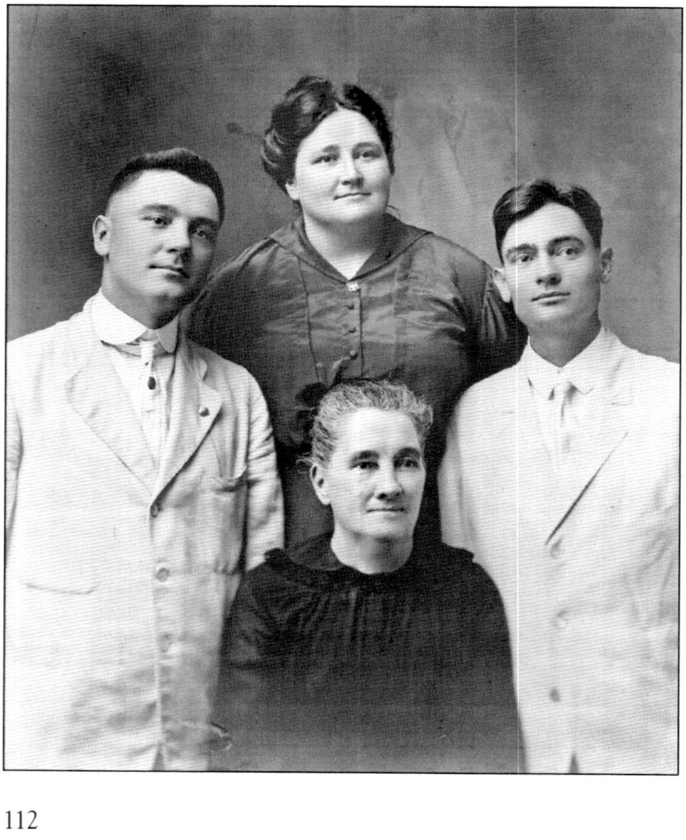

Paulina Albritton (seated) is pictured with three of her children, from left to right, Oliver Albritton Sr., Pearl Albritton Burson, and Claude Albritton Sr. Oliver Albritton was an educator, rancher, and banker, and was a leader in the founding of Navarro Junior College in 1946. Pearl Burson was co-owner of Burson and Pearson Florists, and Claude Albritton was a rancher and educator involved in oil development. (Courtesy of Jane Miller.)

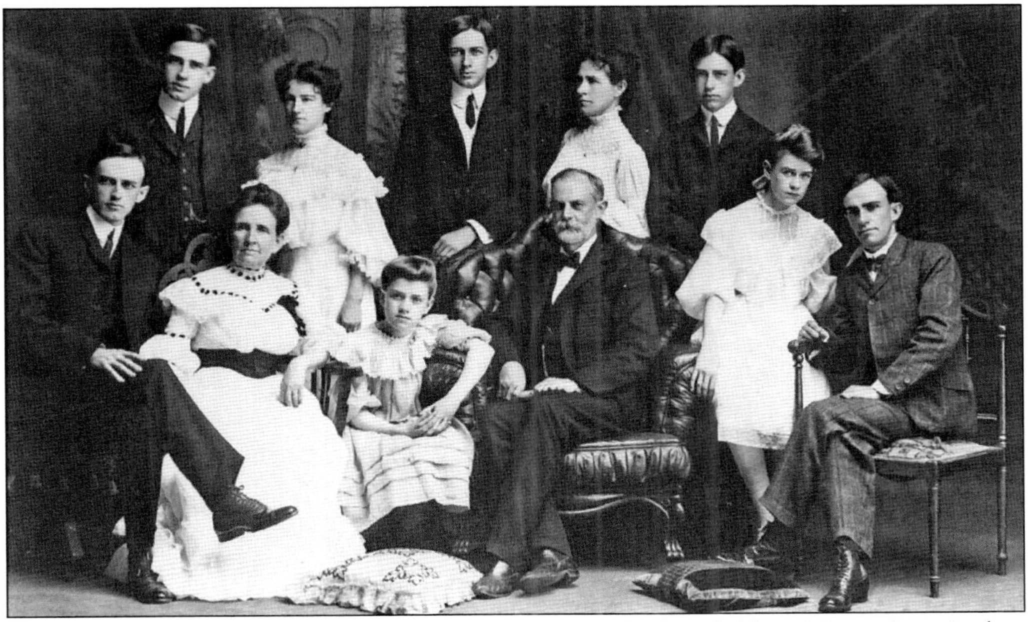

E. Wiley Johnson and his wife, Frances McMillan Johnson had 12 children, Mattie, Lora, Luther, James, Ernest, Frances, Lillian, Robert, Wiley, William, Jerry, Sloan, and Minnie. They came to Navarro County from his native state of Georgia following the Civil War. He engaged in the mercantile business and was also involved in banking. The family home was at 420 West Sixth Avenue and is currently occupied by the Magnolia House. Johnson was active in the Third Avenue Presbyterian Church and was instrumental in establishing the YMCA.

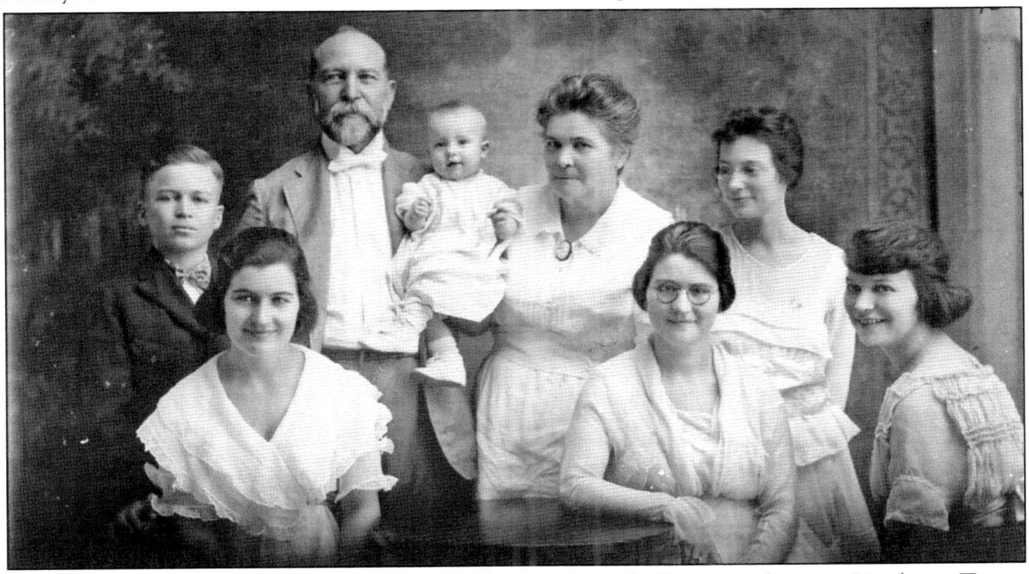

John S. Callicutt, shown here with his wife, Evie, and six children, was born in Pittsburg, Texas, in 1865. He earned a bachelor's degree from Southwestern University in Georgetown, Texas, and a law degree from the University of Texas. In addition to his law practice and his duties as district judge, Callicutt was involved in banking and the wholesale grocery business. The family home was at 1244 West Fourth Avenue.

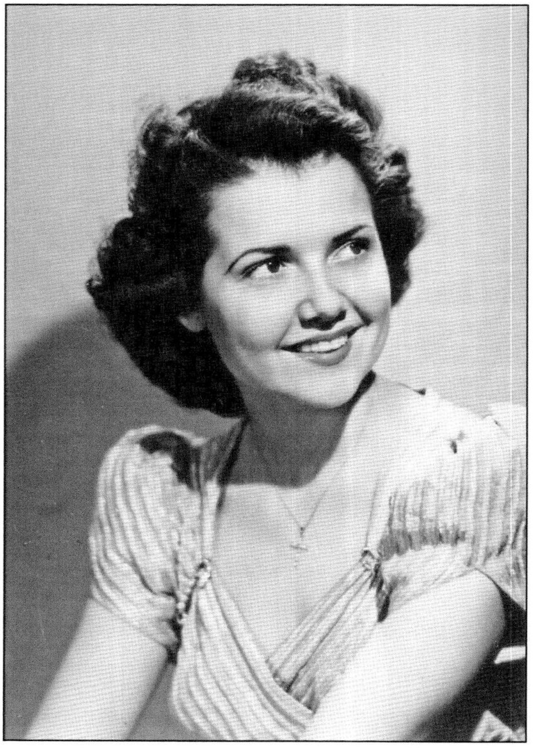

Bonnie Ruth Slauson, daughter of Wolf Brand Chili owner, Fred Slauson, won numerous awards and honors as a student at Baylor University, including being named Queen of Queens at the State Fair of Texas. After a successful Hollywood screen test, she declined contract offers from movie producers and returned to Texas. In 1943, she was diagnosed with polio and died at the age of 22. (Courtesy of Al Hopkins.)

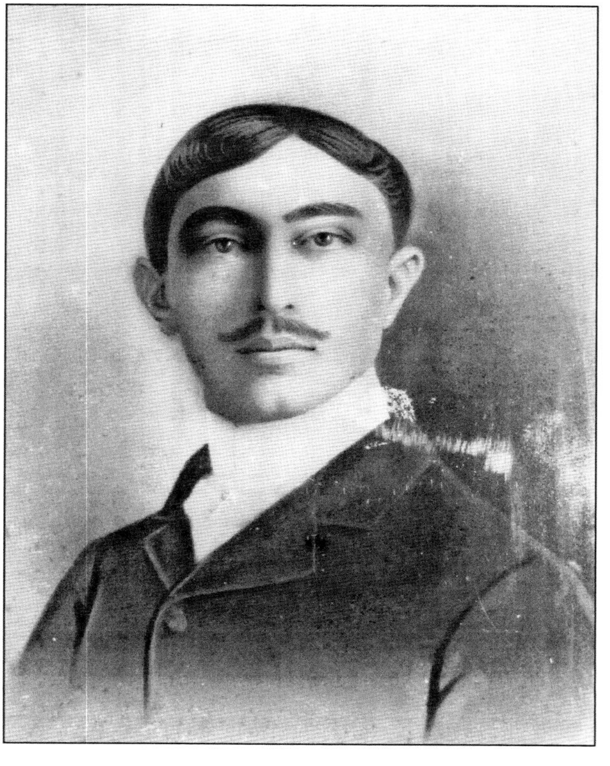

Jake Miller was born in Latvia in 1855. Like thousands of immigrants in the late 19th century, Miller fled to the United States, seeking a better life for himself and his family. Lacking enough money to bring his wife and six children, he worked for five years before he was able to send for his family. Two years after the family was united, Miller died, and his wife passed away the following year. Moses Miller, one of the orphaned children, eventually came to Corsicana, where he operated a grocery business. (Courtesy of Sidney and Jane Miller.)

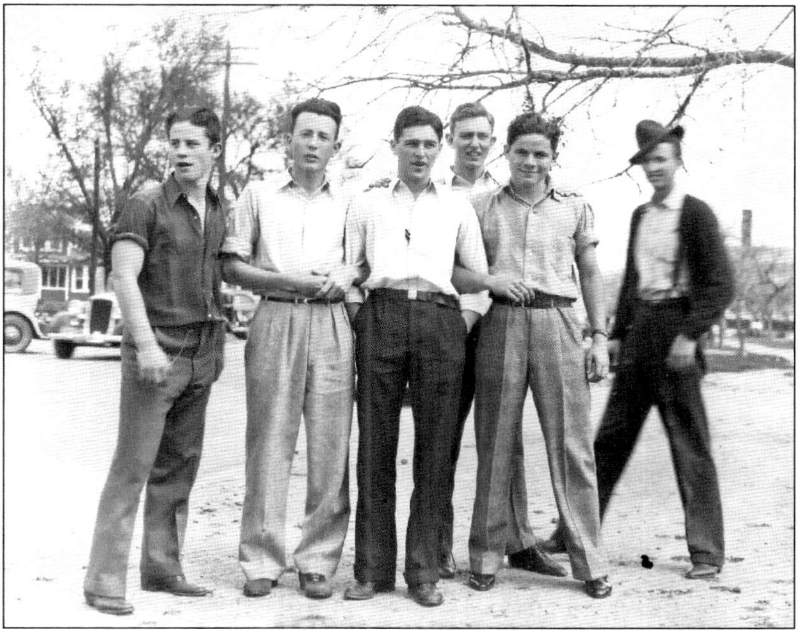

"Hanging out" has long been a popular pastime for young people, regardless of the time period. Shown in this 1936 photograph, taken on the campus of Corsicana High School, are, from left to right, Jack Sroube, Frank Keathley, David McElwrath, Harry Ezell Jr., H. R. "Reno" Stroube, and Wallace Bates. (Courtesy of Jon Ketcham.)

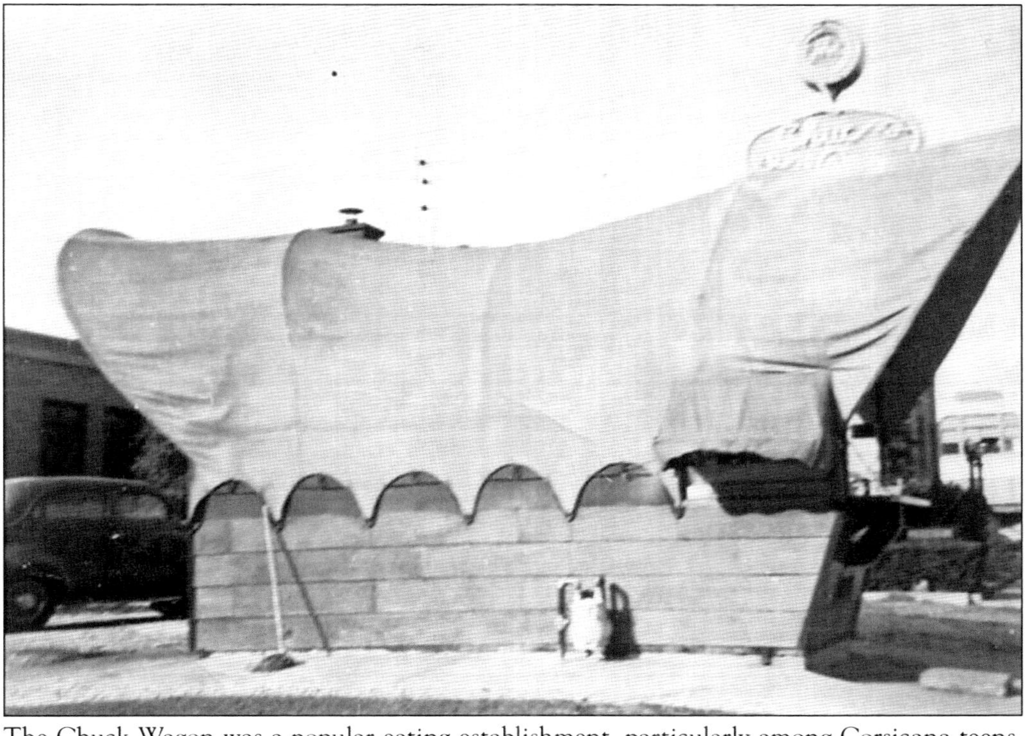

The Chuck Wagon was a popular eating establishment, particularly among Corsicana teens. Part of a chain of restaurants owned by Rex Lanier of Fort Worth, the Chuck Wagon came to Corsicana in 1948. First located on a parking lot behind the post office, it later was moved to Seventh Avenue at the current site of HEB Grocery. Howard Oliphant was the manager. (Courtesy of Tommy Oliphant.)

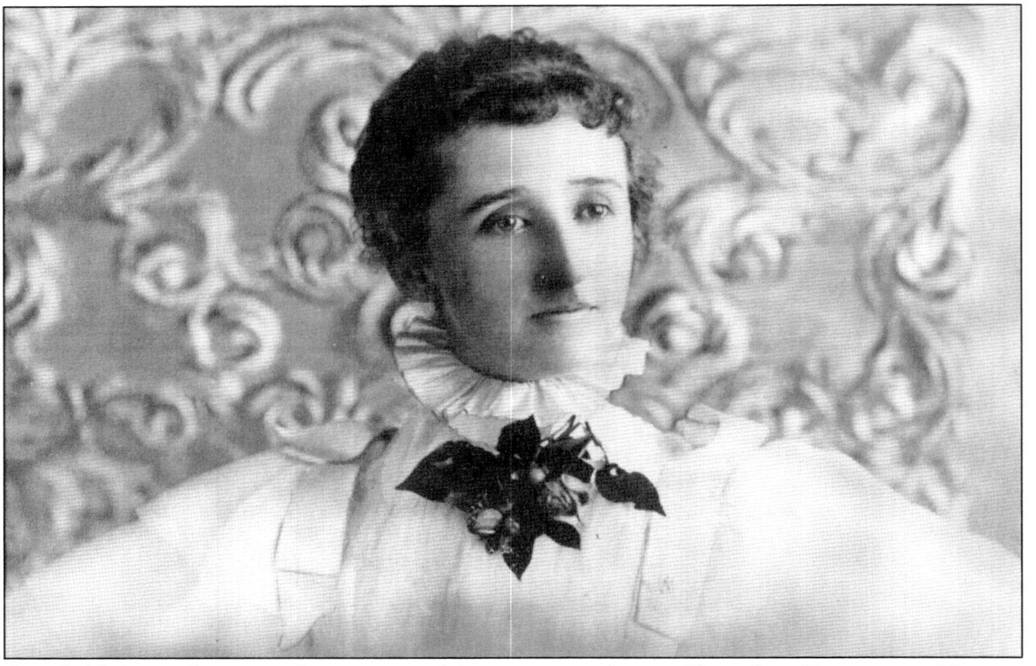

As a child, Annie Carpenter Love came with her parents and nine siblings from Tennessee to Navarro County in 1876. Prior to her marriage to William B. Love in 1901, she taught in rural Navarro County schools. She gathered historical artifacts to display in a museum room in the courthouse, and in 1933, she published a book-length history of Navarro County. She died in 1943.

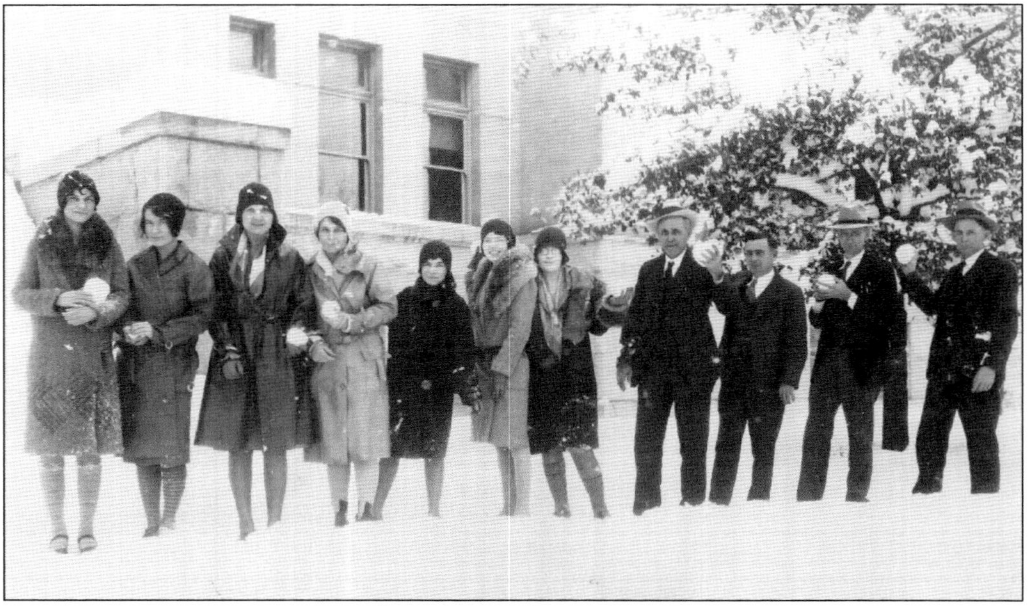

Because winters in Corsicana are usually mild, a 12-inch snowfall that came in 1929 generated excitement among the local residents, including courthouse officials and employees. Shown in this photograph are, from left to right, Lottie Blake, Leatha Keathley, Jessie Cook, unidentified, Elsie Houston, Iva Whitten, Lydia Reed, Frank Young, Andrew Steel, Bridge Morgan, and unidentified.

Four

Home Is Where the Heart Is

Historic Homes in Corsicana

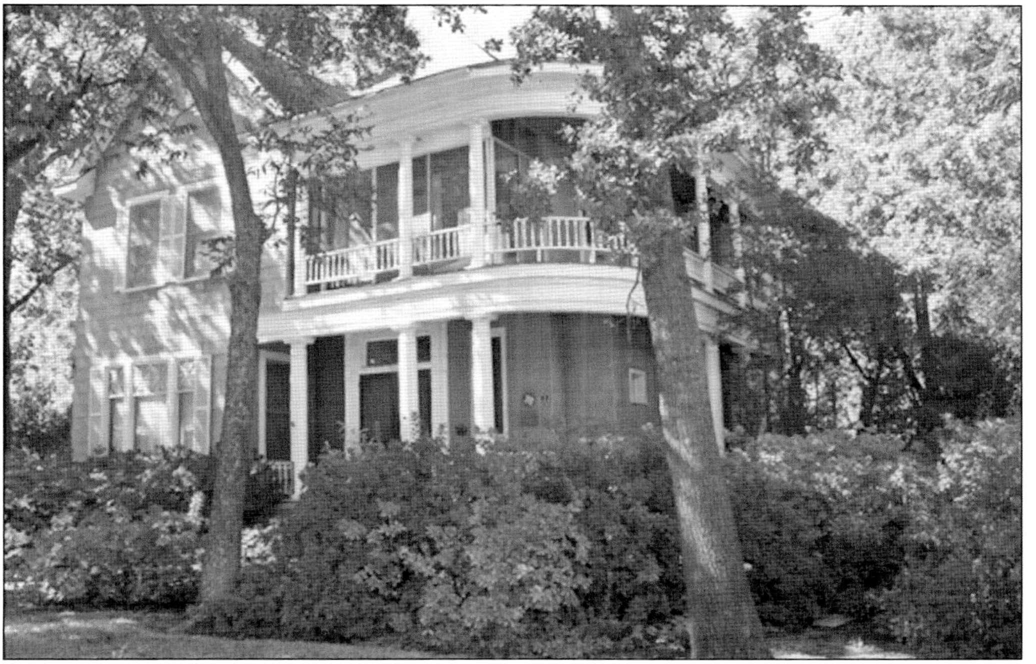

Located at 504 West Second Avenue, this home was built in 1900 by James H. Woods. A respected attorney, Woods served as mayor of Corsicana, as well as a state legislator. T. C. Perry purchased the house after Woods's death and gave it to his granddaughter, Frances Edens. She and her husband lived in the house almost 60 years. (Courtesy of Janet Jacobs.)

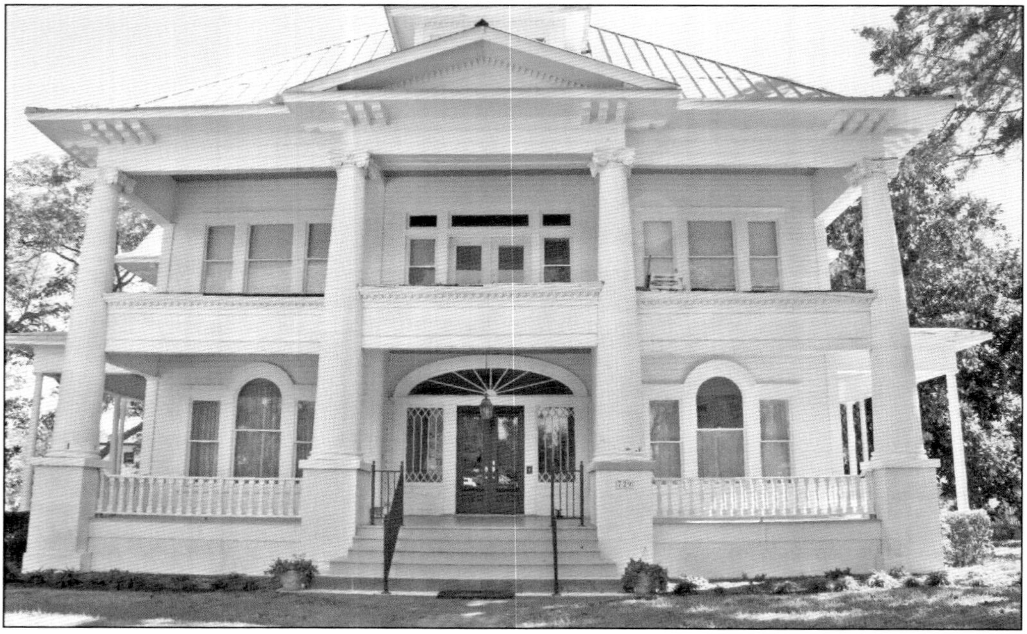

William Tatum, a local hardware merchant, built this home at 729 West Third Avenue in the 1890s. With 7,000 square feet of floor space, the residence has seven fireplaces with a dining room, a music room, and a parlor on the lower level, and five bedrooms upstairs. When constructing the house, Tatum included a type of central heat with ductwork connecting every room in the house to a coal-burning boiler in the basement. (Courtesy of Janet Jacobs.)

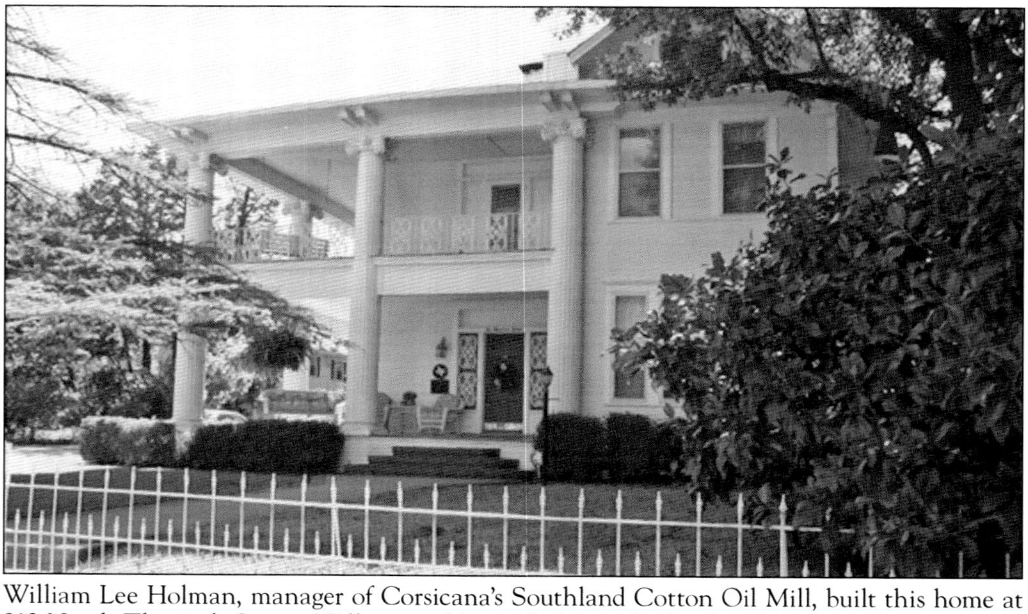

William Lee Holman, manager of Corsicana's Southland Cotton Oil Mill, built this home at 212 North Thirtieth Street. William and his wife, Lucie, had eight children, including Sarah Holman, a longtime principal at Robert E. Lee Elementary School. In 1935, Corsicana Tiger football coach Johnny Pierce purchased the house. Today it is the home of Charles and Lana Orsak. (Courtesy of Janet Jacobs.)

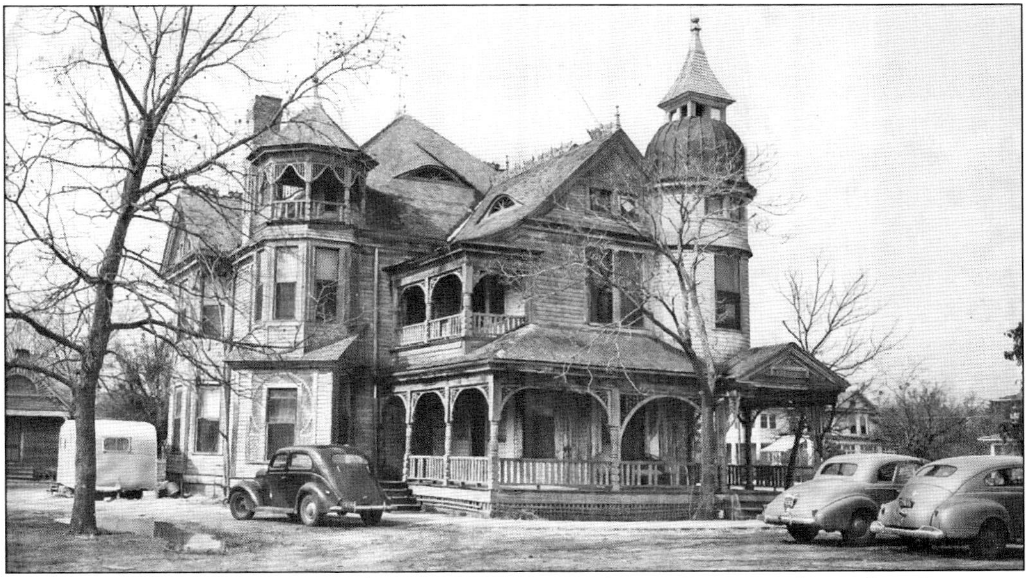

The home of Texas legislator and lieutenant governor George Jester was located at the corner of Seventh Avenue and Fifteenth Street, a site currently occupied by a CVS Pharmacy. Texas governor Beauford Jester was born in this house in 1893. Over time, the house fell into disrepair and was demolished in the 1950s. Prior to CVS acquiring the property, the studio of KAND Radio broadcast from this location.

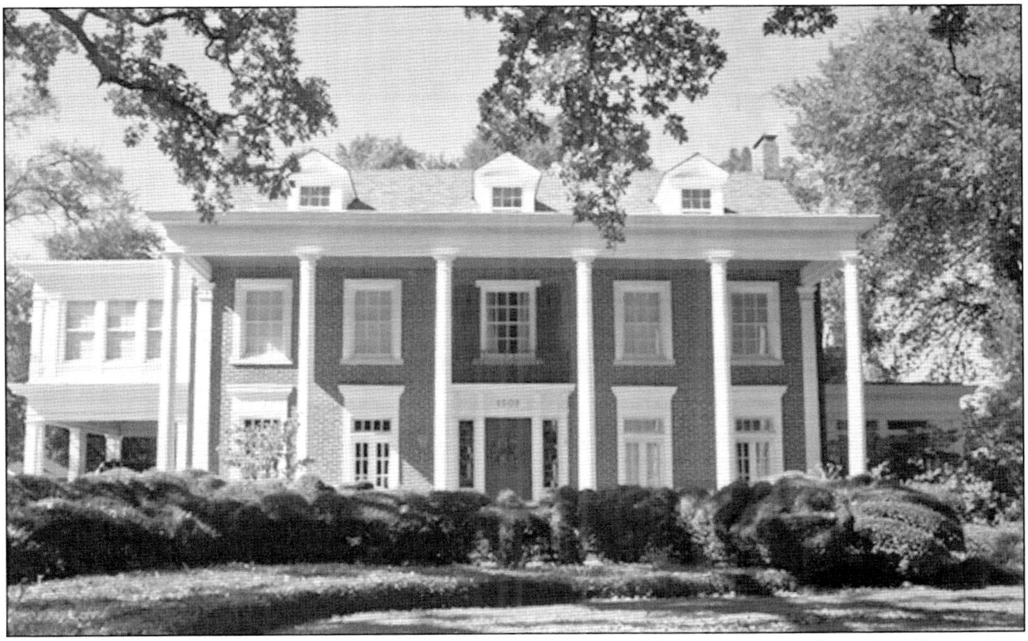

This residence at 1508 Sycamore Avenue was the home of Texas governor Beauford Jester. His father, George Jester, acquired the lot in 1902, and it served as the Jester Dairy for many years. Beauford Jester built this home in 1923. He and his wife, Mabel, lived here until his death in 1949. She sold the home the following year, and it is currently the residence of Lance and Karen Cook. (Courtesy of Janet Jacobs.)

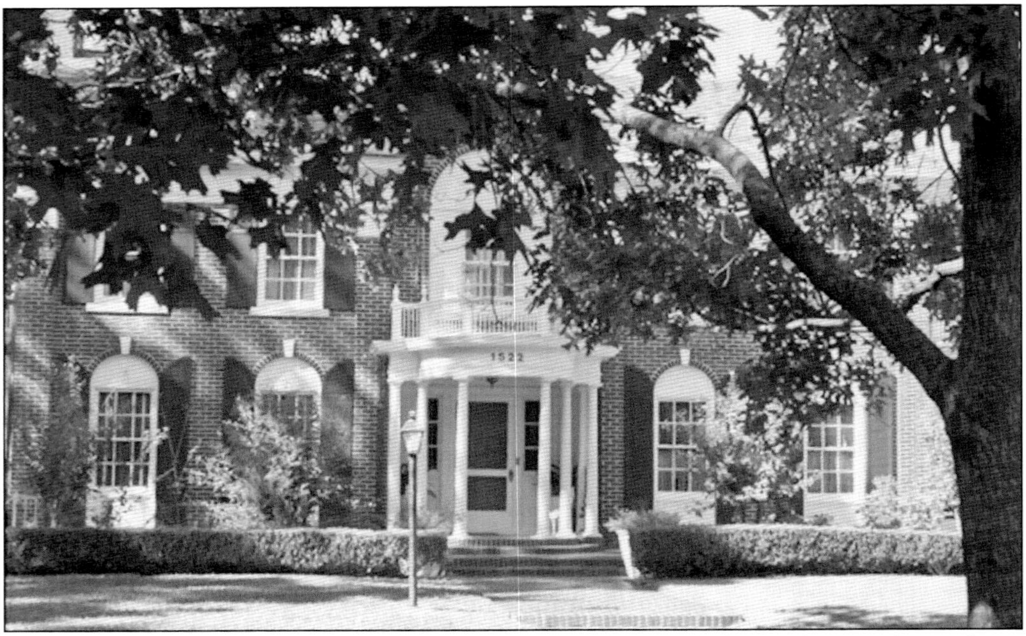

At 1522 Sycamore Avenue and immediately next door to the Beauford Jester home is the residence constructed by his brother Charles G. Jester. The house was built in 1924. Corsicana oilman Joe Butler and his wife purchased the house from the Jesters and lived there for 45 years. The current owners are Dr. Gerthon and Dorthy Morgan. (Courtesy of Janet Jacobs.)

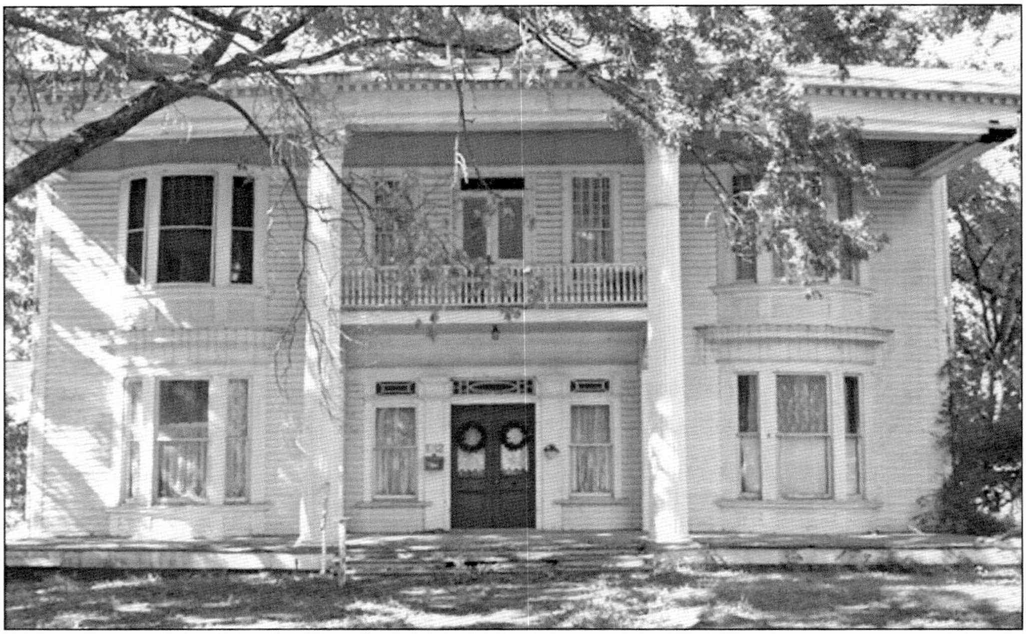

H. G. Damon was instrumental in the development of the Corsicana oil field in the 1890s. A native of Florida and a Civil War veteran, Damon came to Corsicana in 1873, where he "read law" and was admitted to the bar. He was also a pioneer in the real estate mortgage business. His home, which is located at 1012 West Third Avenue, was built in 1900. (Courtesy of Janet Jacobs.)

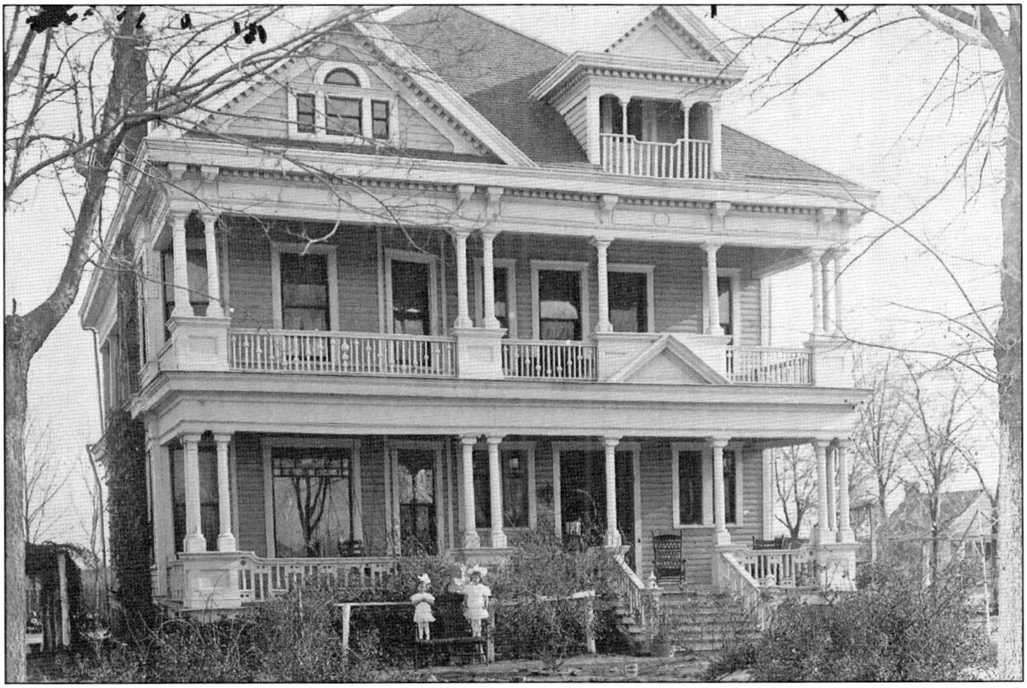

Sam Frost came to Navarro County as an infant with his parents. After serving in the Confederate army during the Civil War, Frost returned to Corsicana. Following his admission to the bar, he was appointed county attorney and later served as county judge, district judge, and state legislator. Two of his nine children are pictured on the front porch of the home, which was located on South Fifteenth Street.

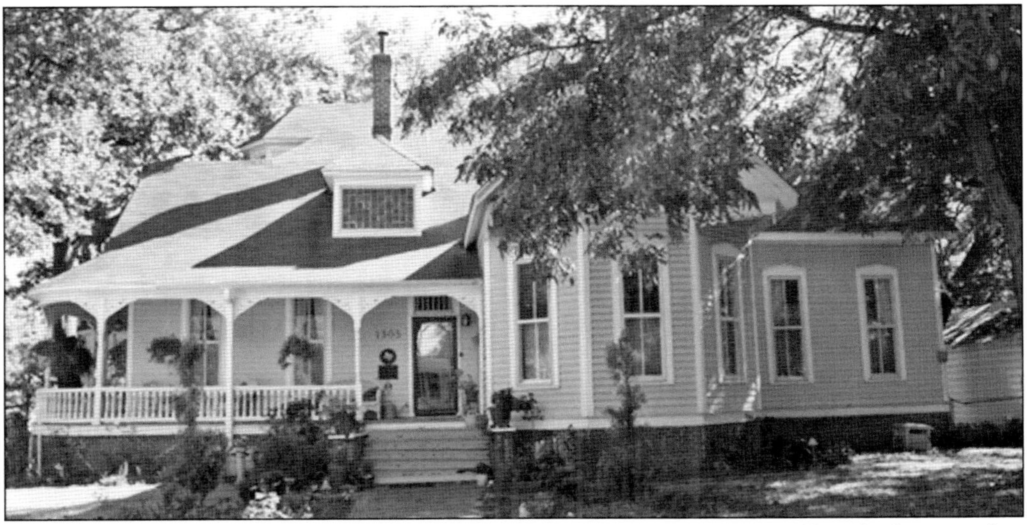

Navarro County sheriff E. E. Dunn built this house in 1866 at 1303 West Fourth Avenue after he returned from service in the Confederate army during the Civil War. A "shotgun" house, it had three large rooms, a kitchen, and a large center hall leading to the back porch. Corsicana grocery man Sam Ransom bought the house in 1890, and he and his wife and five children lived there until his death in 1920. (Courtesy of Janet Jacobs.)

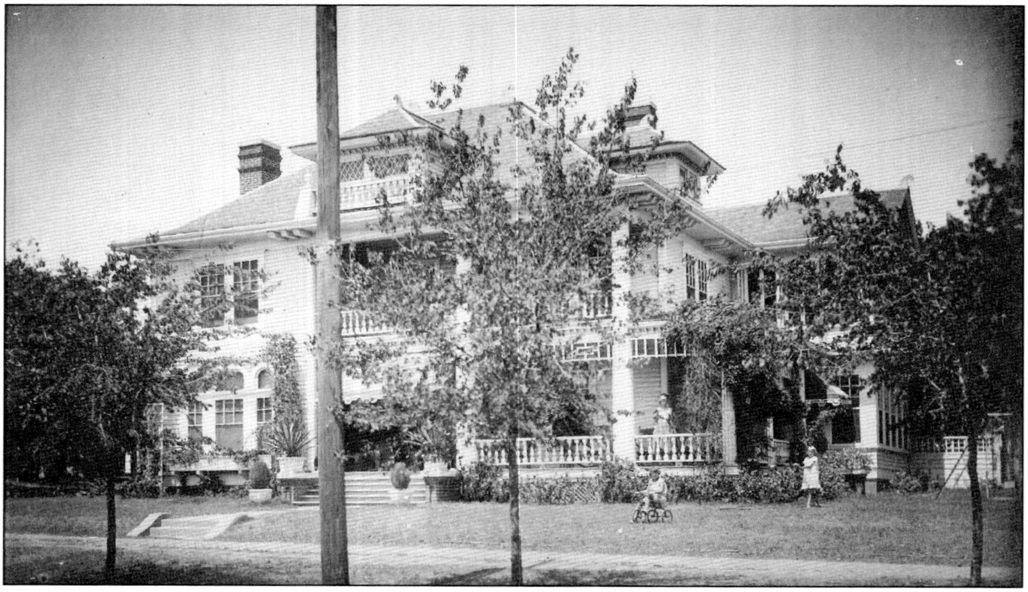

Joel A. Kerr was among the first property owners in Corsicana. He built this house, which was located at 220 West Fourth Avenue, in 1867. The 12 rooms provided a comfortable and spacious residence for Kerr, his wife, and four sons. The youngest son, John Mortimer (Morty), acquired the house after his father's death. He owned a hardware store on Beaton Street, and he and his wife were active in various social and civic groups. The house was demolished in 1966.

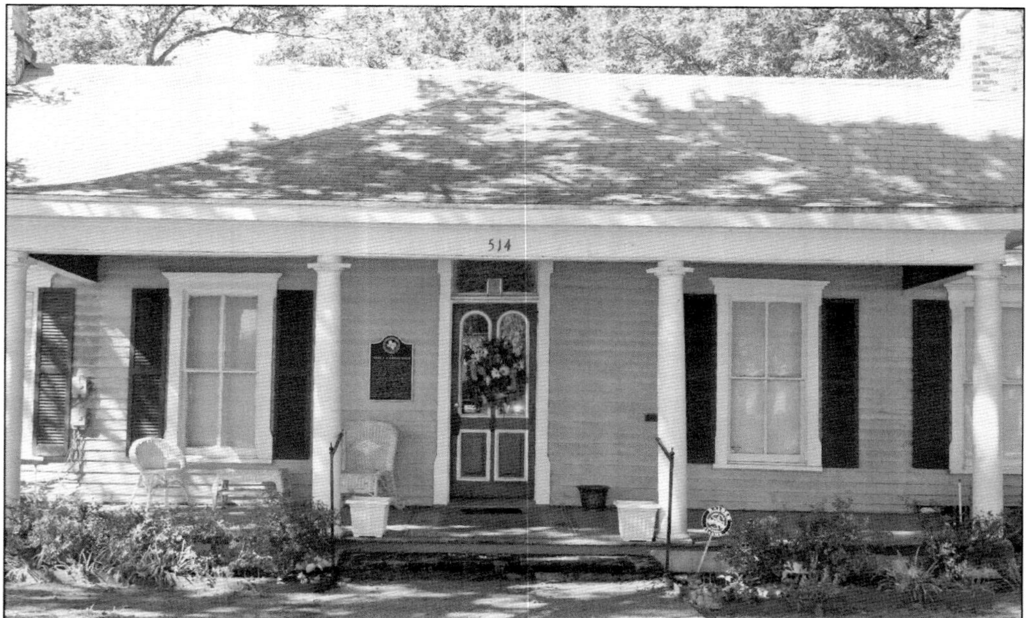

One of the oldest homes in Corsicana was built in 1873 by Eldred J. Simkins, a local attorney. He also served as district attorney, as a member of the board of regents at the University of Texas, state senator, and justice on the court of criminal appeals. Located at 514 West Second Avenue, it is currently occupied by Holmes Photography Studio. (Courtesy of Janet Jacobs.)

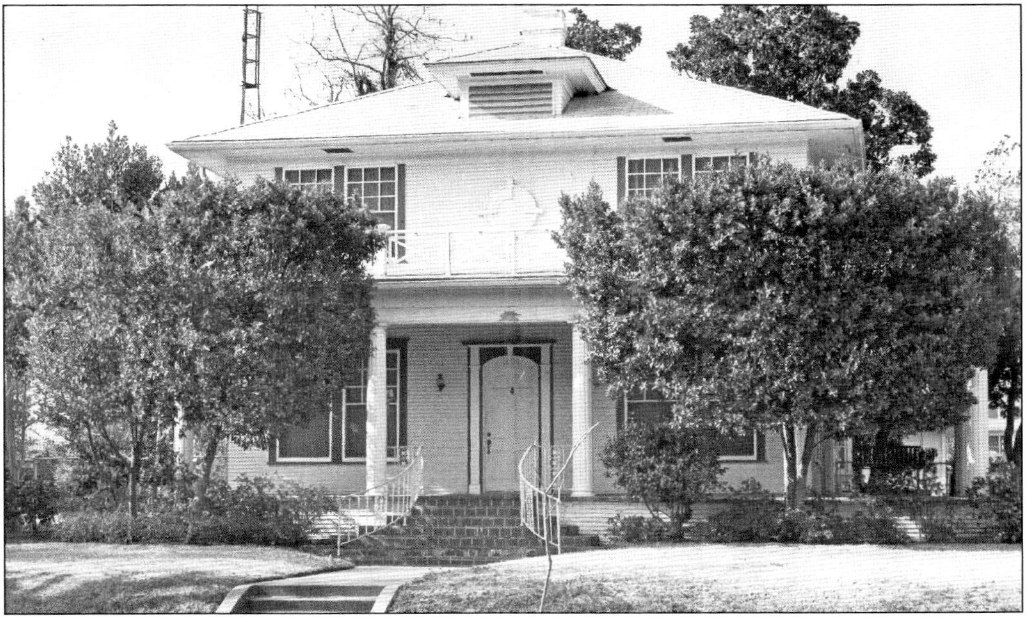

Ben Rosenberg was a leader in the Corsicana Jewish community. He owned Rosenberg Implements, where he sold International Harvester Farm Equipment. Known for his philanthropy, Rosenberg contributed to the Navarro Regional Hospital and many other charitable endeavors. His home at 1206 West Fourth Avenue was noted for its attractive landscaping. (Courtesy of Janet Jacobs.)

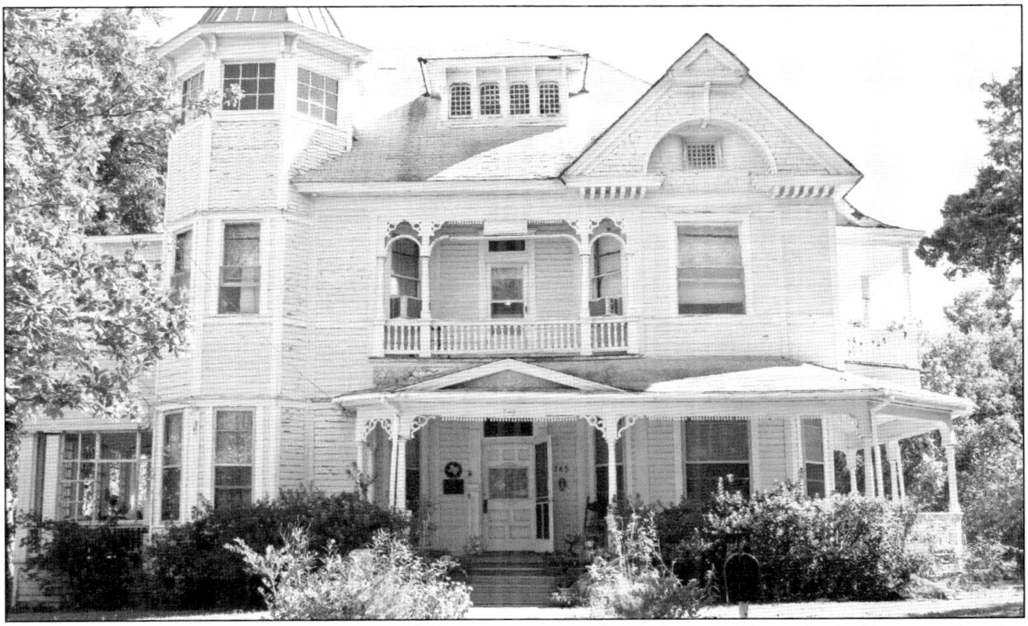

In 1894, A. D. Abraham purchased a lot at 745 West Third Avenue from S. A. Pace under the condition that he build a house on the property within the year at a minimum cost of $2,500. The residence shown in this photograph was completed in 1895. It was built of cypress hauled by wagon from Louisiana. J. W. Edens purchased the home in 1902, and it remained the Edens family residence until 1946. (Courtesy of Janet Jacobs.)

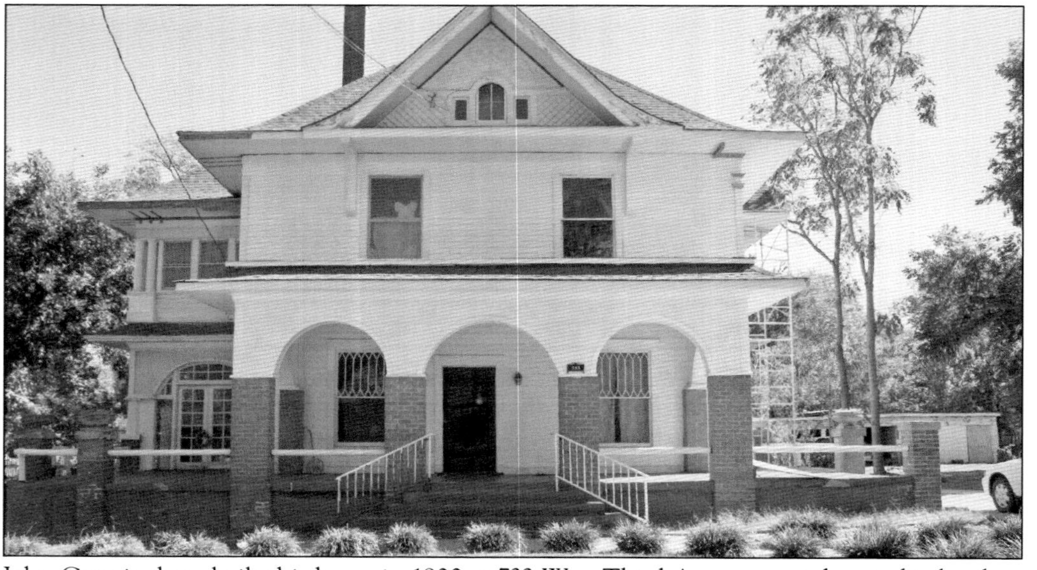

John Cunningham built this home in 1900 at 733 West Third Avenue next door to his brother-in-law, William Tatum. The two men were partners in a Corsicana hardware business. The house was constructed by noted Corsicana builder Whiteselle Lumber Company. It has six fireplaces that originally burned coal. The fireplaces in the parlor and the dining room are back-to-back. (Courtesy of Janet Jacobs.)

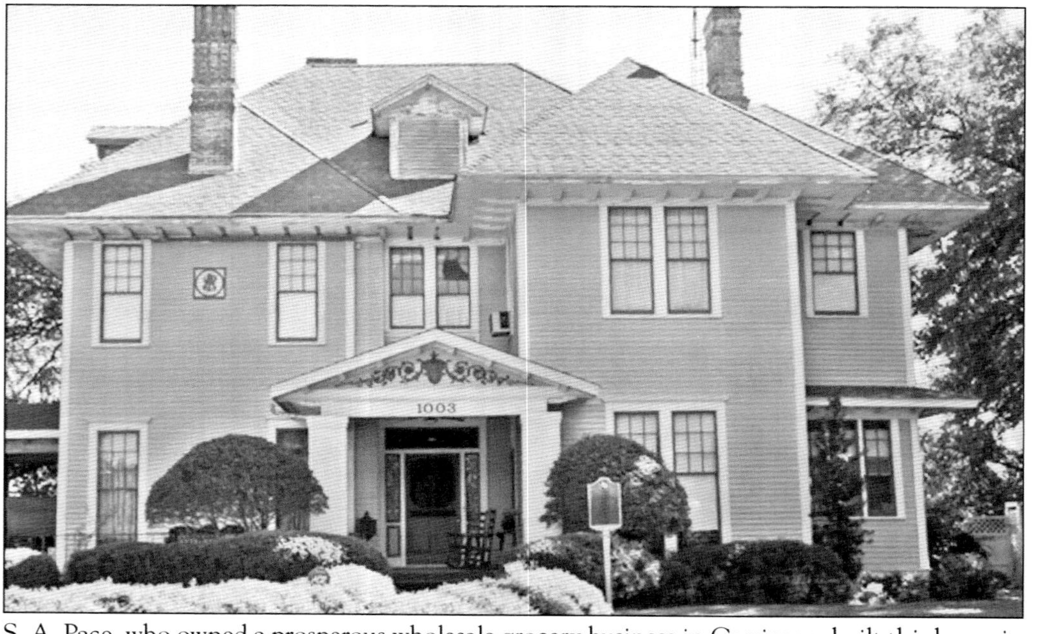

S. A. Pace, who owned a prosperous wholesale grocery business in Corsicana, built this home in 1887 at 1003 West Third Avenue. A meticulous man, Pace is said to have personally supervised the construction of the house, watching every nail being driven into the structure. Originally the house had no closets, with wardrobes used instead to hold clothing and other household items. In 1958, it was acquired by the owners of the Hamilton House, a home-decorating business. (Courtesy of Janet Jacobs.)

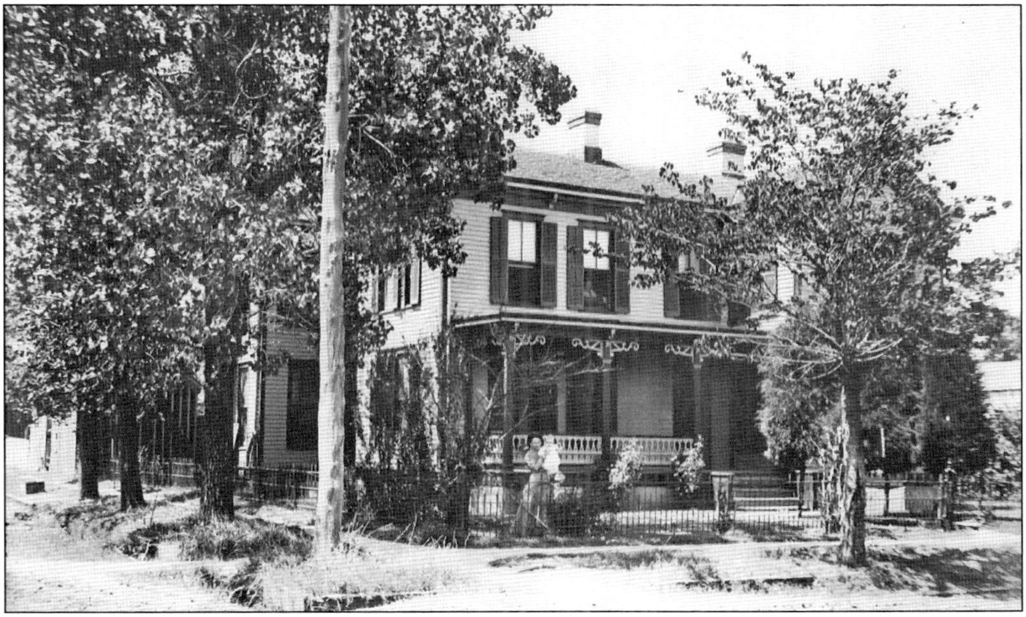

Emil Frey established a photography business shortly after he arrived in Corsicana in the early 1870s, a business he operated for half a century. In addition to his photography career, Frey was a talented musician, teaching and composing music and playing a variety of instruments. His home (pictured here) was at 1304 East Seventh Avenue, which had two oil wells in the yard during the boom of the 1890s.

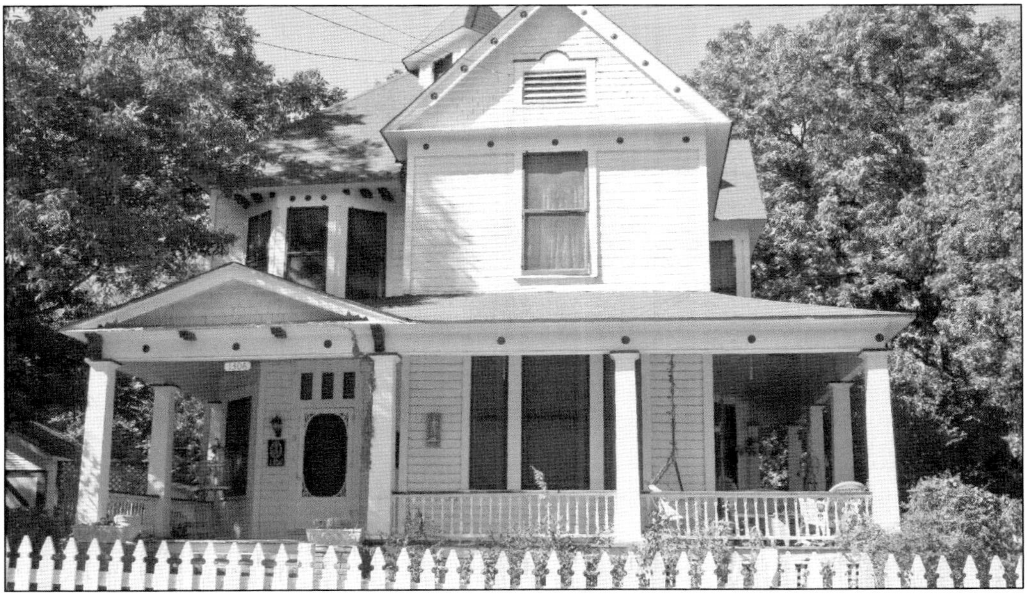

Dr. John R. Smith, who served as mayor of Corsicana from 1883 to 1885, built this home at 1306 West Fourth Avenue. Smith was instrumental in organizing the fire department in 1883. Susan McCrery, a widow, purchased the residence in 1898 as a home for herself, her 10 daughters, and her mother-in-law, and it remained in the McCrery family for more than 60 years. (Courtesy of Janet Jacobs.)

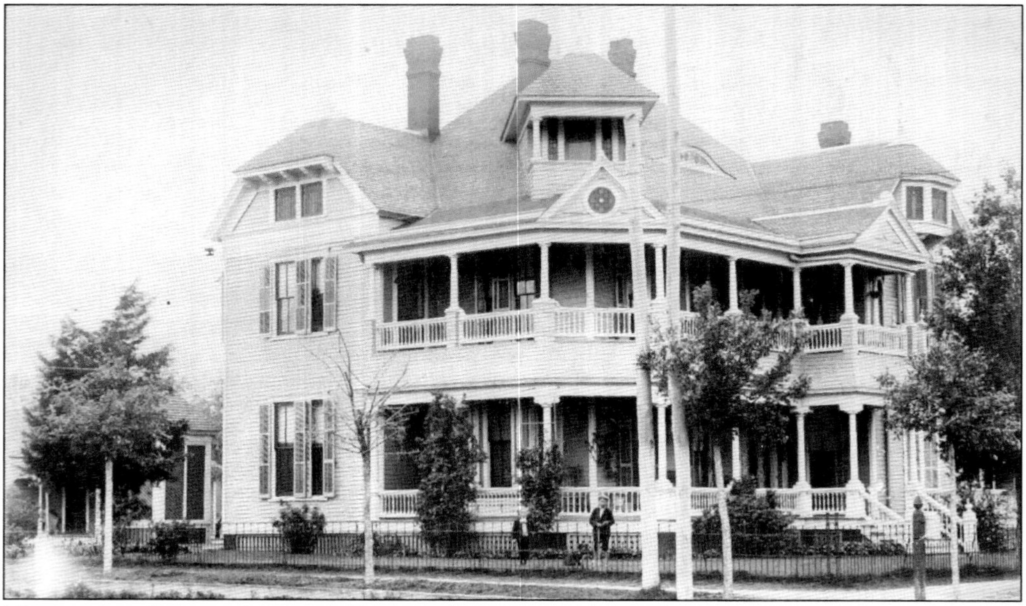

This majestic home at 214 South Fourteenth Street was the residence of Charles Allyn. In addition to serving as a city councilman and mayor, Allyn was the first president of the Corsicana Country Club. He also served on the school board and the library board, and was first vice president of First National Bank. After his death in 1918, his widow moved to a new house at 708 West Seventh Avenue.

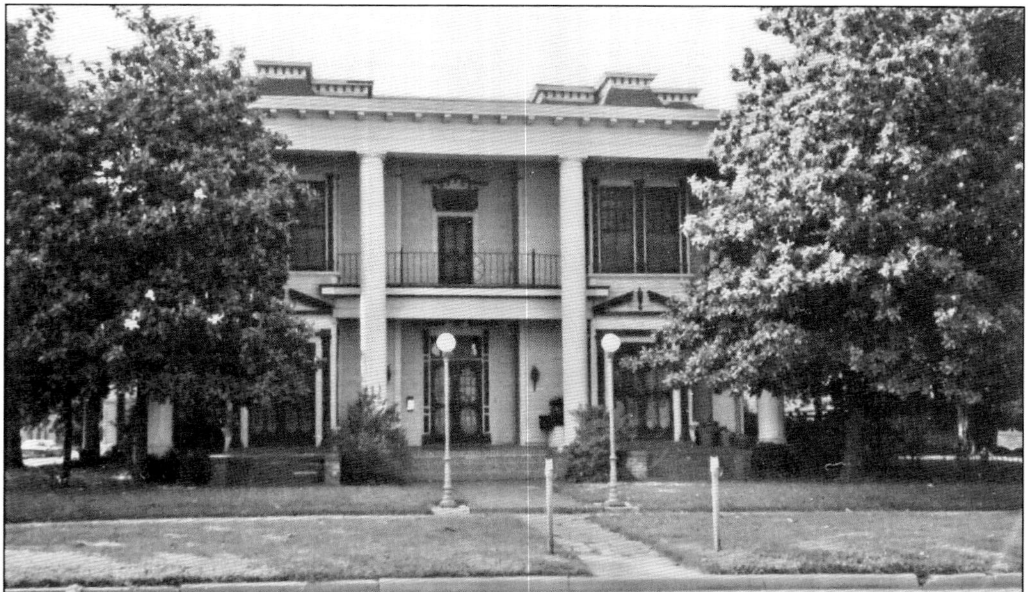

This home at 420 West Sixth Avenue was the family residence of E. Wiley Johnson. Built in 1883, the 10-room house is believed to be one of the oldest remaining residences in Corsicana originally built as a two-story structure. Johnson's son-in-law, W. C. McCammon, acquired the house the house in 1922 and used it for his funeral business. By the 1970s, it was vacant and in disrepair, but it has been restored. Today it is a bed-and-breakfast called the Magnolia House.

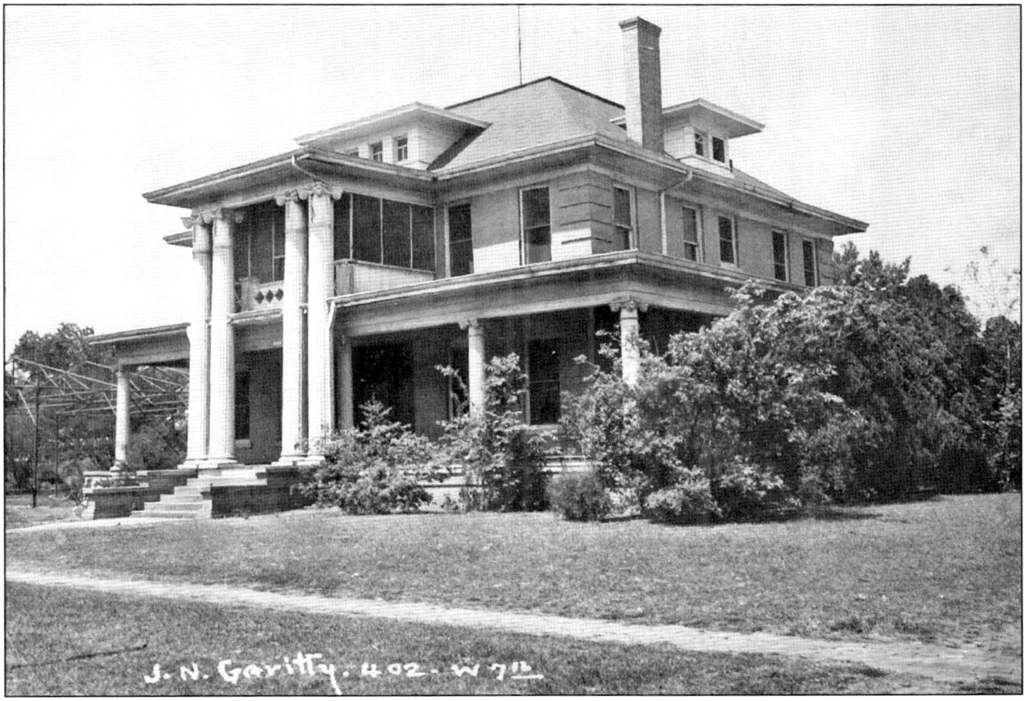

Born in Ireland in 1842, James Garrity spent his early years in New Orleans. He came to Corsicana after serving in the Confederate army during the Civil War. He founded the First National Bank in 1871. This house, which was the family residence, was built in 1910 at 402 West Seventh Avenue. Like many Corsicana homes, it was constructed by the Whiteselle Brick and Lumber Company. The house was demolished in 1964.

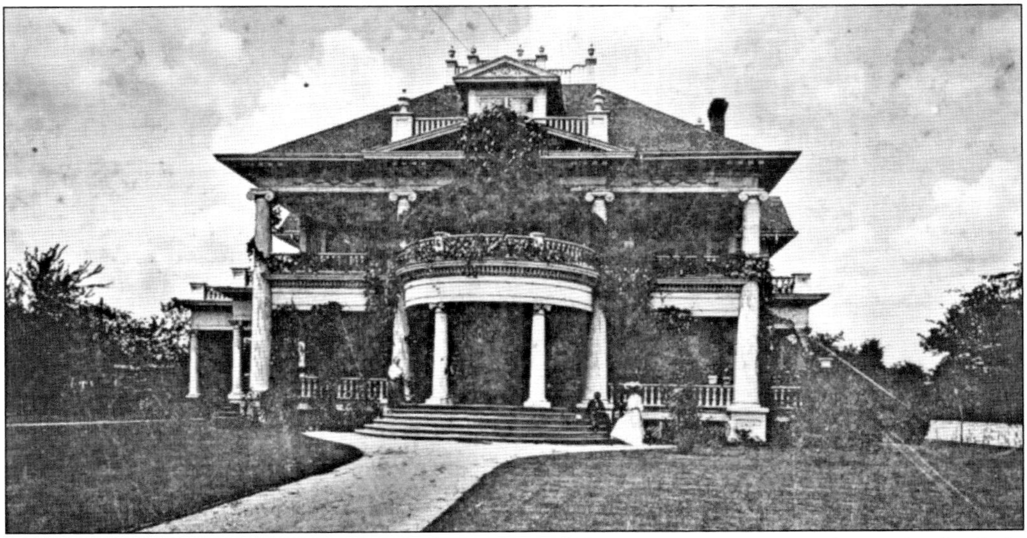

Built in the 1892 by Fannie Halbert, the widow of Corsicana attorney and civic leader J. L. Halbert, this home was a Corsicana showplace. It occupied an entire block with gardens, barns, and stables. The house fell into disrepair and was targeted for demolition, but it has been fully restored to its original splendor. (Courtesy of Helen Albritton.)